Strategisches Kompetenz-Management

S K M

AF756791

Der Resource-based View und – in enger Verbindung dazu – das Management von (Kern-)Kompetenzen haben in den vergangenen Jahren die Unternehmensführung nachhaltig beeinflusst. Wissenschaft und Praxis beteiligen sich gleichermaßen an Fragen der ressourcenorientierten Unternehmensführung und des Knowledge Managements. Die Schriftenreihe greift diese Entwicklung auf und schafft ein Forum für wissenschaftliche Beiträge und Diskussionen.

Saša Šarić

Competitive Advantages through Clusters

An Empirical Study with Evidence from China

With a foreword by Prof. Dr. Dr. h.c. Hans-Christian Pfohl

Springer Gabler

RESEARCH

Saša Šarić
Shanghai, P.R. China

Doctoral thesis, Technische Universität Darmstadt, 2011

D 17

ISBN 978-3-8349-3553-3 ISBN 978-3-8349-3554-0 (eBook)
DOI 10.1007/978-3-8349-3554-0

The Deutsche Nationalbibliothek lists this publication in the Deutsche Nationalbibliografie; detailed bibliographic data are available in the Internet at http://dnb.d-nb.de.

Springer Gabler

Cover design: KünkelLopka GmbH, Heidelberg

Printed on acid-free paper

Springer Gabler is a brand of Springer DE.
Springer DE is part of Springer Science+Business Media.
www.springer-gabler.de

Za moju familiju

獻給我的家人

Foreword

Never since Alfred Marshall first introduced the concept of the industrial district into economic thought in 1890, has the cluster discourse been more vibrant than today. Never since the Italian District School revived his ideas and brought them back into the scientific spotlight, has there been more rigorous research about it. And never since Michael E. Porter elevated "the cluster" to stardom, has there been more attention brought to it by politicians, non-governmental organizations, CEOs, consultants, and the scientific community alike.

Yet, Mr. Saric argues, despite all our research and knowledge about the ability of clusters to promote innovation, regional economic development, and national prosperity, we know surprisingly little about the firms that operate from within these clusters and drive their success. It is here where his greatest contribution to the current cluster-discourse lies as he asks: how do firms create competitive advantages through the cluster they are located in?

And this, more than ever, is an important question. As governments keep on pouring money into once successful industrial regions to stop and turn over their decline and help grow promising upcomers, these initiatives often tend to fail, because many have forgotten that it is the cluster-firms that ultimately drive their success. And only a few seem to know what these firms really need in order to create a thriving, vibrant, and healthy cluster. This leaves executives, employees, workers, and the general public frustrated thus endangering the support of future generations for the concept as a whole.

As an educated student of Strategic Entrepreneurship, Mr. Saric uses a rigorous exploratory approach with evidence gathered from China to tackle this question. China is particularly well suited for this research as its economy is organized around strong industrial clusters.

In a nutshell, his findings suggest that the most successful firms achieved to instill in their companies an entrepreneurial orientation of proactiveness, innovation, and risk-taking to identify the opportunities that exist in clusters and exploit their value generating potential through a well developed cluster-capability. It consists of the ability to gather information and spread it throughout their organization, build and maintain access relationship with other nearby located firms, and recruit, develop, and retain highly skilled personnel and entrepreneurial executives.

Mr. Saric's findings are a first step in our endeavor to learn more about the firms that operate within clusters. They provide an important orientation for politicians in helping them identify those cluster-firms worthy of governmental support. To executives they highlight the importance of capability for entrepreneurship, as the latter is useless in clusters without the former.

What remains after reading this carefully conducted piece of research is the hope, that Mr. Saric's findings become part of the current discourse on clusters and to some extent even alter its future direction. Politicians and executives would be well advised to take these insights and critically ask themselves what they mean for their own daily practice.

The author has done so for himself and decided - at least for now - to leave the academic career path and again venture out into the unknown to explore the world of industry. Yet, he remains a passionate lecturer of management dedicated to use his newly gained insights to become a better teacher for his students.

Prof. Dr. Dr. h.c. Hans-Christian Pfohl

Acknowledgements

"There is no such thing as a 'self-made' man. We are made up of thousands of others. Everyone who has ever done a kind deed for us, or spoken one word of encouragement to us, has entered into the make-up of our character and of our thoughts, as well as our success."

George Burton Adams

When the first thought of pursuing a doctor's degree appeared in my mind, I envisioned myself sitting at a desk, in an office, alone, thinking about the next great thing and writing passionately about what I thought is right. Very much like the archaic image of the scientist, who is like a lone wolf spending his hours in solitude only to appear after weeks, months, or years with an idea that changes the world. I also envisioned myself writing about competition, as I was fascinated by the idea of the survival of the fittest.

Little did I know that years later this vision would prove to be plain wrong! Although I did spent many hours in solitude and wrote about competition, this book as well as the topic I chose, are rather a tale of cooperation, mentorship, loving support, friendship, and family. As much as a cluster is unthinkable without the community of firms it is made up of, so too this book is unthinkable without my community of mentors, students, colleagues, friends, and family who have helped me reaching the stars.

First I would like to thank Prof. Hans-Christian Pfohl for admitting me as his doctoral candidate, but much more for being my most important role model when it comes to ethical behavior in business and in the classroom. As it is with many young mentees, in the beginning I simply tried to imitate his attitudes towards performance, integrity, honesty, and leadership. Of course, in the years that passed since my own first classroom experience I have changed considerably, yet, sometimes I notice how much I still resemble his style when I engage with my students.

I would also like to thank my second supervisor Prof. Ralf Elbert for teaching me the virtues of good theory when I was his Masters student in Darmstadt and for introducing me to the cluster topic. Our exciting discussions during that time and later on during our joint academic work eventually resulted in this research.

Prof. Gang Yang deserves my gratitude for being my closest mentor throughout the three years I spent under his supervision at Tongji. Highly analytical by nature, he forced me again and again to think first, then draft, and only at the end start putting things to paper, or better to say power point. A way of problem solving, I still profit from highly.

Next, I would like to thank the best "triple-blind" reviewers of the world: Prof. Alexander Bode, Dr. Holger Köhler, and my brother Milan. Their highly qualified feedback, stemming from repeatedly going through my script, greatly improved the quality of my work. My brother in particular made me descent from the all too cozy "ivory tower" and think about the practicality of my results. In addition, Holger and I spent countless hours on discussing each others' research and going jointly through the manic-depressive ups and downs of writing a dissertation. Without him, I would never have been able to finish my work in this time.

My research also greatly benefitted from the many students I mentored during my time at Tongji. These are Björn Schmeisser, Katharia Hix, Shulin Zhao, Manuel Bäuml, Lauren Matthews, Simon Alig, Claudius Centner, and Nikos Moraitakis. All of them directly or indirectly shaped my understanding of the cluster phenomenon, the theoretical frameworks I am making use of, and the statistical methods employed. During the many discussions with these young, bright, and enthusiastic people, I often lost track of who is the teacher and who is the student. They belong to the happiest moments I had during my time at the university.

Thanks to my closest friend Dominik Reinhard for enlightening my mood and encouraging me when the going got tough. I am deeply grateful for his ability to bringing me "back to the moment" and for going with me through all the ups and downs of life.

I am also thankful for the loving support I received from Sherry Hsu and her mom Diana throughout the years I was working on this project. Sherry in particular deserves special praise for her support during the good times and the tough times. Writing a dissertation in itself is hard enough, doing so in such a foreign culture and so far away from home, is a daunting challenge. Without her I never would have brought this project to an end.

I would like to again thank my brother Milan for his many advises and feedbacks regarding my script, career, and important decisions in life. My mother Darivojka instilled in me the desire for intellectual development and her influence has helped to solidify my wish of pursuing a doctor's degree. From my father Nikola I learned that in the long run, there is no shortcut to the top, but that it is hard work and nothing else that makes a man successful. It is this attitude that prevented me from getting up from my desk during those long hours of solitude.

Thank you, to all of you!

Saša Šarić

Outline

Contents

List of Figures

List of Tables

List of Abbreviations

AHP	Analytical Hierarchy Process
AVE	Average Variance Extracted
CBSEM	Covariance-Based Structural Equation Modeling
CSIC	Classification for National Activities of China-Code
DID	Degree of Industry Dominance
EO	Entrepreneurial Orientation
FDI	Foreign Direct Investment
GDP	Gross Domestic Product
GIOV	Gross Industrial Output Value
GREMI	Groupe de Recherche Européen sure les Milieux Innovateurs
ICT	Information and Communication Technology
IPO	Initial Public Offering
ISIC	International Standard Industrial Classification of All Economic Activities
JV	Joint Venture
LQ	Location Quotient
MIMIC	Multiple Effect Indicators for Multiple Causes
MNC	Multinational Company
MSA	Metropolitan Statistical Area
NPV	Net Present Value
PLS	Partial Least Squares
R&D	Research and Development
RBV	Resource-Based View of the Firm
ROA	Return on Assets
ROS	Return on Sales
SEM	Structural Equation Modeling
SEZ	Special Economic Zones
SIC	Standard Industry Classification
SME	Small and Medium Sized Enterprise
SOE	State Owned Enterprise
VIF	Variance Inflation Factor
WTO	World Trade Organization

1 Introduction

"When an inventor in Silicon Valley opens his garage door to show off his latest idea, he has 50 percent of the world market in front of him. When an inventor in Finland opens his garage door, he faces three feet of snow."

J.U. Niemen, former CEO of Nokia-Mobira[1]

The world over, clusters are home to leading firms and institutions that compete on the edge of technology. They can be found in developed and developing countries alike and comprise such famous ones as Silicon Valley, London's financial center, ceramic tile and fashion in north Italy, wine in Bordeaux, automotive in Stuttgart and Munich, software in Bangalore, and manufacturing in China's Pearl-river delta.[2]

Today they are studied by a variety of scholars from different fields including economists, social scientists, and strategists, but also by a growing number of business practitioners and policy makers.[3] As a result, knowledge on the capacity of clusters to promote regional economic development and national prosperity and the role of local industrial policy in creating new clusters has increased rapidly in recent years.[4]

Yet, this came at the expense of the individual firm. As many cluster scholars assume (implicitly or explicitly) a high level of homogeneity among cluster-firms up to the degree of total interchangeability, the attention had turned away from the individual firm and towards the cluster as a whole[5]: "*Throughout most of the literature there is a tacit assumption that all cluster firms are relatively homogeneous and that they do not merit attention in their own right.*"[6] Thus, there is little account of specific firm-level characteristics such as resources, processes, or strategies that may help firms create and defend competitive advantages through clusters.

A newly emerging stream of research studies, however, attempts to change this. They can be divided into two streams. The first stream focuses on the examination of structural differences among cluster-firms. It shows that clusters "*are not populated by homogeneous communities of*

---

1 van Tulder (1988), p. 169.

2 See Enright (2003), p. 100; Rosenfeld (1997), pp. 3f.

3 See for example Martin/Sunley (2003), p. 6; McCann/Sheppard (2003), p. 650; Porter (1990), pp. 144ff.; Rocha (2004), p. 368; Roelandt et al. (1999), pp. 315ff.; Rosenfeld (1997), pp. 8f.; St. John/Pouder (2006), p. 141.

4 See for example Amin (1989); Becattini (1989); Brusco (1992); Beaudry/Breschi/Swann (2002); Enright (1996); European Commission (2002); Feser/Bergman (2000); Piore/Sabel (1984).

5 See Porter (1998a), p. 86; Molina-Morales/Martinez-Fernandez (2004), p. 475. Illustrative examples provide Piore and Sabel in their description of firms in Italy's industrial districts in Piore/Sabel (1984), p. 32 and Sabel (1995), p. 155.

6 Lazerson/Lorenzoni (1999), p. 237.

entrepreneurs and technicians sharing both technical know-how and generic information."[7] Rather, firms show significant differences in their structural characteristics and the roles they obtain in the cluster hierarchy. Lazerson and Lorenzoni for example, examine several Italian industrial districts and show how larger firms orchestrate production using groups of smaller firms, explore new markets, and perform the majority of the research and development (R&D) that takes place in the districts.[8] In a similar study, Molina-Morales and Martinez-Fernandez expose significant differences in the way firms participate in these networks and gain access to the available resources.[9]

It is here that the second research stream focuses on the types of firms that are able to turn the opportunities that abound in clusters into competitive advantages. Here scholars have largely examined the effect of firm size and age on the relationship between clusters and firm performance, while others have focused on the firm resources that differentiate high from low-performing cluster-firms.[10]

At this point, however, it remains unclear what mechanisms are at work that actually produce these benefits. Consequently, there is also no account of how these mechanisms are influenced by distinct cluster-contingencies. In an effort to shed light on this lack of insight, this study attempts to answer the following overriding **research question**:

How do firms create and defend competitive advantages through clusters?

To this end, it shifts the focus of analysis from the cluster-centered view that has dominated the cluster discourse for so long back to a firm-centered view. It combines the fields of entrepreneurship and strategic management into a theoretical framework of analysis to identify the elements through which firms explore new opportunities and turn them into competitive advantages. In particular, it emphasizes the importance of firm-level characteristics and environmental contingencies to perceive opportunities in clusters, mobilize the required resources in response, and defend competitive advantages in the long-run. Derived from this framework of analysis, three related research questions will be addressed sequentially throughout this study and together provide an answer to the overriding research question:

(1) *What internal characteristics allow firms to create and defend competitive advantages through clusters?*

(2) *How do these internal characteristics influence firm performance under different cluster-contingencies?*

(3) *How can these internal characteristics be implemented into organizational reality?*

---

7 Molina-Morales/Martinez-Fernandez (2008), p. 39.

8 See Lazerson/Lorenzoni (1999), p. 258.

9 See Molina-Morales/Martinez-Fernandez (2004), p. 484.

10 See Kukalis (2010), p. 22; Wennberg/Lindqvist (2010), pp. 235-236; Zhang/Li (2008), p. 625; McCann/Folta (2011), pp. 120f.; Liao (2010), pp. 166f.

In order to understand the research process that will guide the search for answers, the next section stresses the scientific-theoretical positioning of this study.

1.1 Scientific-Theoretical Positioning

The present research is best described as being **exploratory** in nature. It *elaborates* and *extends* existing theory. By doing so, it takes up a distinct position within scientific theory that is defined by three levels of analysis: (1) the meta-methodological level, (2) the methodological level, and (3) the theoretical level.[11]

Meta-methodological level

The meta-methodological level is related to the question of "*why*" to research and touches on human beings' core assumptions on the nature of reality (ontology), knowledge (epistemology), and the pre-determination of human actions (human nature). These core assumptions delineate the subjective and objective approach to science, which make up the polar ends of a continuum with varying philosophical positions between them (see figure 1).[12]

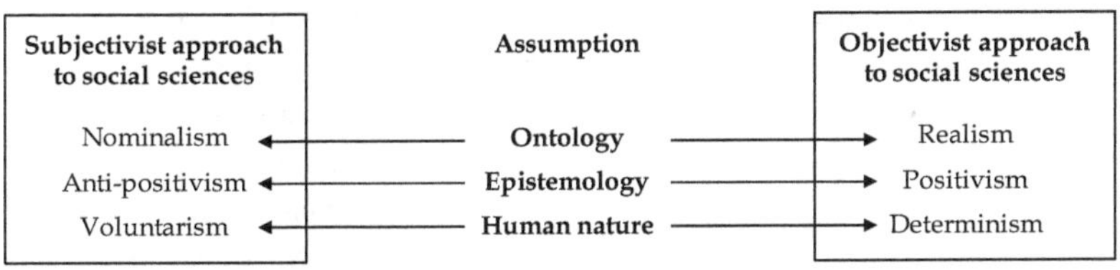

Figure 1 - The dimensions of research on the meta-methodological level
(Source: Adapted from Holden/Lynch (2004), p. 399)

The *subjectivist* view on ontology is nominalism. It assumes that reality is individually constructed and exists only in one's own mind. Thus, what one person perceives as reality differs for another as multiple realities exist as a projection of human imagination. The epistemological standpoint is therefore anti-positivistic in that knowledge cannot be discovered, but only subjectively created since it depends on personal experience. From this perspective, understanding the true and full nature of a phenomenon requires getting personally involved with it as every person perceives reality in different ways. In line with these assumptions is the view of voluntarism in that human beings are autonomous and free-willed, able to shape their environment.[13] Hence, within subjectivism there is no such thing as "objective data" or "the truth". Rather there are multiple truths and all depend on the individual standpoint of the observer. Subjectivists argue that researchers cannot and should not sepa-

11 See for the following discussion Peters (2010), pp. 9ff.; Kuhn (1996), pp. 182ff.; Stokes (1995), pp. 27ff.

12 See Burrell/Morgan (1979), pp. 21ff.

13 See Morgan/Smircich (1980), p. 494.

rate themselves from the object they are studying. The goal of science from a subjective standpoint is to understand and explain a problem within its distinct contextual setting.[14]

By contrast, proponents of the *objectivist* approach to science are realists. They argue that reality predates individual observers and thus exists as an empirical fact, a hard, tangible, measurable, and relatively immutable entity. Therefore, knowledge is perceived positivistic. It can be discovered through observation and measurement, classified according to regularities, and used for prediction based on causal relationships. This entails a view of individuals as being born into a deterministic world made up of causal regularities that shape the patterns of social behavior. Therefore, objectivists believe that their own interests, values, and beliefs are independent of and neither affect nor are affected by the object under study.[15]

Given that these two positions represent extreme assumptions, most business research today has been from a more moderate *pragmatist* position.[16] Similar to objectivism, pragmatism views reality as being existent and tangible, but at the same time also shaped by the behavior of human beings. As a consequence, while reality can be objectively measured, it is also subject to continuous change. What holds true today does not necessarily have to hold true tomorrow. Facts, explanations, and theories are therefore chosen according to one's own belief and replaced by others when they are better at producing results that are anticipated or desired.[17] While pragmatism acknowledges the existence of causal relationships, they are chosen by subjective beliefs, values, and interests and therefore cannot be completely separated from chosen explanations of or theories about reality. Hence from a pragmatist view, there exist multiple explanations or theories that all carry a sense of truth in them. Human beings are therefore free to choose and by doing so shape and are being shaped by their environment.[18]

This study takes a pragmatist view that is in line with the view of *management research as an applied social science*. The aim is to analyze human agency and its outcomes within complex social systems.[19] In this context, the pursuit of competitive advantages takes place within the realm of management and in systems of social life comprised of individual firms and the clusters they are embedded in. As both systems are in a constant state of interaction shaping and reshaping one another, causal relationships are formulated based on the more stable elements of reality. This acknowledges the fact that the behavior of complex social systems cannot be fully controlled for and that there may exist answers for the overriding research question other than those provided here.

---

14 See Holden/Lynch (2004), p. 404.

15 See Remenyi et al. (1998), p. 33 and Gordon (1991), p. 664.

16 See Holden/Lynch (2004), p. 402.

17 See Cherryholmes (1992), p. 14.

18 See Morgan/Smircich (1980), pp. 494f.

19 See Ulrich/Hill (1979), p. 163; Fülbier (2004), p. 267.

Methodological level

The second, methodological level of scientific research relates to the question of "*how*" to research and concerns procedures and rules for theory development and testing. It differentiates between an inductive and deductive research approach. *Inductive research* is generally ascribed to a subjectivist stance and used for building theories and exploring the phenomenon under investigation. It starts from empirical experience and attempts to abstract theory from observed intentions, motives, and human actions as well as patterns and regularities.[20] *Deductive research* on the other hand, represents the objectivist position of positivism and is used for theory testing. The aim is to first formulate hypotheses about the nature of things and then try to falsify incorrect hypotheses.[21] The key lies in isolating causes and effects, identifying underlying relationships, and measuring their outcomes in order to arrive at models for explaining real-world phenomena.[22]

Given that there is little account of how firms create and defend competitive advantages through clusters, this research applies both methodologies in an alternating fashion, yet puts particular emphasis on *induction through exploration*. This is in line with the pragmatist view taken on the meta-methodological level halfway between subjectivism and objectivism. The exploratory research stage uses existing theory and empirical evidence based on case studies to identify constructs and relationships that may be of relevance for firms in clusters. Subsequently grounding these insights in literature provides a substantive basis for deductive hypothesis development and testing. The empirical results are then used to elaborate and extend existing theory by exploring a new set of relevant literatures and link the empirical evidence back to existing concepts.

Theoretical level

Finally, on the **theoretical level**, which relates to questions of "*what*" to research, stands the choice between single, pluralistic, or eclectic approaches to theory. *Pluralistic* approaches use multiple theories and apply each theory in its regular form to explain a single aspect of the phenomenon under study. *Eclectic* approaches on the other hand, combine individual elements of multiple theories based on what seems best to holistically explain the phenomenon being studied.[23] This study makes use of both approaches. It first applies the fields of entrepreneurship and strategic management independently from one another using a pluralistic perspective. It then applies the emerging theory of Strategic Entrepreneurship using an eclectic approach.

Entrepreneurship deals with how firms explore new short-lived economic opportunities, while strategic management explains how firms create strategic defenses to exploit already

---

[20] See Eisenhardt/Graebner (2007), pp. 25ff.

[21] See Popper (2002), pp. 7ff.

[22] See Remenyi et al. (1998), p. 32.

[23] See Kirsch (1990), p. 114.

existing competitive advantages. As entrepreneurship and strategic management are complementary to one another, recent literature suggests the need to combine elements from both fields into a unifying Strategic Entrepreneurship theory. It emphasizes that firms need to simultaneously be entrepreneurial in order to explore new opportunities and strategic to exploit the value that is being created. The pluralistic and eclectic approaches lead to somewhat competing hypotheses. The question which one suits the cluster context better is resolved in an empirical study that was conducted in China.

The scientific-theoretical positioning of this study is summarized in figure 2.

Meta-methodology	• This study is related to a pragmatist view of science • It recognizes the existence of causal relationships that can be tested, if the elements are stable over time • Because social systems are complex, there may be answers to the research questions other than those provided here
Methodology	• The research process is exploratory in nature aiming at elaborating and extending existing theory • It alternates between inductive theory building and deductive theory testing, always linking results to existing concepts
Theory	• Entrepreneurship, strategic management, and Strategic Entrepreneurship are applied as theoretical frameworks • The fields are combined in a pluralistic and eclectic theory approach, independently

Figure 2 - Scientific-theoretical positioning of this study

1.2 Outline of this Research

Based on its scientific-theoretical positioning and the underlying research questions, figure 3 illustrates the broad outline of this research study. A more detailed outline is provided in appendix 1.

Chapter 2 presents a comprehensive discussion of the current literature on clusters. The first part reviews some of the concepts and definitions that are commonly associated with the cluster phenomenon and exposes the absence of an agreement regarding a meaningful definition of clusters. Therefore, part two takes a step back and retraces the historical evolution of the cluster concept and the main Schools of Thought that have contributed to its current understanding. Based on the elements on which all Schools of Thought agree, part three then develops a meaningful definition of clusters, which serves as foundation for the remainder of this study. Part four then reviews studies on the effect of clusters on firm performance and leads to the first set of hypotheses. It also exposes the need for the exploration of further internal characteristics that enable firms to create and defend competitive advantages through clusters. Chapter 2 closes with the baseline model of this study.

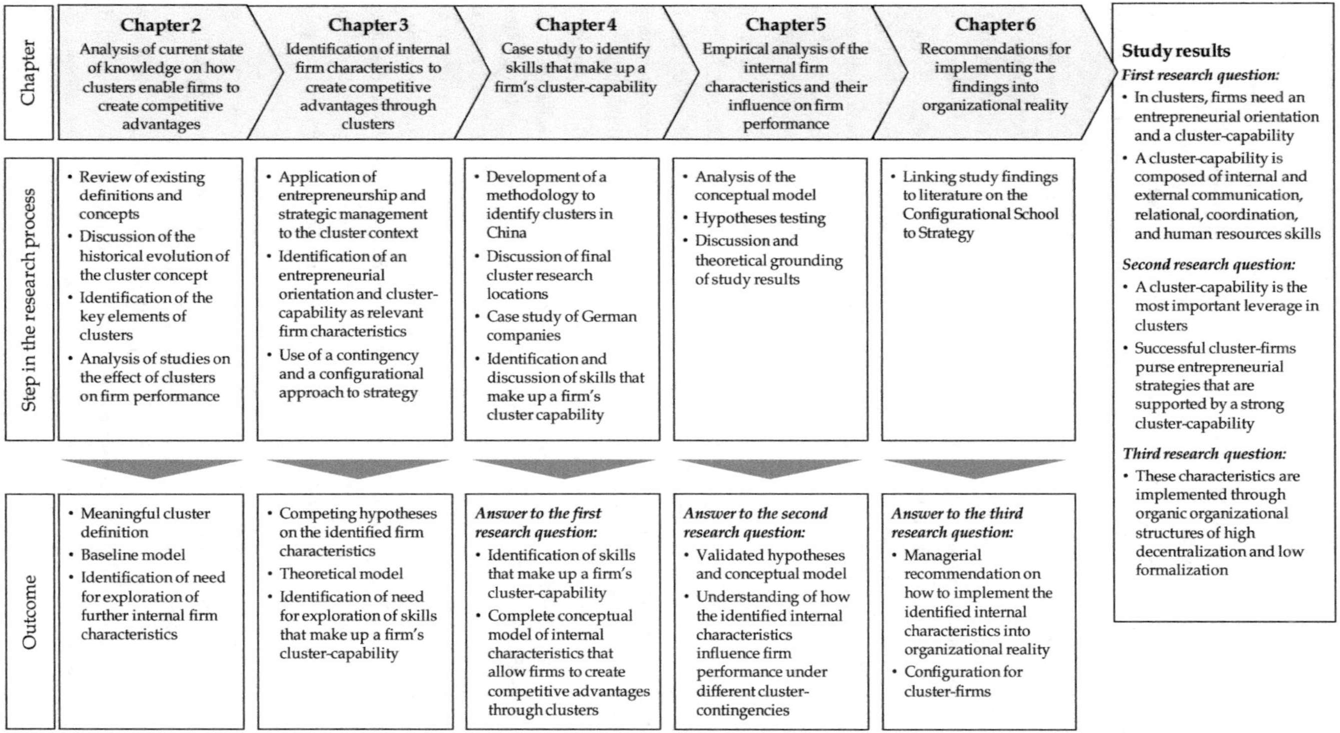

Figure 3 - Outline of this research study

Based on the identified need for further exploration, *chapter 3* applies the fields of entrepreneurship and strategic management to the cluster context to develop a theoretical model of internal characteristics that enable firms to create competitive advantages through clusters. To this end, the first two parts apply both fields in a contingency mode to the cluster context, that is, independent from one another. Part one identifies a firm's entrepreneurial orientation as critical for exploring the continuous stream of opportunities that is generated in clusters, while part two shows that firms need a strong cluster-capability to exploit existing advantages by utilizing the resources that abound in clusters. As literature calls for a balance between exploration and exploitation to continuously renew a firm's competitive advantages, the third part integrates both fields into a process model of Strategic Entrepreneurship. It is then applied to the cluster context and results in the configurational hypothesis that firms need to simultaneously pursue entrepreneurial strategies in clusters and develop a distinct cluster-capability to turn opportunities into competitive advantages. Chapter 3 closes with the theoretical model of this study. While the concept of an entrepreneurial strategy is already well established, literature has yet to come up with a set of skills that actually make up a firm's cluster-capability. This results in the need for exploration of these skills through a case study based research.

Based on the identified need for the exploration of skills that make up a firm's cluster-capability, *chapter 4* presents the first empirical fieldwork, a case study about German companies in China's industrial clusters. The aim is to explore the elements of a distinct cluster-capability by investigating the competitive behavior of firms in clusters. Part one introduces China as research setting and shows that the country's current industrial organization centers on highly competitive industrial clusters. Yet, as an emerging market country China lacks a consistent statistical data set and reliable evidence on the boundaries of its clusters and their industry composition. Therefore, part two introduces the methodology that was followed to identify specific clusters that may serve as research locations. It is based on the previously developed cluster definition. Part three then provides a description of the methodology that was followed during the fieldwork. Part four presents the findings that were derived from the data analysis. In doing so, it gives a detailed account of the skills that make up a cluster-capability and that firms need to create competitive advantages through clusters. Part five consolidates these findings in the conceptual model of this study and provides an answer to the first research question.

Chapter 5 presents the second empirical study that is used to test the previously developed conceptual model. Part one introduces the general methodology that was applied during the design stage and provides a description of the sample characteristics. Part two introduces partial least squares as the methodology to analyze the data and validate the conceptual model. Then, part three and four present the two-step approach that was followed during the testing stage. Part five critically discusses the results in the light of distinct cluster-contingencies, the sample characteristics, and existing literatures. It concludes by providing an answer to the second research question.

Chapter 6 then attends to the third research question. The results of this study point to the validity of the configurational perspective, which integrates the fields of entrepreneurship and strategic management into a unified theoretical framework. Although not initially investigated, the Configurational School to strategy suggests distinct organizational structures that provide practical recommendations on how to implement the identified internal characteristics into organizational reality.

Finally, *chapter 7* summarizes the results of this study and provides a consolidated answer to the overriding research question. It closes with a discussion of some of its limitations and an outlook on further research.

2 Current State of Knowledge on how Clusters Enable Firms to Create Competitive Advantages

Clusters appear in varying forms, shapes, and sizes, are home to all types of industries and exist in different lifecycle stages. They can be found in developed and developing countries and comprise such famous ones as Silicon Valley, Las Vegas, London's financial center, India's information and communication technology (ICT) and China's manufacturing clusters, ceramic tile and fashion in north Italy, and wine in Bordeaux. This variety causes a problem of definition and has led to a multiplicity of interpretations, terminologies, and Schools of Thought, each of which treats the cluster phenomenon somewhat differently. This chapter therefore develops a framework that integrates these different conceptualizations. The underlying research process is depicted in figure 4.

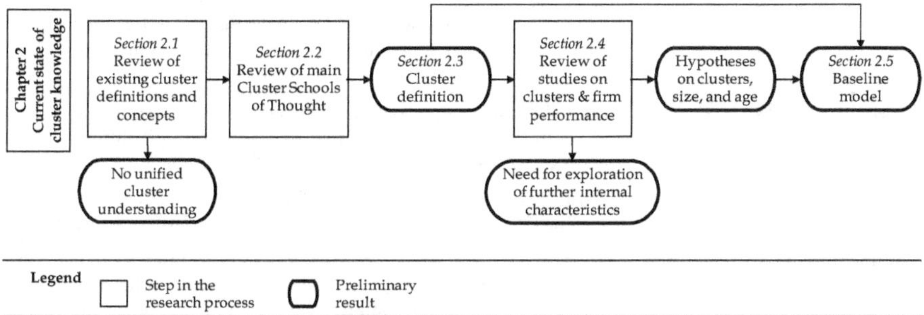

Figure 4 - Outline of chapter 2

Section 2.1 first shows how a vast proliferation of definitions and concepts resulted in a variety of understandings of what clusters actually are. To develop a meaningful definition of clusters, section 2.2 reviews the historical evolution of the concept and the main Schools of Thought that have provided different, but complementary insights about clusters. Section 2.3 then develops a definition of clusters based on their key dimensions that will serve as foundation for the remainder of this study. Based on this understanding, section 2.4 reviews studies that have investigated how clusters influence firm performance and derives the first set of hypotheses. It also exposes the need for exploration of further internal characteristics that serves as key rationale for the subsequent research process. The chapter concludes with the summary of the findings in a baseline model.

2.1 Clusters – A Seemingly Chaotic Concept[24]

Within the literature on clusters there is a large **proliferation of definitions** that has caused much confusion and difficulties when one tries to communicate about it (see table 1). [25] The main reason for this situation is that due to their popularity clusters are studied by a variety of scholars from different fields such as economists, social scientists, and strategists, but also by a growing number of business practitioners and policy makers. All of them tend to approach the phenomenon differently, adding their specific views, terminologies, theoretical and practical frameworks, and languages to the cluster discourse. While it certainly adds richness to it, this circumstance also makes it incredibly difficult to delineate what constitutes the core of the cluster concept and where its boundaries should be drawn.

Author(s)	Definition
Crouch/Farrell (2001), p. 163	"The more general concept of 'cluster' suggests something looser: a tendency for firms in similar types of businesses to locate close together, though without having a particularly important presence in an area."
Feser (1998), p. 26	"Economic clusters are not just related and supporting industries and institutions, but rather related and supporting institutions that are more competitive by virtue of their relationship."
Pietrobelli/Barrera (2002), p. 542.	"A cluster is defined as a group of enterprises spatially close, and specialized in the development of a similar or the same product."
Simmie/Sennett (1999), p. 51	"We define an innovative cluster as a large number of interconnected industrial and/or service companies having a high degree of collaboration, typically through a supply chain, and operating under the same market condition."
Rosenfeld (1995), p. 7.	"A [cluster is] a geographically bounded concentration of interdependent businesses with active channels for business transactions, dialogue, and communications, and that collectively shares common opportunities and threats."
Swann/Prevezer/Stout (1998), p. 1	"A cluster means a large group of firms in related industries at a particular location."
van den Berg/Braun/ van Winden (2001), p. 187.	"The popular term cluster is most closely related to this local or regional dimension of networks...of specialized organizations, whose production processes are closely linked through the exchange of goods, services and/or knowledge."

Table 1 - An overview of different cluster definitions

Additionally Porter for example, defines clusters as "*a geographically proximate group of interconnected companies and associated institutions in a particular field, linked by commonalities and*

[24] The title of this chapter is based on Martin and Sunley's (2003) highly influential review of the cluster concept in which the authors critically examine its definitions, theorizations, empirics, and benefits.

[25] The aim of this discussion is to show the vast proliferation of cluster definitions and concepts, which serves as basis to develop a workable definition in section 2.3 and that will guide the remainder of this study.

complementarities."[26] Clusters encompass a large array of specialized suppliers, service companies, related downstream and upstream industries, producers of complementary products, specialized infrastructure providers, governmental agencies and other institutions providing specialized services such as training, education, market research as well as technical support. Porter's definition highlights that clusters consist of a variety of actors from different fields which are somehow linked to each other. These links can be horizontal and vertical. Clusters can be centered on small firms and large firms or a mix of those. Important for cluster formation is that these actors are geographically close to each other as this represents a key defining dimension.

Echoing Porter, Hakanson underlines that clusters *"consist of and are defined by [related] value-adding activities in a set of linked companies and institutions"*[27], where relatedness stems from similarity and complementarity of activities. In a similar way, Maskell and Lorenzen see clusters as *"co-localization of separate economic entities, which are in some sense related, but not joined together by any common ownership or management."*[28] Picking up the notion of relatedness, Feser and Lugar define clusters as *"concentrations of businesses that co-locate because of trading (buyer-supplier) relationships and/or to share common factor markets (including infrastructure, knowledge resources, and labor) and/or common goods markets."*[29]

While in the former definitions clusters can encompass institutions and firms from related industries, other authors take a more narrow view on clusters. Hill and Brennan for example define clusters as *"concentrations of competitive firms or establishments in the same industry."*[30] This type of clusters is also known as sectoral or industry clusters. As Romanelli and Khessina explain, firms in these clusters tend to produce the same or similar goods and services.[31]

Feser and Bergman on the other hand, completely dismiss the geographical dimension. Instead they define clusters *"as sectors related through formal production linkages, regardless of geographical proximity."*[32] The geographical dimension is also absent in Roelandt and colleagues' very broad definition of clusters *"as economic networks of strongly interdependent firms linked in a value-adding production chain. In some cases, clusters encompass strategic alliances with agents in the knowledge infrastructure, such as research institutes, universities, engineering companies and firms of consultants."*[33] New in this definition is that firms in clusters can be organized in specialized networks as opposed to loosely defined relationships or related activities.

26 Porter (1998b), p. 199.
27 Hakanson (2005), p. 443.
28 Maskell/Lorenzen (2004), p. 991.
29 Feser/Luger (2003), p. 3.
30 Hill/Brennan (2000), p. 67.
31 See Romanelli/Khessina (2005), p. 346.
32 Feser/Bergman (2000), p. 3.
33 Roelandt et al. (1999), p. 315.

Thus, the lack of a common understanding about the key characteristics of clusters has given authors ample opportunities to come up with their own definitions and applications of the concept.

Recognizing that clusters appear in different forms and sizes, some authors propose to group clusters into ideal types or to classify them according to their evolutionary stage. Based on their empirical work, Gordon and McCann identified three different **types of cluster**. That is, a model of pure agglomeration, an industrial complex model, and a social network model (see figure 5).[34]

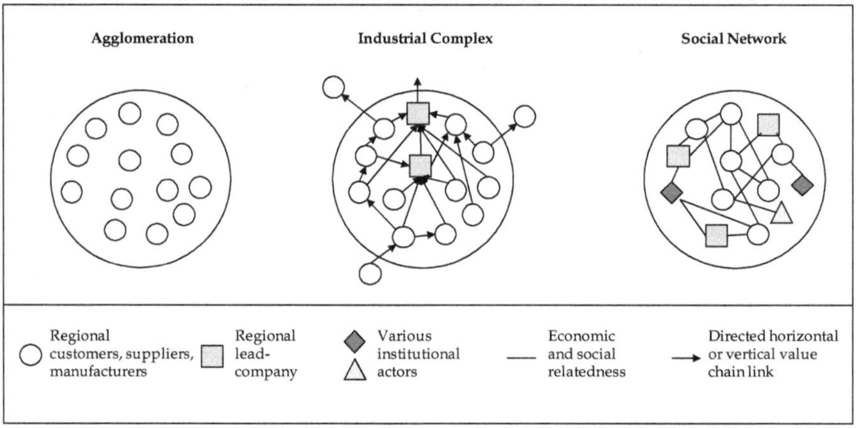

Figure 5 - Cluster typology according to Gordon and McCann

In a *pure agglomeration* model firms, although they are geographically concentrated in a given location, are neither related nor do they have any links with each other. In *industrial complexes* on the other hand, small firms are grouped around large firms in hierarchical buyer-supplier relationships. Finally, *social networks* are characterized by mutual trust relations between key decision-making agents in different organizations.

While Gordon and McCann based their typology on different theoretical perspectives, Rosenfeld distinguishes clusters according to their performance implications. *Working or overachieving clusters* represent the most sophisticated and beneficial clusters as they are the most productive ones due to a high-degree of self-awareness and dense inter-firm networks. *Latent or underachieving clusters* present opportunities that have yet not been exploited to their fullest extent, while *potential clusters* have some of the ingredients necessary to be successful, but lack some key inputs and a critical mass.

Particularly problematic about all such cluster typologies is that none of the concepts itself can explain clusters as they appear in real life, because elements of each of them can co-exist

34 See Gordon/McCann (2000), p. 515.

in certain industries and/or regions.[35] Hence, it is difficult to judge under which particular circumstances one cluster type should be more applicable than another. Assigning a real life cluster to one of these types would therefore inevitably be an arbitrary process, which significantly reduces the practical applicability of such typologies.

As an alternative, Aziz and Norhashim propose to identify clusters according to their evolutionary development. Drawing heavily from technology, product, and industry lifecycle concepts[36], these authors develop a **cluster lifecycle model** consisting of six stages (see figure 6).

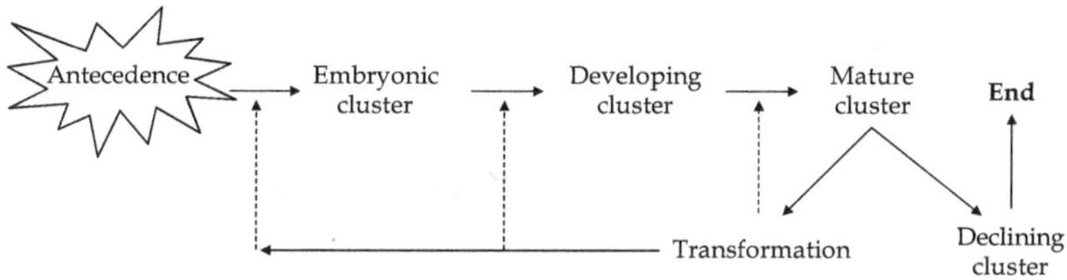

Figure 6 - Cluster lifecycle
(Source: Aziz/Norhashim (2008), p. 367.)

The *antecedent stage* is the early phase of a cluster where growth is either endogenous or exogenous initiated by industrial policies. In the *embryonic stage* a cluster shows first signs of agglomeration without the existence of links and networks between firms. *Developing clusters* have reached a critical mass in which links in clusters develop and become active. *Mature clusters* reach their peak stage in which the common industry or technology denominator has matured and growth and performance show no signs of further growth. *Declining clusters* have already peaked and are now in a state of decreasing returns. Clusters in the *transformation stage* are mature or declining clusters that have successfully avoided their demise by finding new growth opportunities.

The authors base their arguments on the notion that firms in clusters share similar resources and technologies or target similar markets thus belonging to similar industrial sectors. Therefore, their approach requires to first identify the common denominator of a cluster that causes firms to co-locate and then to assess its maturity. This then serves as evidence to determine the evolutionary stage of the cluster as a whole.[37] The main contribution of lifecycle models is the idea that besides different structural characteristics clusters also undergo certain development stages that have specific consequences for firms and policy makers. In practice however, it is very difficult to determine the exact development stage of a given real life cluster, as it is very likely that its firms will share more than one common resource or technology and also belong to more than one industrial sector. How then should a researcher

35 See vom Hofe/Chen (2006), p. 15.

36 See for example Cainarca/Colombo/Mariotti (1992), pp. 49ff. and Anderson/Zeithaml (1984), pp. 6ff.

37 See Aziz/Norhashim (2008), pp. 367f.

decide which one of the various possible denominators is responsible for the current growth of a cluster and at what point in time it may turn into a rigidity?

As a result of this vast proliferation of different cluster definitions, typologies, classifications, and models, many researchers tend to (accidently or deliberately) confuse the cluster concept with other related and antecedent concepts of geographical proximity. Silicon Valley, which is one of the most studied regions in literature, was already referred to as "*regional network*"[38], "*industrial district*"[39], "*technology district*"[40], "*new industrial space*"[41], "*innovative milieu*"[42], "*agglomeration*"[43], and "*learning region*"[44] among others.

It is equally not unusual to see studies in which authors regularly switch between the "cluster" and one or more of the other related concepts.[45] For this reason, it is important to first understand the evolution of the cluster concept and its theoretical foundation before any useful definition can be derived and before any meaningful discussion about its impact on firm performance can be led. Therefore, the next section reviews the main Schools of Thought that have contributed the most to today's understanding about clusters, that have provided valuable answers about their key constituting characteristics, and that have explicated the types of competitive advantages they provide.

2.2 Review of the Main Cluster Schools of Thought

2.2.1 Overview of the Historical Evolution of the Cluster Concept

The following sections retrace the historical evolution of the cluster concept and the main Schools of Thought that have contributed the most to its current understanding. All Schools arose against the background of distinct historical events that have significantly altered the competitive landscape and the way in which firms interact with their local environment. Their distinct historical context, basic premises, and main propositions regarding the competitive advantage of firms through clusters are summarized in table 2.[46]

---

38 Saxenian (1990), p. 91.

39 Markusen (1996), p. 306.

40 Storper (1997), p. 156.

41 Scott (1988), p. 4.

42 Castells/Hall (1994), p. 144.

43 Audia/Rider (2010), p. 362.

44 Florida (1995), p. 531.

45 See for example Shaver/Flyer (2000); Canina/Enz/Harrison (2005); Folta/Cooper/Baik (2006); McCann/Folta (2011).

46 See for the following discussion also Rocha (2004), pp. 368ff.

Table 2 - Summarized overview of the main cluster Schools of Thought

	19th century	1970s to 1980s		1990s onwards				
Historical context	Emergence of the vertically integrated firm	Suspension of fixed exchange rates, oil crisis, increased liberalization and competition		Declining trade barriers, globalization, rapid technological change				
School of Thought	Marshallian	Italian School	Californian School	Porter's Competitiveness School	New Economic Geography	Geography of Innovation	The Innovative Milieu School	Nordic School of Innovation and Learning
Concept	Marshalllian Industrial District	New Marshallian Industrial District	Californian Technology District	Cluster	Industrial concentration	Innovation concentration	Innovative Milieu	Learning region
Basic premises	Local concentration of specialized labor, presence of related industries	Community of firms based on socio-cultural and institutional context	Externalization of production steps and vertical disintegration	Competitiveness depends on national diamond	Local concentration of industrial activity	Local concentration of Innovation activity	Interaction between territories and regional actors	Localized learning and innovation activity
Competitive advantages	External economies of scale, localized learning due to industrial atmosphere	Flexible production due to industrial atmosphere and cooperative relationships	Reduced transaction costs due to lower risk and untraded interdependencies	Increased productivity, innovativeness, and commercialization of new businesses	Increasing returns due to specialization and scale	Increased innovation due to knowledge spillovers	Increased innovation due to regional innovation networks	Increased innovation due to local knowledge infrastructure and spillovers

For many, the conceptual starting point of modern research about clusters is Marshall's notion of **industrial districts** in England at the end of the 19th century.[47] During this time Marshall witnessed the dawn of a new age and a paradigmatic shift in production that Piore and Sabel would later call the *"first industrial divide"*[48]. A manifestation of this divide was the emergence of the large, vertically integrated corporation that drew its success from internal economies of scale and the production of standardized goods. As new powerful competitors these corporations threatened to replace the small craft-based firm. Yet to the surprise of Marshall, all over England and Europe small firms not only survived this transition, but also continued to thrive in environments that would come to be known as industrial districts. Besides a lively and vivid description of the industrial districts of his time, Marshall was also able to convincingly explain how they enabled small firms to successfully compete with large corporations. His arguments rest on two mechanisms that he observed during his studies: *external economies of scale* and an *industrial atmosphere* that was present among the firms in the district; both are subject to discussion in section 2.2.2.

After Marshall's initial contribution, industrial districts received little to no attention. This lack of scholarly interest can be explained by the widening of the industrial divide due to the ongoing success of the vertically integrated firm. What followed was the construction of institutions designed to create and support predictable mass-markets based on rigid labor laws, product regulation, widening of the welfare state, controlled capital flow, and centralized governments.[49]

This situation was prevalent until in the early 1970s and 1980s a series of drastic events demanded economic, social, and institutional changes which together led to a general crisis of the industrial system, i.e. mass-production through large independent firms. Increased uncertainty about the future prospect of individual markets arose mainly due to external shocks such as the declining power of organized labor, the suspension of fixed exchange rates and the introduction of floating currencies, the oil crises of the 1970s and 1980s, and a shift in public policy towards increased liberalization and competition. The resulting demand crisis led to slow growth and low productivity gains, which made it difficult for large firms to profit from economies of scale. This caused a reduction of the efficiency advantage of mass production relative to craft production.[50]

At this time highly competitive industrial regions in central and north-east Italy and in southern and central California emerged that were characterized by vertically disintegrated production, dense inter-firm networks, and local labor markets. They were said to be concrete manifestations of flexible and specialized production models whose emergence

47 See Marshall (1920) and Marshall (1927).

48 Piore/Sabel (1984), p. 5.

49 See Marangoni/Solari (2006), p. 80.

50 See for a summary of the events Piore/Sabel (1984), pp. 165ff.

represented the "*second industrial divide*"[51], that leads back to craft methods of production and the comeback of the region as the center of economic activity.[52]

While setting out to explain their remarkable success in recessionary times, Italian and American scholars re-discovered Marshall and his concept of industrial districts. Known as **Italian Industrial Districts** and **Californian Technology Districts**, these scholars argued that one factor that contributed to the success of these regions was precisely their *vertically disintegrated production* in inter-firm networks. The other factor that was perceived as being even more important, however, was the way in which these firms were embedded in the *social and institutional context* of their regions. An atmosphere of mutual trust and cooperative relationships allowed them to flexibly adjust their production to fluctuating demand and thereby avoid the high fixed costs that plagued the vertically integrated firm. As a consequence, for the first time in the history of the research of competitiveness the focus shifted from the individual firm to the socially embedded collective of firms, i.e. the industrial district. This decisive transition and the impact it had on the cluster discourse is discussed in the sections 2.2.3 and 2.2.4.

If the 1970s and 1980s were characterized by dramatic changes that led to increased environmental uncertainty within nation states, then the 1990s saw the simultaneous advent of two powerful contextual forces that drastically altered the global competitive landscape: **the globalization of markets** and **rapid technological change**.[53]

At the beginning of the 1990s, *deregulation* and *liberalization* of industries and markets took on a global scale and led to a sharp decline of artificial trade barriers. Increased foreign direct investment (FDI) and the widening of international trade agreements helped to spread these trends. They set in motion a process of macro-regional integration in many parts of the world that gave rise to new emerging market economies. As a consequence, it became easier for firms to do business within and across national borders.[54]

Rapid technological change in ICT on the other hand, caused an increased pace of innovation that led to shortened product life cycles. This eroded competitive advantages that previously have been assumed as being sustainable.

These changes created a new competitive landscape that has been associated with "*hypercompetition*"[55] and "*high velocity markets*"[56]. For many researchers and practitioners the advent of this **new competitive landscape** represents the ultimate transition to a highly dynamic environment from the 1990s onward.[57] It has even prompted some to proclaim the "*death of*

---

51 Piore/Sabel (1984), p. 6.

52 See Storper (1997), pp. 3f.

53 See Held/McGrew/Goldblatt (1999), p. 13 and Longhi/Keeble (2000), p. 45.

54 See Dunning (2000), p. 11.

55 D'Aveni (1994), pp. xiii and 217f.

56 Eisenhardt (2000), p. 1106.

57 See the overview in McNamara/Vaaler/Devers (2003), pp. 262f.

distance"[58] as geographical proximity is perceived as becoming increasingly obsolete: why, after all, should geographical proximity matter when advances in ICT and falling trade barriers have so drastically reduced the costs of transporting goods and information across geographical space?

Yet, at the same time as the geographical dimension has been put to rest in some areas, it has also sparked renewed interest in others. Despite all counter arguments, geographical concentrations of firms in electronics and high-tech in Silicon Valley, film industry in Los Angeles, ceramic tile and fashion in north-east Italy, automotive and machinery in south-western Germany, pharmaceuticals in north Switzerland, medical devices in Massachusetts, services in Bangalore, and manufacturing in south and east China to just name a few still serve as highly cited success stories for vertical disintegration and local specialization. How, one could ask, can the mere existence and success of these specialized regions be explained in a highly dynamic environment amidst globalization and advanced ICT?

To find an answer, a traditional explanation for the co-existence of globalization and local specialization would rest upon Adam Smith's seminal insight that *"the division of labor is limited by the extent of the market."*[59] This means that globalization provides increased incentives for firms to specialize in certain economic activities as it extends the size of the market and thereby increases the likelihood that they can find a buyer for their specialized products. Therefore, globalization will lead to more, rather than less, regional specialization and by consequence will lead to an increase in geographical concentration of economic activities.[60]

While explaining its persistence, the theory of specialization does not explain what kind of activities are most likely to be geographically concentrated. To examine this question, traditional trade theories of the Ricardo and Heckscher-Ohlin type suggest that nations will specialize in those industries in which they hold a comparative advantage. The initial endowment with immobile production factors like capital and labor are therefore the main drivers for national and international trade. The theories argue that those countries who hold dissimilar resource endowments will exchange dissimilar goods with each other.[61]

In reality, this story-line only explains part of world trade, that is, inter-industry trade that takes place between developed and developing countries. Much of the world trade, however, is intra-industry trade that happens between high-income countries that show a striking similarity in their industry composition and that hold similar resources.[62] Moreover, they also exchange similar products with each other that are highly differentiated and knowledge-intensive.

---

58 Cairncross (1997).

59 Smith (2007/1776), p. 24.

60 See Dunning (2000), p. 15.

61 See Rocha (2004), p. 373f.; Ricardo (1817); Heckscher (1919); Ohlin (1933).

62 See Brülhart (2008), p. 19.

As shown in the sections 2.2.5 to 2.2.9, specialization and geographical concentration assist firms in this new competitive landscape by providing opportunities to accumulate valuable knowledge stocks in a specialized field of expertise; a process which depends on social interaction and that to some degree is spatially sticky. Learning and the accumulation of knowledge increases firms' ability to compete on innovation, productivity, and technological sophistication rather than on low-cost. Thus, globalization triggers regional concentration of knowledge-intensive activities by making them a key source of competitive advantage.

Within this context, the literature has divided into two streams: the **economic** one focusing mainly on the external economies highlighted by Marshall, and the **socio-economic** one, which highlights the social, cultural, and institutional dimensions of clusters (see figure 7).

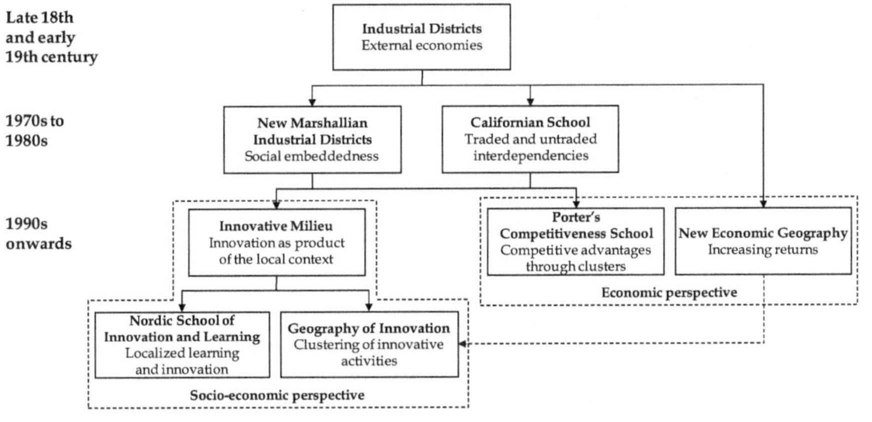

Figure 7 - Historical evolution of the cluster concept

The first stream encompasses Porter's Competitiveness School (section 2.2.5) and Krugman's New Economic Geography (section 2.2.6), while the Geography of Innovation (section 2.2.7), the Innovative Milieu School (section 2.2.8), and the Nordic School of Innovation and Learning (section 2.2.9) fall into the second stream.

The next sections provide an intensive discussion of the different Schools of Thought, the historical context of their theoretical development, and their main contributions to the cluster discourse.

2.2.2 Marshall's Industrial Districts

The starting point of modern research about clusters is Marshall's work on industrial districts. Based on his observations about the location pattern of economic activity in 19th century England, he defines an industrial district as "*the concentration of large numbers of small businesses of a similar kind in the same locality.*"[63] The historical reference of comparison is the internal economies of scale of large companies that thrived during the second industrial revolution.[64]

According to Marshall, industrial districts enable small and medium sized enterprises (SMEs) to profit from **external economies of scale.** They increase their efficiency through a high degree of division of labor and allow each firm to focus on one step of the production process.[65] In this way, industrial districts represent an alternative form of industrial organization as compared to the production on a large scale performed by vertically integrated firms. In his work, Marshall identified several external economies and diseconomies when locating in industrial districts (see table 3).

External economies	External diseconomies
• Presence of skilled labor • Availability of specialized related industries • Industrial atmosphere • Access to market information	• Higher wages • Higher ground rents • Threat of competitive rigidity and economic decline

Table 3 - Economies and diseconomies of industrial districts

Industrial districts offer an attractive **market for skilled labor** that benefits employers and employees alike by minimizing the economic risk for both parties as compared to isolated locations. While employers gain access to "*a good choice of workers with the special skill which they require*"[66] employees benefit from the presence of many potential employers, which give them and their families higher chances of finding a new or better job should they need or wish to look for one.

Similar forces also favor the "*growth in the same neighbourhood of industries of a supplementary character*"[67] that allow for dividing the process of production into several small steps. Due to extensive division of labor, firms in districts can even make economical use of highly specialized production factors, although they might be difficult to purchase or maintain in the first place.[68] Ultimately, these effects lead to internal and external economies that mutually reinforce each other. **Specialized manufacturers** of intermediate goods are able to operate at

63 Marshall (1920), p. 277.
64 See Rocha (2004), p. 369.
65 See Marshall (1920), p. 271.
66 Marshall (1920), p. 271.
67 Marshall (1920), p. 272.
68 See Marshall (1920), p. 271.

higher capacity, while supplying industrial districts with their specialized inputs.[69] This provides the scale needed for suppliers to further invest into refining and upgrading their skills and work for the productive advantage of the final manufacturers.[70]

Trust and a shared culture in industrial districts on the other hand, enhance the flow of technical knowledge among skilled workers and specialized suppliers creating an **industrial atmosphere**. It emerges "*in districts in which manufacturers have long been domiciled, a habit of responsibility, of carefulness and promptitude in handling expensive machinery and materials becomes the common property of all.*"[71] It represents the fertile ground for the development of new ideas and innovations that are taken up, upgraded, and then diffused by other members of the district. It is as "*the mysteries of the trade become no mysteries; but are as it were in the air.*"[72]

Similar processes are at work when it comes to the acquisition of **market related information** regarding products and services. For certain transactions potential buyers usually have to conduct personal research about suitable price-quality combinations. The required effort increases quickly, if the transactions are complex and/or non-standardized or if the buyer has not much time available. In these cases, personal contact and inspections are necessary to ensure a successful purchase. Yet, even for long-established supplier-buyer relations agglomerations can be beneficial. When production steps have to be frequently adjusted or are difficult to predict both sides rely on timely and effective contact. And the higher the number and intensity of required changes the more beneficial agglomerations become.[73]

Besides these economies, industrial districts also impose certain **external diseconomies** on their member firms such as higher wages and ground rents. In addition, industrial districts that depend mainly on one industry are in a constant threat of decline in case demand falls or supply runs out.[74] Therefore, Marshall favors industrial districts that are comprised of a variety of distinct industries as they increase their resilience against economic shocks.

Summing up, Marshall's biggest contribution was the notion that proximity generates significant efficiency advantages for SMEs, which enable them to profit from similar economies as large corporations. And secondly, by introducing the socio-cultural dimension of industrial districts he set the basis to analyze their non-economic dimension that has received so much attention since the New Industrial District School sparked renewed interest into the phenomena in the 1970s.[75]

---

69 See Hoover (1971), p. 78.

70 See Cortright (2006), p. 8.

71 Marshall (1920), p. 271.

72 Marshall (1920), p. 271.

73 See Marshall (1927), p. 285.

74 See Marshall (1920), p. 227. A modern example represents the automotive industry in Detroit, USA, which experienced a sharp decline in demand due to the economic crisis in 2008 followed by a massive restructuring of the whole sector and a partial takeover by the state.

75 See Rocha (2004), p. 369.

2.2.3 New Marshallian Industrial Districts

In the 1970s Italian scholars re-introduced Marshall's concept of industrial districts as a framework to explain the economic success of central and north east Italian regions. These regions, labeled by some as "*Third Italy*"[76], were home to a **large number of SMEs** specialized mainly in the higher-quality end market of light, labor-intensive industries such as clothing, textile, and furniture and related metalworking and machine tools sectors.[77] Although the majority of the firms were very small and partly employed less than ten workers, the share of their products in Italy's overall manufacturing export accounted for 27,7 % in 1977.[78] Due to their success in recessionary times, the concept was also applied to certain other regions in countries such as Germany, Denmark, Spain, and the USA.[79]

Although definitions of what exactly constitutes a Marshallian industrial district vary, some important recurring themes can be identified. These themes center (a) around the appropriate unit of analysis and (b) the complex mix between social, cultural, and institutional factors that facilitate trust and cooperation and curb excessive competition between actors in the district.[80]

According to Italian scholar Becattini, the success of the firm is deeply rooted in the territory and can thus not be analyzed without reference to its regional origin. He defines an industrial district as "*a socio-territorial entity which is characterized by the active presence of both a community of people and a population of firms in one naturally and historically bounded area.*"[81] Firms located in such districts profit from an industrial atmosphere, which was already noted by Marshall, and that constitutes their socio-economic dimension in which "*community and firms tend to emerge*"[82]. As a result, a shared set of common norms, values, and a body of knowledge links firms to one another and creates a balance between cooperation and competition. This is further extended by formal regional and local institutions that serve to resolve conflicts and provide real services to the large base of SMEs such as worker associations, technical schools, credit co-operatives, networks of local banks, and development agencies.[83] It is this **thick institutional context** which is seen as a key feature of industrial districts and which differentiates them from other forms of network production (see figure 8).

---

76 Brusco (1990), p. 13.

77 See Zeitlin (1992), p. 282.

78 See Amin (1989), p. 114.

79 For a comprehensive review see Sabel (1989).

80 See Whitford (2001), p. 40.

81 Becattini (1990), p. 38.

82 Becattini (1990), p. 38.

83 See Brusco (1992), p. 178 and Whitford (2001), pp. 41f.

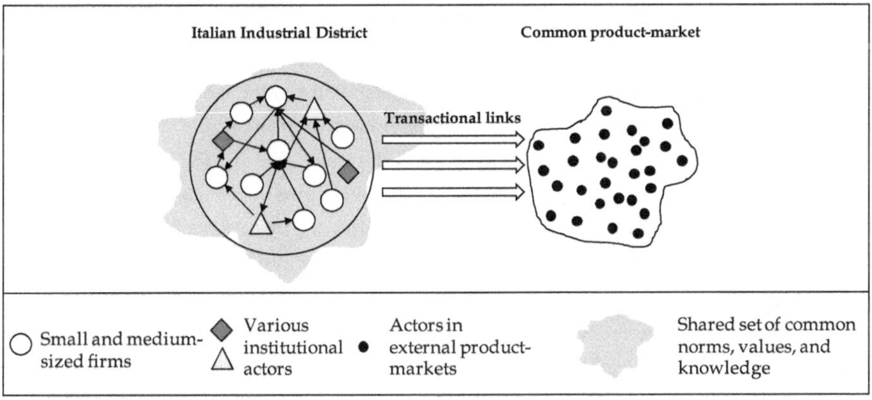

Figure 8 - The Italian Industrial District

Through a rich body of empirical examples and case studies several other structural characteristics have been identified:[84]

- An extensive division of specialized labor that serves a **common narrowly defined product-market** and which facilitates the exchange and integration of technical knowledge;
- The existence of an **information network** about supply and demand markets due to geographical proximity that contributes to convert individual knowledge to collective capabilities for the district as a whole;
- A **highly skilled workforce** which is the result of inter-generational transfer of knowledge and formal training at technical schools and larger firms.

Together these characteristics lead to a highly interdependent network between small and larger firms as well as between merchants who serve as middle-men responsible for marketing and distribution of intermediate and final goods. These networks, as Amin in his analysis notes, rely on intensive subcontracting between their actors based on short-term contracts. As a consequence, production runs are short and highly flexible, costs and risks can be spread out, and demand even for small batches of customized products can be met. Vertical disintegration introduces market mechanisms into the production process and forces firms to specialize, exploit economies of scale, cut costs, and allocate resources to places where they can be used most efficiently. It is this latter phenomenon, which is responsible for the co-existence of cooperation and competition within industrial districts.[85] The success of the district firms rests on their interdependence; one firm alone, regardless how competent it is, would not be able to achieve the maximum of economies possible. Therefore, Becattini ar-

84 See Asheim (2000), p. 418.

85 See Amin (1989), pp. 115ff.

gues that the proper unit of analysis should not longer be the single firm, but the industrial district as a whole.[86]

With their rich empirical and theoretical revival of Marshall's initial work, the New Marshallian Industrial District School provided three main **contributions** to the literature on clusters.[87] First, it extended the focus of analysis from the individual firm to the community of firms. Second, the success of the district and its member firms relies not only on economic and financial factors, but also on socio-cultural ones. Third, firms are deeply embedded into their regional context and therefore need to be capable to tap into and exploit their economic potential.

A major **weakness** of the concept however, is the fact that its theoretical insights are heavily dependent on the Italian example, its complex historical and cultural roots, the dominance of a vast number of SMEs, and its focus on traditional craft based industries. These shortcomings significantly limit the generalization and application of the New Marshallian District School's insights to other contexts such as countries that show a strong tendency to more competitive norms of economic behavior or advanced and innovative high-tech industries.[88] This inability triggered the emergence of the Californian School of Thought, which based its premises on a general theory of the firm.

2.2.4 The Californian School

The second School of Thought that emerged in the 1980s was the Californian School.[89] It focused its attention on successful technology districts in southern and central California that were comprised of geographically concentrated, specialized, and vertically disintegrated networks of firms and institutions. Due to the very different institutional environment in these regions, this school chose a different theoretical perspective in explaining the existence of these districts, namely through a transaction cost based analysis.

The main argument rests on the assumption that certain external factors give rise to increased uncertainty, which is met by **externalization of production steps** to minimize the risk of creating overcapacity and to maximize the benefits of specialization. **Vertical disintegration** of production leads in turn to an increased number of external transactions based on input-output relations. Under specific circumstances these transactions are more frequent, less predictable, and more complex leading to an increase in transaction costs. Geographical distance also increases costs and at some point the feasibility of vertical disintegration diminishes. Yet, **flexible production systems** such as the just-in-time or product customization concepts require a dense set of inter-firm links between selected sets of producers.[90] This en-

86 See Becattini (1989), p. 123ff.

87 See Rocha (2004), p. 372 and Bahlmann/Huysmann (2008), p. 308.

88 See Storper (1997), pp. 7f.

89 The main representatives of this School of Thought are Scott (1988), Scott/Storper (1992), and Storper (1997).

90 See Storper/Allen (1989), p. 26.

courages agglomeration, which is the result of firms' pursuit to reduce transaction costs, and subsequently increases the advantages of flexibility, risk minimization, and specialization (see figure 9).[91] These advantages are external economies, because they lower input costs and increase the probability of successful sales and purchases within the regional network of firms.

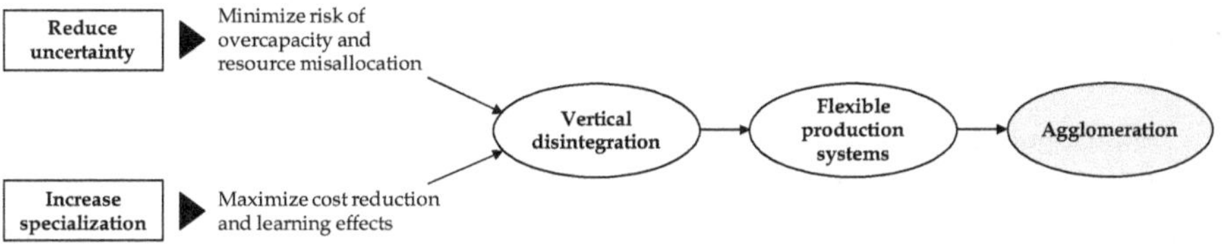

Figure 9 - Core logic of the Californian School

The fact that the Californian School based its analysis on a general theory of the firm leads to a greater coverage of the model and represents a major extension to the Marshallian Industrial District School. It allows the inclusion of firms of all sizes, different sectors including the services industry, and regions of different historical and institutional contexts. Yet, a major weakness of this approach is its focus on measurable **traded interdependencies**. As Storper himself, a major representative of the Californian School, acknowledges, in some instances *"the direct local input-output relationships between firms are not dense enough to account for either the size of the agglomerations or for a high proportion of what goes on in the sector."*[92]

This is particularly evident in the case of the San Francisco Bay area, a region that encompasses Silicon Valley and that is known for being home to a large array of knowledge intensive high-technology sectors. In a survey among small high-tech firms Oakey, Rothwell, and Cooper found that more than 45 % and 70 % of their respondents acquired their inputs and sold their products primarily outside their home region, respectively. This led them to conclude, that the cost advantages of intraregional input-output links are not the only reasons for locating in these clusters.[93] To account for the additional effects, Storper introduced the concept of **untraded interdependencies**. That is, region-specific socially constructed assets such as conventions, norms, and informal rules that are responsible for most of the transaction cost savings generated through clusters.[94] Under this institutional regime firms learn about each other's habits and capabilities over time and this learning substitutes to some extent the need for hierarchical coordination. Any free-rider or defector, that violates these

---

91 See Storper (1997), p. 9.

92 Storper (1997), p. 12.

93 See Oakey/Rothwell/Cooper (1988), pp. 68f. This modest impact of input-output linkages on geographical clustering has also been shown by Erikson's (1974) and Pred's (1976) studies of older industrial regions as well as Chapman and Walker's (1987) study on high-technology production spaces.

94 See Storper (1997), p. 5.

unwritten codes of conduct, faces the risk of punishment and exclusion from the community together with the associated economic costs.[95]

Using the motion picture industry of Los Angeles as an example, Storper was able to show how trust and experience regulate repeated transactions among firms and significantly reduce the likelihood of opportunistic behavior. As a result, these institutionalized norms and conventions determine what constitutes good behavior and "*make possible levels of vertical and horizontal disintegration that would not be possible in the presence of other sorts of actions frameworks*".[96]

Again, the purely economic perspective, which is manifested in the transaction cost based analysis, is augmented by the analysis of untraded interdependencies to grasp the socio-cultural factors of technology districts. So, the Californian School came "*full circle to rejoin the initial authors of the flexible-specialization thesis (and the Marshallian theme of 'atmosphere')*."[97]

What remains is the fact that the Californian School contributed to extend the model of agglomerations, industrial districts, and clusters beyond the Italian example. It showed not only how the externalization of economic activities leads to dense inter-firm networks, which give rise to untraded interdependencies, but also how exactly this industrial atmosphere contributes to the efficiency of its member firms.

2.2.5 Porter's Competitiveness School

Porter's concept of clusters draws heavily on his competitive strategy framework in which he explains how firms and nations through their respective industries can achieve and sustain competitive advantage.[98] It is through this perspective that Porter "accidently discovered" clusters as a valuable research avenue. Based on his studies on "*The Competitive Advantages of Nations*"[99], Porter identified clusters as main drivers of a nation's competitiveness.[100] Accordingly, in his subsequent work he repeatedly centers his arguments on the themes of competitiveness, productivity, and upgrading.[101] Competition, Porter argues, imposes pressure on firms and forces them to constantly upgrade their activities and innovate in order to stay ahead of their rivals. Clusters are central to firms and nations, because they enhance their competitiveness, that is, their economic success relative to their rivals.[102] Therefore, it is essential to first understand his approach to competition, strategy, and competitive advantage before turning to a detailed discussion of his conceptualization of the cluster phenomenon.

---

95 See Storper/Allen (1989), p. 30.

96 Storper (1997), p. 101.

97 See Storper (1997), p. 11.

98 See Caves/Porter (1977); Porter (1980); Porter (1985); Porter (1991).

99 See Porter (1990).

100 See Porter (1990), p. 152.

101 Porter (1991), p. 111.

102 See Porter (1991), p. 96.

Porter's Approach to Competition

Central to Porter's competitive strategy framework is his view that the sources of competitive advantage lie outside the firm, that is, in the structure of its industry. The industry structure itself is perceived as being constant and shaped by five competitive forces, which define its relative attractiveness.[103] The firm on the other hand is defined as a bundle of value activities, which determine its cost structure and ability to create value.[104] A firm's performance is the result of how a firm utilizes its value activities to gain a favorable position within its industry compared to its competitors. The better the firm's position, the higher is its competitiveness, for it can realize competitive advantages and gain monopoly rents. A favorable position can arise either from cost advantages or from the firm's ability to differentiate itself from its competitors and demand a premium price for its products and services that exceeds the additional costs. For Porter, **strategy is a configuration of value activities** aiming at creating competitive advantage based on differentiation or low cost where much *"depends on a sophisticated understanding of industry structure."*[105] Successful implementation of value activities, however, is costly and requires tangible and intangible assets such as capital, technologies, and human resources as well as information, knowledge, and skills.[106] Clusters, then, represent an attractive opportunity to increase the productivity and innovative capacity of a firm's value activities, because they *"help any company in any industry to compete in the most sophisticated ways."*[107] Therefore, the next section discusses in detail Porter's view on clusters.

Porter's Cluster Concept

Given his theoretical background, it is not surprising that for Porter *"much of competitive advantage lies outside a given company or even outside its industry, residing instead in the locations of its business units."*[108] What is new, however, is the latter part in his statement. In this new way of thinking competition is dynamic and does not longer take place on a local, but on a much broader, global scale. While globalization has rendered comparative advantages in labor and capital almost obsolete, it increased the importance of innovation and productivity for the competitiveness of firms, industries, and even whole nations. From this perspective, links to buyers, suppliers, and institutions, all of which are intensely local, are decisive to create new skills and capabilities to improve and upgrade.[109] Hence, competitiveness depends as much on the local business environment as it does on managerial choices and the sophistication of

103 These five forces are the power of suppliers and buyers, the threat of substitutes and new entrants, and industry rivalry (see Porter (1980), p. 4).

104 See Porter (1985), p. 37.

105 Porter (1991), p. 104.

106 See Porter (1991), p. 102.

107 Porter (1998a), p. 86.

108 Porter (2000a), p. 254.

109 See Porter (1990), p. 158.

company operations[110]: "*The environment shapes how activities are configured, which resources can be assembled uniquely, and what commitments can be made successfully.*"[111]

This **business environment** is created through six attributes that have the greatest influence on a firm's ability to innovate and upgrade and which converge in what he calls the "*diamond*"[112]. The diamond shapes "*the information firms have available to perceive opportunities, the pool of inputs, skills and knowledge they can draw on, the goals that condition investment, and the pressures in firms to act.*"[113]

The most **important country specific attributes** are factor and demand conditions, related and supporting industries, and firm strategy, structure and rivalry (see figure 10). *Factor conditions* comprise human, capital, and natural resources as well as infrastructure. The presence, quality, and specialization of these factors results in improved productivity. Innovative *related and supporting industries* facilitate transfer of knowledge between firms and also positively influence productivity. *Demand conditions* are characterized by local presence of sophisticated and advanced buyers who continuously stimulate innovations. And finally, *firm strategy and competition* force companies to produce innovations and improve their productivity. Further influences on the environment for competitive advantage within clusters are *chance events* and *government*.

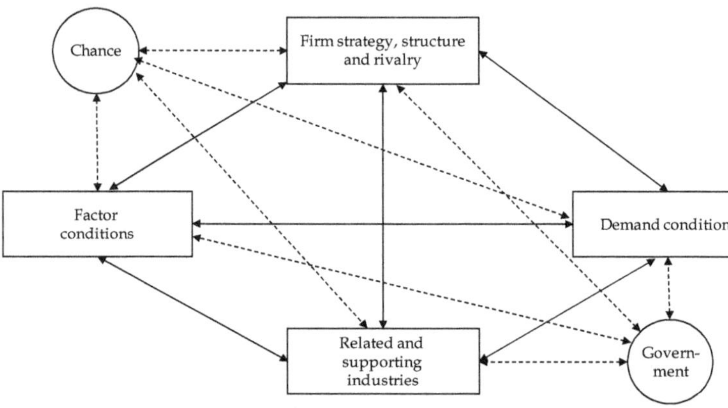

Figure 10 - The diamond of national competitive advantage
(Source: Porter (1990), p. 127)

For Porter, the diamond constitutes a dynamic system. The attributes are mutually reinforcing: positive effects of one determinant depend on the state of others.[114] Geographical con-

110 See Porter (1998a), p. 80.
111 Porter (1991), p. 110.
112 Porter (1990), p. 72.
113 Porter (1991), p. 111.
114 See Porter (1990), pp. 144ff.

centration in clusters enhances these effects and amplifies the pressures on firms to innovate and upgrade. Moreover, for Porter *"a cluster is the manifestation of the diamond at work."*[115] In this way, clusters improve the productivity of their members firms, increase their innovation capability, and stimulate the creation of new ventures.[116]

These benefits are also the key determinants for the **formation of clusters**. Once the diamond facilitates the establishment of a successful industry, it's mutually reinforcing process helps to develop other related and supporting industries through the provision of technology, skills, and demand. The benefits of clusters spread downstream and upstream within and horizontally across industries. Spin-offs and new entrants from other industries increase rivalry and stimulate upgrading through R&D and the introduction of new skills. Knowledge and information tend to move more freely and innovations diffuse throughout the cluster. Links among suppliers, buyers, and institutions help entrepreneurs identify new opportunities and diversify into new industries. Once a critical mass is achieved, the cluster development accelerates by attracting highly skilled talent and the attention of government institutions. Then the economy's resources start to flow towards the cluster and away from less developed and/or isolated locations. This process is further strengthened as the cluster gets exposed to international competition, because the more industries achieve a favorable global position the more sustainable their competitive advantages become.[117]

On the other hand, the diamond may also work in reverse. **Clusters decline** when upgrading and innovation are no longer supported due to external chance events or internal rigidities that undermine local rivalry. For example, inward-looking cluster participants can develop a groupthink that results in competitive inertia. Governments can harm clusters as well by suspending or intervening in competition. For Porter, competition is so essential to a cluster's long-term success that he develops a somewhat simplistic view on the advantages of competition; competition in Porter's view seems always to be good even if its leads to failure of some firms: *"Though some local rivals may go bankrupt and some mergers and consolidation may take place, the process of local rivalry produces stronger survivors."*[118] Therefore, firms and governments should try everything to maintain a competitive environment.[119]

This is also one of the main reasons why Porter, although generally acknowledging the importance of cooperation and socio-cultural factors, treats them more or less only on a side note when compared to his extensive discussion of the economic and more competitive dimensions of clusters. While cooperation does and should take place in clusters, especially between buyers and suppliers, he cautions against too much of it: *"No firm can depend on another firm for skills and assets that are central to its competitive advantage. If it does, the firm runs*

115 Porter (2000b), p. 21.
116 See Porter (1998a), p. 80.
117 See Porter (1990), pp. 149ff.
118 Porter (1990), p. 119.
119 See Porter (1998a), p. 85.

a grave risk of losing its competitive advantage in the long run."[120] Instead, cooperation in clusters is better pursuit through informal networks based on personal face-to-face meetings.[121]

After reviewing the Schools of Thought that precede Porter's cluster concept in the previous sections, one has to agree with vom Hofe and Chen that it is "*more a synopsis of accepted agglomeration phenomena rather than new groundbreaking insights explaining the reasons for firms to group in space.*"[122] On the one hand, his work clearly mirrors Marshall in his notion on the specialization advantages of clusters.[123] On the other hand, the emphasis on the remaining economic factors can already be found in Scott's and Storper's early work on new industrial spaces and technology districts.[124] Furthermore, his later writings on the network dimension of clusters reflect a central theme in the literature on New Marshallian Industrial Districts and the Italian School of Thought. Nevertheless, with his writings on national competitive advantages and competitiveness, Porter brought the notion of geographical concentrations and clusters into the mainstream of economics and business literature. Although his concept is more intuitive and largely centers on what can already be found in the literature, his work is still worth reviewing because it had so much influence on academics, practitioners, and governments alike.

2.2.6 Krugman's New Economic Geography

The second School of Thought that falls into the economic stream of clusters is Krugman's New Economic Geography.[125] Recognizing that the most striking feature of the geography of economic activity is concentration[126], Krugman sets out to explain this phenomenon through the effect of **increasing returns**. They occur due to economies of specialization and scale at the plant level. These scale economies, which are rooted in Marshall's external economies, affect firms of all kind and motivate producers to specialize and concentrate geographically. In addition, transport costs for transactions that happen across space force producers to locate close to demand and supply markets. Once a region develops a comparative advantage against other regions, favorable conditions lead to uneven, self-reinforcing patterns of economic activity, market dominance, and specialization.[127] Without increasing returns, Krugman argues, producers would have no incentive to concentrate their activities at one location. Instead, they would supply their target markets from many local plants, for an extension of the market would have no influence on their returns to scale.[128]

---

120 See Porter (1990), p. 613.

121 See Porter (1998a), p. 81.

122 vom Hofe/Chen (2006), p. 14.

123 See Marshall (1920).

124 See for example Scott (1988) and Storper/Allen (1989).

125 See for example Krugman (1991a); Krugman (1991b); Krugman (1998); Krugman (2000).

126 See Krugman (1991b), p. 5.

127 See Krugman (1991b), p. 98.

128 See Krugman (1998), p. 10.

Besides these **centripetal factors**, Krugman also introduces **centrifugal factors** (see table 4). Differences in factor endowments, increased land rents, and congestion costs tend to oppose geographical concentration. Otherwise, as he notes, we would *"all live in one big city."*[129] It is due to these differences in economic patterns that producers within and across nations tend to specialize in the production of certain goods and that lead to national and international trade. In this sense, geographical agglomerations and clusters do not only profit from the ongoing globalization process, but also serve as one of its most important drivers.

Centripetal factors	Centrifugal factors
• Economies of scale	• Differences in factor endowments
• Economies of specialization	• Increased land rents
• Reduced transportation costs	• Congestion costs
• Market size effects	
• Labor markets	

Table 4 - Factors affecting geographical concentration

A clear contribution of Krugman's efforts is the explanation and mathematical formalization of why production and labor can be found clustered in particular places. Yet, as a downside of his rigorously formalized models he deliberately ignores other important factors such as the socio-cultural dimensions and technological spillovers among firms. He emphasizes that they *"are invisible; they leave no paper trail by which they may be measured and tracked"*[130] and therefore dismisses them as assumptions that can and should not be modeled.

To give further support to his argument, Krugman examines the location pattern of new and traditional industries in the USA. His analysis reveals that not only are high-tech industries clustered in regions such as Silicon Valley and Boston's route 128, but that so are many other more traditional industries like automotive in Detroit and *"low technology industries"*[131] like textile in the Piedmont area. Assuming that a shared culture and spillovers are not important for these kinds of industries Krugman concludes that *"whatever drives industries to concentrate in one place, it is not solely a matter of technological spillovers."*[132] However, the previous remarks on the success of Third Italy's industrial districts and the notion of untraded interdependencies clearly serve to dismiss Krugman's argument as even "low technology industries" profit greatly from socio-cultural effects.[133]

Yet, despite the fact that his models fail to acknowledge the importance of the "softer" factors, Krugman is nevertheless able to show that even with falling transportation costs and

129 Krugman (1998), p. 8.

130 Krugman (1998), p. 53.

131 Krugman (1998), p. 59.

132 Krugman (1998), p. 59.

133 This fact is even more disturbing as Krugman himself shows that under certain conditions expectations, conventions, and boosterism can play a significant part in regional development by leading to irrational self-fulfilling prophecies (see Krugman (1998), pp. 30f.; Krugman (1991c), p. 651; Martin/Sunley (1996), p. 273).

reduced trade barriers geographical agglomerations and clusters still matter.[134] And it is from this perspective that his contributions should be valued.

2.2.7 Geography of Innovation

Unlike the previous Schools of Thought, the representatives of the Geography of Innovation are less interested in why geographical concentrations of firms exist and how they form in the first place. Instead, they focus their research exclusively on **knowledge spillovers** and their impact on the innovation process.[135] Although this school extensively studies the phenomenon of knowledge spillovers, there is no clear definition of what exactly constitutes them. Implicitly it is assumed that knowledge represents a truly public good. This means that once a firm generates new knowledge it is not able to completely appropriate it. Due to spillover effects, knowledge tends to leak out and thereby enables other firms to access and make use of it. This process of appropriating another firm's knowledge is furthermore assumed to be largely costless and effortless.[136]

The Geography of Innovation School emerged as a direct critique to Krugman. As brought up earlier, he argues that economists should abandon research about knowledge spillovers as they leave no paper trail. Challenging this, representatives of the Geography of Innovation disagree, because *"knowledge flows do sometimes leave a paper trail, in the firm of citations."*[137]

Thereby, the Geography of Innovation resorts to a widely used classification of different types of knowledge that was developed by Polanyi. He distinguished between codified/explicit and tacit knowledge. **Codified knowledge** involves know-how that is easily transmittable between two or more actors using formal communication artifacts such as spoken or written language. It does not require direct experience and interaction and can easily be transmitted over long distances. **Tacit knowledge** on the other hand, cannot be communicated in any codified way. Its transfer requires direct interaction between actors in the form of informal take-up and learned/observed behavior and procedures (see figure 11).[138] Tacit knowledge is therefore deeply embodied in and non-separable of individual agents, groups of agents, and firm's processes and routines.

---

134 See Armstrong/Taylor (2000), p. 138.

135 See the studies of Jaffe/Trajtenberg/Henderson (1993); Audretsch/Feldman (1996); Gilbert/McDougall/Audretsch (2008); Tappeiner/Hauser/Walde (2008); McCann/Folta (2011) as main representatives of this School of Thought.

136 See Howells (2002), pp. 874f.

137 Jaffe/Trajtenberg/Henderson (1993), p. 578.

138 See Polyanyi (1967), pp. 12ff.

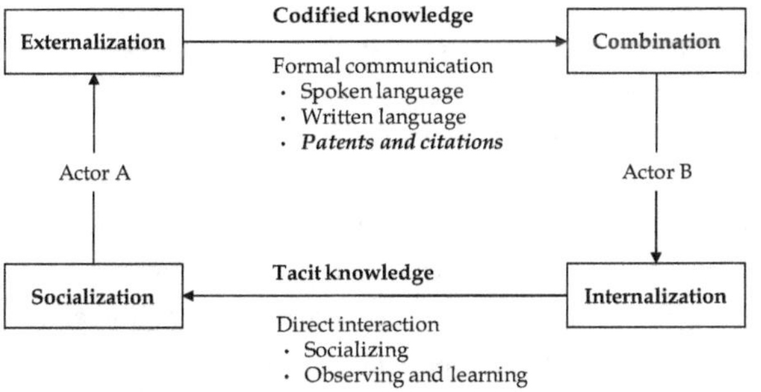

Figure 11 - The process of knowledge transmission

And it is this characteristic of tacit knowledge on what the main argument of the Geography of Innovation rests. Tacit knowledge, it is said, is so deeply embedded in the situational, social, and institutional context of its production that its transmission cannot completely occur outside of it. This then serves as main rationale to argue that agents need to be geographically close to transfer tacit knowledge between each other as proximity is a condition for sufficiently frequent and intense direct interaction.[139]

Since knowledge spillovers cannot be directly observed, the Geography of Innovation School employs proxies to indirectly measure their existence and effect. By using econometric methods of analysis, two main methods can be distinguished.

The first type of studies uses an **innovation production function**, which relates expenditures in public and private R&D to innovation output measures such as patents or innovation counts:

$$I_{si} = IRD^{ß_1} * UR_{s_i}^{ß_2} * \epsilon_{si}$$

where

- *I* is the measure of innovative output,
- *IRD* is private corporate expenditures on R&D,
- *UR* is the research expenditures undertaken at universities, and
- β_1 and β_2 indicate the elasticity of the innovation output with respect to corporate and university research expenditures.[140]

A distinction is then made between inputs which come from outside and those that come from inside of a given geographical observation unit. Significant differences in the above parameters are then interpreted in favor for or against the existence of knowledge spillovers. Using patent data from US states, Jaffe for example found that patents occur more often in

139 See Breschi/Lissoni (2001), p. 980.

140 Values of e.g. $\beta_1 = 1$ and $\beta_2 = 2$ would indicate that the innovation production function exhibits constant returns to scale and increasing returns to scale of corporate and university R&D expenditures, respectively.

those states, where public and private R&D expenditures were the greatest.[141] In addition, Audretsch and Feldman by using US-based data that provides direct measures of industries' innovative activities show that geographical concentration of the innovation output is positively related to the R&D intensity of the industry. According to the authors, this reveals the *"propensity for innovative activity to cluster spatially."*[142] Further studies with similar results include the work of Acs, Audretsch, and Feldman as well as Feldman and Florida among others.[143] As Feldman puts it, the basic conclusion derived from these studies is that *"geographic regions with greater amounts of knowledge-generating inputs produce more innovation."*[144]

The second type of studies makes use of **patent citations** as an instrument of transferring codified knowledge (see figure 11). It explores the temporal and geographic influence of a patented innovation on other patented innovations. It does so by linking an originating patent to other patents that reference or cite it. The most influential studies tracked direct codified knowledge flows between academic research institutions and firms' R&D output.

Jaffe, Trajtenberg, and Henderson for example in a cross-industry comparison found that innovative firms are more likely to quote research from nearby universities than from similar universities elsewhere.[145] A similar study was carried out by Almeida and Kogut within the semiconductor industry in which the authors came to the same conclusion thereby strengthening the evidence that firms tend to pay more attention to the research of nearby universities.[146] Comparable results have also been reached in the studies of Maurseth and Verspagen as well as Verspagen and Schoenmakers. These authors count the numbers of citations between pairs of regions and then estimate an econometric model where these counts are related to the geographic distance between these regions. The results show that the number of cross-citations drops as the distance increases.[147]

All of these studies as well as the growing body of subsequent research that is based on the same or similar methods provide significant evidence that innovative performance is indeed geographically concentrated. However, what they do not prove despite their claim is the existence of knowledge spillovers as a truly public good, because *"there is no understanding of the way in which spillovers occur and are realized at the geographic level."*[148]

Building on this limitation, Breschi and Lissoni have articulated the most sophisticated **critique** of the Geography of Innovation School. It centers on the notion of knowledge spillovers *"as if it could encompass any kind of localized knowledge flows, no matter whether such flows are the outcome of economic transactions, free sharing agreements or some agents' failure to appropriate the*

141 See Jaffe (1989), p. 968.
142 Audretsch/Feldman (1996), p. 638.
143 See Acs et al. (1994); Feldman/Florida (1994).
144 Feldman (2000), p. 378.
145 See Jaffe/Trajtenberg/Henderson (1993), p. 595.
146 Almeida/Kogut Bruce (1997), p. 28.
147 See Maurseth/Verspagen (2002), p. 542 and Verspagen/Schoenmakers (2000), p. 17.
148 Feldman (2000), p. 378.

outcome of their innovation efforts."[149] The authors argue that, instead of being a public good flying freely around in their air, even tacit knowledge requires specific channels in order to be transmitted and that these channels depend on traded interdependencies and pecuniary externalities. Inter-firm mobility of highly skilled employees, for example, can be restricted by firms providing incentives to their employees to stay or simply by prohibiting their star-employees to become employed by nearby firms, whether they are competitors, suppliers, or former clients. In addition, unless a sharing agreement has been put in place that motivates employees to offer their knowledge to colleagues, knowledge remains a private good. Furthermore, the authors caution against the conclusion made by patent cross-citation studies regarding the university-firm linkage because in reality *"much of knowledge transmitted from universities to firms has nothing to do with the public results of basic science, but consists of consultancy services to firms."*[150] Therefore, what might first appear as knowledge spillovers of a public good type depend more often on trade interdependencies between cluster agents.

Despite its significant shortcomings, the Geography of Innovation School has convincingly shown that (1) innovation tends to cluster and (2) that it is more frequent in those regional concentrations of firms where the presence of a sophisticated learning infrastructure such as universities and R&D laboratories is the greatest. Its main shortcoming, however, is its inability to explain why innovative activity shows the observed location pattern. It is here that the two remaining Schools of Thoughts have contributed the most to the literature on clusters.

2.2.8 The Innovative Milieu School

The Innovative Milieu School was founded by the *"Groupe de Recherche Européen sure les Milieux Innovateurs"* (GREMI); a group of scholars rooted in economics and the social sciences.[151] The starting point of their inquiries was the question what differentiates competitive and innovative regions from less successful ones. Early on, this group hypothesized that there is *"'something', localized on the regional level, [that] made it possible to understand why certain regions were more dynamic than others."*[152]

Henceforth, the discussion centered on the role of the **territory** in the innovation process of the firm. The term "territory" is often interchangeably used with the term "region" and expresses the view that it is more than just the locus of economic activity. Instead, a territory is created through interaction between individual and groups of economic agents and the space in which they live/act.[153] These agents comprise industrial and service firms, financial

149 Breschi/Lissoni (2001), p. 976.

150 Breschi/Lissoni (2001), p. 994.

151 See Aydalot/Keeble (1988); Camagni (1991a); Ratti/Bramanti/Gordon (1997); Crevoisier (2004) as main representatives of this School of Thought.

152 Crevoisier (2004), p. 368 in reference to the early work of Aydalot (1986) and Aydalot/Keeble (1988) (emphasis added in the original).

153 See Bramanti/Ratti (1997), pp. 4f; Quévit/van Doren (1997), p. 348.

institutes, research and training centers, industry and trade associations, as well as political authorities and administrations. Territories generate resources through the economic activity of their agents that are necessary for innovations, i.e. labor, machinery, infrastructure, know how, etc., for example through various training and research activities as well as supporting institutions that are located in the territory.[154]

Territories, which beyond these "hard factors" encompass a community with similar cultural values, conventions, a collective identity, and a mindset of mutual assistance that pushes its agents towards innovation, are defined as **innovative milieus**. To illustrate this latter point, Maillat et al. for example define an innovative milieu as "*a territorialized, outwardly-open complex which incorporates know-how, rules and a relational capital. It is attached to a collection of players and to human and material resources. It is by no means a closed world; on the contrary, it is constantly interacting with its environment.*"[155] Bramanti and Ratti on the other hand define it as "*a territorialized whole, in which the interactions of economic and local agents develop, by learning, from multilateral transactions which generate externalities specific to innovation, by the convergence of learning on more and more advanced forms of common resource management.*"[156]

These definitions serve as representatives for the concept of an innovative milieu as they encompass its **constituting dimensions**:[157]

- A territory as locus of innovation.
- A network of heterogeneous actors related to each other in this territory.
- A set of values and norms that coordinates the interaction between these actors.

The innovative milieu is essentially a context for economic development and renewal. It empowers and guides its agents to be able to coordinate their actions with other agents towards innovation. This is because for the Innovative Milieu School, innovation is fundamentally a complex and collective learning process. It takes place in networks of actors which are embedded in their milieu and that creatively utilize its resources, and the milieu provides the members of these networks with the know-how and resources they need for successful innovation. Therefore, the firm's innovation process can neither be seen as an individual process nor as independent from its territory/innovative milieu.[158] More precisely, it is supposed to take place in two stages (see figure 12).

---

154 See Crevoisier (2004), pp. 371f.

155 Maillat et al. (1997), p. 112.

156 Bramanti/Ratti (1997), p. 29.

157 See Cova/Mazet/Salle (1996), p. 654.

158 See Bramanti/Ratti (1997), p. 5.

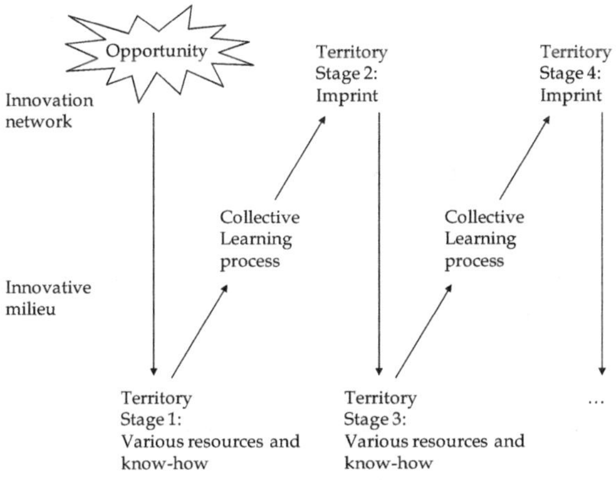

Figure 12 - Innovation process of innovative milieus
(Source: Adapted with changes from Crevoisier (2004), p. 373)

In the first stage, the firm perceives an economic opportunity that has gone unnoticed. To develop an innovation targeted at exploiting this opportunity, it must engage in an innovation network to mobilize the necessary resources that are located among the agents of the territory. Second, shared values and norms then serve as coordinating mechanisms to direct the innovation process towards the desired outcome. Once the project is completed and the project-based network resolved, the accumulated learning experiences of the individual agents become imprinted into the innovative milieu and this is how the milieu evolves and stays dynamic.[159]

Yet, although **spatiality** is a decisive element in this creative process and the notion of it is held to be important for understanding innovation, its definition is kept enormously vague: "*The spatiality of innovative milieus thus naturally includes physical space, institutional space, and the like, but it also includes the space of consciousness, space as it is perceived and experienced.*"[160] With such an arbitrary conceptualization one could ask how an innovative milieu should be identified in the first place. The answer lies in its definition: innovation occurs because of an innovative milieu, and a milieu is what exists in regions where there is innovation: "*A survey of innovative milieus begins with the – relatively easy – identification of the new products or technologies that have been developed in a region. The process then moves on to the networks and milieus.*"[161] This methodology, however, reveals a major flaw, because it does not identify the economic logic by which the resources and know-how, that are so important to the innovation process,

159 See Crevoisier (2004), pp. 373f.

160 Crevoisier (2004), p. 372.

161 Crevoisier (2004), p. 375.

are generated in the first place. Instead, as Storper notes, the Innovative Milieu School seems not to be able *"to specify the logic or content of the intangible they are after."*[162]

Yet, besides these shortcomings, the Innovative Milieu School provides an important alternative to the primarily economic views offered by the earlier Schools of Thought who view *"the local relationships mainly in terms of locational efficiency."*[163] In this way, it resembles the theory of flexible production and specialization. It also adds clarity to the arguments put forth by the New Marshallian Industrial District School about the importance of inter-firm networks. How economic agents pursue their goals and interact with each other, they argue, is ultimately a product of their local context. And the influence this local context has on its agents is likely to be increased in case of proximity. Therefore, in their pursuit of creating knowledge and resources individual firms have to engage in face-to-face contacts, social relations, and networks to foster innovation through collective local learning processes.[164]

2.2.9 Nordic School of Innovation and Learning

The Innovative Milieu School has also triggered and influenced the development of a variety of related concepts such as *"learning economies"*[165], *"regional systems of innovation"*[166], *"learning regions"*[167], and more broadly the evolution of a *"knowledge-based view on clusters"*[168]. These concepts have come to be known as the Nordic School of Innovation and Learning. It argues that today's economy is characterized by permanent change and the continuous erosion of competitive advantages. Therefore, innovation is seen as the most important factor to ongoing success as it renews the competitive base of the firm, while learning and the production of new knowledge represent its key processes. Innovation involves the synthesis and creation of different types of knowledge, most importantly informal and tacit knowledge. As a consequence, innovation cannot longer be seen as a linear process, where new technology develops as a linear function of new investment into the scientific base. Instead, as already shown by the Innovative Milieu School, innovation is a creative, disruptive, and interactive process that is enhanced by inter-firm relationships and that relies on a resource rich environment that facilitates trust and cooperation, i.e. learning regions or regional systems of innovation.[169]

Therefore, innovative actors strive to create a **knowledge infrastructure** that allows them to produce and transfer knowledge between each other in a more efficient way (see figure 13). A knowledge infrastructure may consist of intangible and physical institutions such as

---

162 Storper (1997), p. 17.

163 Camagni (1991b), p. 2.

164 See Maillat et al. (1997), pp. 135f.

165 Lundvall (1996).

166 Doloreux (2002); Lundvall et al. (2002).

167 Florida (1995).

168 Maskell (2001); Bathelt/Malmberg/Maskell (2004); Bahlmann/Huysmann (2008).

169 See Lundvall et al. (2002), pp. 218f.

norms, rules, and habits as well as public or private research organizations, universities, science and technology parks, and national laboratories.[170] It generates a favorable local and institutional environment that fosters informal personal contacts and that leads to the geographical concentration of innovators in clusters.[171]

Clusters of innovative firms are therefore important manifestations of learning regions and regional systems of innovation. **Geographical proximity** it is argued, allows firms to exchange tacit and informal knowledge more easily as dense relationships between suppliers and buyers foster trust and cooperation. Second, it not only increases the speed of communication between firms, but also its quality as firms that cooperate with each other on a long-term basis are more likely to share sensitive information. Third, proximity also reduces cultural and social insecurities and misunderstandings. Firms in the same locality are more likely to share the same mental models, a common language, and cultural background, which reduce linguistic and organizational constraints to communication. Thus, proximity increases the likelihood that communicated messages will be correctly transmitted and decoded by the receiver.[172]

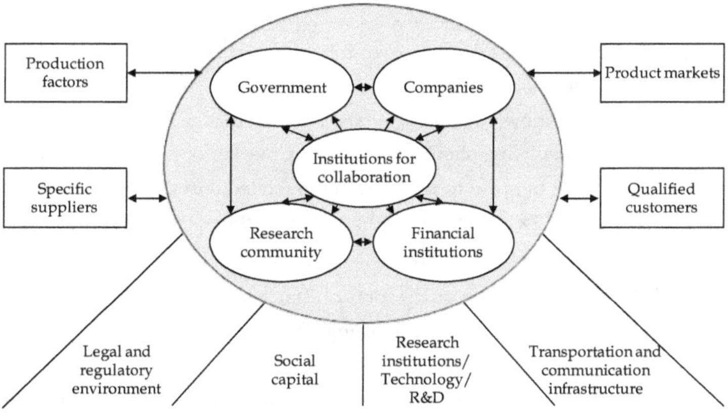

Figure 13 - Example of a regional system of innovation
(Source: Morschett/Schramm-Klein/Zentes (2009), p. 119)

More specifically, Maskell has shown how learning and the production of new knowledge takes place in clusters along the horizontal dimension consisting of firms with similar capabilities and the vertical dimension consisting of firms with complementary capabilities.

170 See Florida (1995), pp. 532f. The notion of a knowledge infrastructure clearly resembles the main idea behind the Geography of Innovation and Innovative Milieu School.

171 See Rocha (2004), p. 376.

172 See Doloreux (2002), pp. 250f.

Along the **horizontal dimension** firms are engaged in similar activities and find themselves often in competing and rival relationships that constrain potentials for direct inter-firm co-operation. Hence, horizontal learning happens indirectly and mainly through observation, comparison, imitation, and variation. Geographical proximity serves as a facilitator of these activities as it creates a communal social culture with similar beliefs, conventions, and values of success. It also eliminates any static advantages firms might gain from different locations such as factor costs or access to a large local market. This encourages firms to directly compare their performance with each other and to find innovative ways to produce new knowledge that successfully differentiates them from their local rivals. One reason why clusters exist, so the argument goes, is because they allow firms to *"monitor each other constantly, closely and almost without effort or cost."*[173] This argument strongly resembles Porter and is at the core of his concept of rivalry.[174]

The **vertical dimension** on the other hand, deals with the type of learning that takes place within the direct input-output relations of suppliers, buyers, and service providers. The key mechanism behind the vertical learning process is vertical disintegration and has already been discussed in the context of the New Marshallian Industrial District and the Californian School. Geographic proximity lowers the costs of input-output relations within the vertical dimension and as these relations develop over time they encourage increased specialization. This in turn creates differences in the knowledge stocks of the specialized actors. Ongoing production of specialized knowledge only serves to widen this gap and as a result firms tend to hold asymmetrical knowledge about products and market opportunities. Firms then engage in inter-firm learning in order to profit from the related, but different knowledge stocks of other cluster members. This then serves to reinforce the specialization process and the achievement of higher levels of knowledge.[175]

Although the oversimplified conceptualization of "tacit knowledge = local" and "codified knowledge = global" seems to be very appealing in explaining the cluster phenomenon, it has not been without critiques. Breschi and Lissoni in their previously mentioned meta-study about knowledge transfer in local innovation systems find that firms are not tied to their local environment when it comes to learning from their main competitors. The reviewed studies show that firms are able to substitute missing tacit knowledge by employing a wide array of mechanisms that have not necessarily anything to do with geographical proximity such as reverse engineering, patent disclosures, trade journals, and fairs. Furthermore, managers rated independent R&D activities as the most effective means of learning about competitors' new technologies.[176] In another study, which was more focused on the tacit-codified distinction of knowledge, Audretsch and Stephan studied the links between biotechnology

173 Maskell (2001), p. 930.

174 See Porter (1998a), p. 119.

175 See Maskell (2001), pp. 930ff.

176 See Breschi/Lissoni (2001), pp. 996f.

firms and the university-based scientists they employed to carry out their scientific research. The authors found that 70 % of these links are non-local. This means that the vast majority of codified and tacit knowledge that is used in innovations is transferred via formal arrangements that do not depend on geographical proximity.[177]

In summary, these studies point indeed to the fact that geographical proximity can and should not be seen as the unique source of tacit knowledge as the latter is not as immobile and confined to the local as it is often suggested. Instead, as demonstrated throughout the earlier chapters of this work, one should look at the tacit dimension of knowledge as being person-embodied, context-dependent, and socially accessible only through direct physical interaction. As pointed out by Morgan, this makes it to some degree spatially sticky, because *"something gets lost, or degraded, when individuals and organizations communicate at a distance, even when they know each other very well."*[178] Therefore, geographical proximity matters when knowledge transfer requires the need to access a localized pool of skilled labor and expertise or to establish transaction-intensive relationships with specialized suppliers and customers. On the other hand, when the need for face-to face contacts is not high enough as to require co-localization or when knowledge can be transmitted through formal arrangements such as contractual networks, joint ventures (JVs), and acquisitions proximity appears to be less important.[179]

At this point and after reviewing those Schools of Thought that had the biggest impact on the cluster discourse, several recurring themes emerge that tend to be most relevant to understand the essentials of the cluster concept. Before this study continues to discuss the effect of clusters on firm performance, the following section will provide a meaningful definition of clusters that is based on the insights gained so far.

2.3 Towards a Meaningful Definition of Clusters

Today's understanding of clusters has come a long way. Since Marshall's seminal work it has inherited a variety of theoretical explanations, rival and opposing views, complementary insights, and an extensive body of empirical work. This builds up to a somewhat chaotic picture in studies about clusters, because different concepts are treated as they were only one, i.e. clusters. This lack of a precise definition makes it increasingly difficult to compare findings with each other as the underlying operationalizations are likely to differ across studies. In order to advance the field and to avoid that the cluster discourse continues to exhaust itself in fruitless discussions that mix arguments and findings from different levels of analysis, it is essential to first develop a precise cluster definition. Only then it is possible to integrate findings from different studies and related fields into a meaningful cluster framework.

177 See Audretsch/Stephan (1996), p. 650.

178 Morgan (2004), p. 8.

179 See Breschi/Lissoni (2001), p. 998.

A conceptual cluster definition that serves this purpose has therefore to be (1) *conservative* in that it is not identical to other concepts, (2) *unique* in that it is not tautological, and (3) *parsimonious* to include only those elements that are the constituting characteristics of the concept under study.[180]

To start with, it is useful to focus on the key elements of clusters on which the previously discussed Schools of Thought agree. That is, (1) economic activity of firms and institutions from different fields tends to specialize and cluster geographically, (2) these actors are interrelated with each other, and (3) this is the precondition to build formal and informal links among each other in order to achieve their goals.

2.3.1.1 Geographic Proximity

The main insight regarding the importance of geographic proximity is that firms and institutions through their actions not only profit from the resources clusters have to offer, but also participate in producing new resources that then become imprinted into its geographic landscape. Geographic proximity is therefore a key dimension of clusters as it defines where local talent pools are located, where formal and informal communication links are established, where transaction-intensive relationships between suppliers, customers, and associated institutions are being built as well as where inter-firm networks engage in joint actions. Geographic proximity also increases the likelihood that cluster agents share a similar cultural background, which fosters mutual trust and understanding. A proper cluster definition has therefore to incorporate the geographical dimension.

It should, however, also be noted that there is again no clear consensus about the appropriate geographical distance around which cluster boundaries should be drawn. This is due to the fact that clusters vary in their size, degree of concentration, and geographical scope. Some clusters are located within city district while others stretch across two or more cities and national and state boundaries, while again others are confined to small or big metropolitan areas. Studies, which aim to identify clusters, have therefore used a variety of different **measures** to delineate their boundaries. Distances used include a range of one square mile[181], zip codes[182], metropolitan statistical areas (MSAs)[183], standard regions[184], and states[185]. It is important to note that all of these measures have their advantages and disadvantages (see table 5).

State measures have the simple advantage of data availability. Except for a few large and advanced countries such as the USA, Canada, and Denmark many others do not offer com-

180 See Wacker (2008), p. 9.

181 See Rosenthal/Strange (2003), p. 380.

182 See Canina/Enz/Harrison (2005), p. 571; Kukalis (2010), p. 463.

183 See Folta/Cooper/Baik (2006), p. 227; Gilbert/McDougall/Audretsch (2008), p. 412; McCann/Folta (2011), p. 110.

184 See Molina-Morales/Martinez-Fernandez (2009), p. 1017.

185 See Shaver/Flyer (2000), p. 1181.

prehensive data on the regional/provincial or city level. Therefore, it is not surprising when studies tend to use states as observation unit. The problem with this measure is that in general states, seen from a geographical standpoint, are simply too large to account for the benefits of clusters. This is especially true in studies that have focused on US states. While it is possible that firms in the state of New York may be able to tap into the same local talent pool, the same cannot hold true in a state such as Texas. It is highly unlikely that a potential employee on his search for work will be willing to commute between its northern and southern state border.

MSAs on the other hand have the advantage that they encompass a geographical region in which employers and employees share a common sphere of life. The downside, however, is that clusters are often not confined to artificially drawn metropolitan boundaries. While this method might identify a cluster within a MSA, it might as well not be able to recognize its full size simply because the cluster extends beyond its boundaries.

Conceptual boundary	Advantages	Disadvantages
Distance-based measures	• Data gathering • Encompass a common sphere of life • Account for cluster benefits • Identification of industry clusters • Theoretical considerations	• Data availability • Arbitrarily drawn boundaries • Difficult to identify resource-based clusters
Zip codes	• Encompass a common sphere of life • Account for cluster benefits • Policy usage	• Data availability • Arbitrary politically drawn cluster boundaries • Unable to identify boundary crossing clusters
MSA	• Data availability • Encompass a common sphere of life • Account for cluster benefits • Policy usage	• Unable to identify boundary crossing clusters • Arbitrary politically drawn cluster boundaries
States and standard regions	• Data availability • Policy usage	• Too large to account for cluster benefits • Assumption of state/region-wide clusters • Arbitrary politically drawn cluster boundaries

Table 5 - Advantages and disadvantages of cluster boundary measures

To account for this issue there is a common agreement in the literature that in order to truly identify a cluster, researchers should go beyond **quantitative** and also include **qualitative measures** such as interviews and surveys. Only then is it possible to realistically determine a cluster's boundaries by carefully analyzing as to what degree firms and institutions in a geographically bounded area share a common ground and have formed links among each other.

A comprehensive approach that is able to overcome some of these shortcomings is based on the cluster identification methodology introduced by the Cluster Mapping Project, an initiative of the Institute for Strategy and Competitiveness at the Harvard Business School (see figure 14).[186]

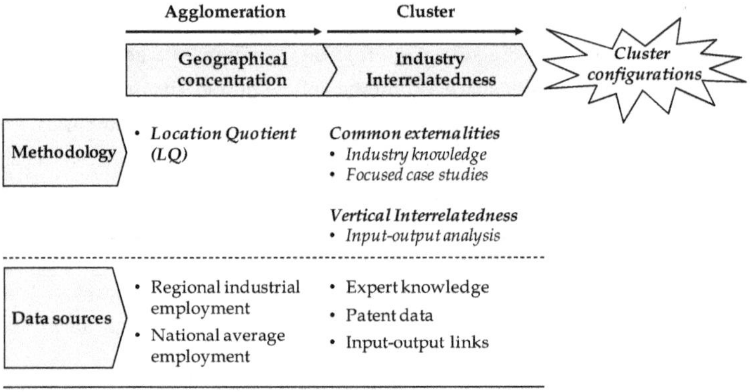

Figure 14 - Cluster identification methodology of the Cluster Mapping Project

The Institute's Cluster Mapping Project employs qualitative and quantitative techniques to analyze the distribution of economic activity in the USA over time with a special focus on the presence of industrial clusters. It uses information on employment, firm plants, and wages by four-digit Standard Industry Classification (SIC) codes drawn from the annual County Business Patterns database. In addition, patent data is analyzed across regions to generate insights regarding the collocation behavior of industries. The aim is to identify a region's main clusters and its boundaries by using the correlation of industry employment within pre-defined geographical areas. The logic behind this approach is that linked and related industries will collocate geographically based on the assumption that they share common externalities such as infrastructure, employees, technologies, and resources. Industries then, that are commonly found to be located in close proximity to each other are grouped together and classified as cluster.

The main methods rely on analytical techniques that use location quotients (LQ) and input-output data to identify geographically concentrated industries.[187] While the *LQ* approach relies on regional and national employment (or firm plant) data to measure industry concentration in a particular region, the *input-output analysis* identifies transactional patterns in the

186 See Porter (2003), pp. 549ff.

187 Both approaches will be subject to a more detailed discussion in section 4.4.

buying and selling behavior of related industries. It is particularly helpful in identifying clusters of industry verticals.[188]

Once regional concentrations of employment are identified, the next steps involve a mixture of quantitative and qualitative techniques to determine the degree of interrelatedness between industries with regards to particular externalities. First, subjective industry knowledge and focused case studies are used to assess as to what degree the identified industries share common externalities with one another. Second, in the case of no apparent links, the analysis of input-output data is used to reveal the degree of vertical interrelatedness. As a result, links are dropped in those cases where neither the qualitative nor the quantitative techniques reveal a meaningful degree of interrelatedness. Applying this methodology resulted in 41 identified clusters in the USA with an average of 29 industries in each cluster.[189]

Summing up, in order to not add to the existing confusion, it is important that researchers clearly specify the purpose of their study and plausibly explain the appropriateness and limitations of their chosen methodology. Only then will they be able to contribute to the advancement of the field.[190]

2.3.1.2 Industry Interrelatedness

Several of the previously discussed Schools of Thought have theorized and empirically studied how clusters come into existence and how they evolve over time. Initially, clusters might form around a successful firm when spin-offs and new entrants co-locate as suppliers or to profit from the advantages of specialization. In this case, the cluster evolves vertically first in response to a market opportunity before attracting horizontal players that over time begin to compete with each other. Such a cluster may develop a strong industry identity in that its firms tend to serve a specific product market. Examples of such **industry-based clusters** can be found in Napa Valley's wine cluster, London's financial services clusters, or Stuttgart's automotive cluster.

On the contrary, there are also **resource-based clusters** that develop due to a common need for infrastructure, technology, skills, labor, or natural resources. In this case, firms co-locate in order to access a similar resource, but with the aim to exploit it through different applications and by targeting different product-markets. For example, biotechnology clusters rest on resources that are simultaneously utilized by firms from the pharmaceutical, analytical instrumentation, medical, and agricultural industries. ICT and electronics clusters also tend to be home to firms from different industries including transistors, semiconductors, consumer electronics, and computers. The same is true for manufacturing clusters in east and south China that rely on the same pool of low-cost labor. Firms in these clusters are far less related

---

188 See Kukalis (2010), p. 11.

189 See for the results and a detailed discussion on the employed methodology Porter (2003), pp. 562f.

190 See Rocha (2004), pp. 384f; vom Hofe/Chen (2006), pp. 21ff.

to each other in terms of industry membership as in terms of dependence on a common resource-base.

Relatedness differentiates clusters from pure agglomerations as firms in the latter are indeed geographically concentrated, but lack any sort of similarity in terms of a common product-market or resource-base. Relatedness is a prerequisite for firms to develop a common culture and form links among each other as they are likely to experience the same problems and challenges when trying to target similar markets or to access the same resource. It also facilitates formal and informal communication among firms. Employees from different firms are likely to share the same language and mental models thereby enabling them to learn from each other either directly or indirectly through monitoring and observation thus contributing to each others' success.[191] Porter for example, has shown how the economic success of the Napa Valley wine cluster depends on a multitude of firms and institutions from related areas such as vineyards, wineries, winemaking, equipment producers, and wine-related education and research.[192] Therefore, relatedness is another important dimension of a conceptual cluster definition.[193]

2.3.1.3 Cluster Links

Interrelatedness is the precondition for building links in clusters. Links can be grouped in formal, informal, vertical, and horizontal relationships. Examples are depicted in figure 15.

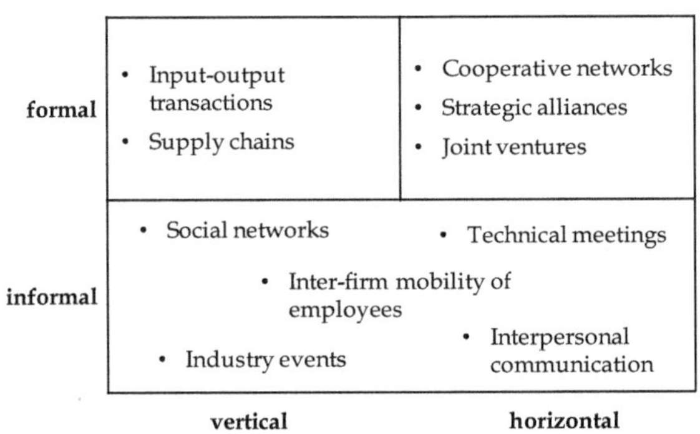

Figure 15 - Examples of links in clusters

[191] See St. John/Pouder (2006), pp. 159f.

[192] See Porter (1998a), pp. 78f.

[193] As is evident from this discussion, relatedness is a complex construct that is based on different notions of similarities among firms. Measuring it therefore requires a multidimensional approach, one of which will be introduced in chapter 4.

Formal relationships comprise direct input-output links between buyers and suppliers as they can be found in supply chains.[194] They represent long-term stable and predictable transaction relations and resemble the cluster's **vertical dimension**. Firms with established vertical links usually show a high degree of relatedness in that they have similar transaction patterns. Due to their specialization they depend on distinctive resources and usually engage in what Maskell calls the vertical learning process.[195] Along the **horizontal dimension** on the other hand, firms share similar resources and target similar product-markets. Links along the horizontal dimension will therefore likely involve competitors that engage in formal cooperation such as strategic networks with the aim to improve their competitive positions.[196] Joint activities might involve lobbying efforts, the development of new products, marketing at fairs and trade shows, sourcing of input factors, and the establishment of education and training centers.[197]

Informal relationships on the other hand, occur outside of formal transactional agreements and represent the relations that are socially embedded in a cluster. They comprise casual encounters of individuals from different firms and institutions in regular and every day spheres of life such as bars, sports and cultural facilities, and trade shows, but also the type of informal relationships amongst engineers that are friends and happen to work in different firms. In her lively description of Silicon Valley, Saxenian showed how entrepreneurs created an environment of informal socialization, which fostered information exchange and speedy diffusion of innovations. One important facilitator of these informal networks is the inter-firm mobility of individuals, which move easily from one firm to another while continuing to meet at trade shows, industry conferences, and similar forums where relationships are formed and maintained.[198] In a similar study, Dahl and Pedersen examined the role of informal networks among engineers in a cluster in Denmark regarding information and knowledge exchange. The authors found that engineers indeed exchange knowledge, which they rate as being of high or medium importance for their own work, through informal social contacts. It involves very specific knowledge about new products, but also more locally confined information about potential employment opportunities as many engineers have found their current job through their social network rather than through formal job channels.[199] This discussion and a closer look at the cluster definitions reviewed in section 2.1 shows that links are a decisive dimension of clusters as they represent its vitality.

---

194 Pfohl (2004, p. 325) defines supply chains as the vertical network of interconnected entities including suppliers, manufacturers, wholesalers, retailers, as well as logistics service providers encompassing the flow of products, services, information, and finances from a source to an end customer.

195 See section 2.2.9.

196 Gulati and colleagues (2000, p. 203) define strategic networks as being "*composed of interorganizational ties that are enduring, are of strategic significance for the firms entering them, and include strategic alliances, joint ventures, long-term buyer-supplier partnerships, and a host of similar ties.*"

197 See Porter (2000b), p. 22.

198 See Saxenian (1990), p. 97 and Saxenian (1994), pp. 32f.

199 See Dahl/Pedersen (2004), p. 1685.

With this in mind, it is now possible to come to a **meaningful definition of clusters** that encompasses its key dimensions:

> *Clusters are a geographical concentration of linked firms and institutions that are related to each other in terms of a common resource-base and/or product-market.*

This definition fulfills the necessary requirements in that it is short, significantly different from other concepts such as agglomerations or innovative milieus, and not tautological. It is also considerably simpler than the definitions reviewed in section 2.1 and yet, it includes the key dimensions of clusters on which all Schools of Thought agree. It does, however, not imply that there are no networks in clusters or that their firms do not share a common cultural background, but that these factors are not there by definition. They are rather potential consequences of the structural cluster characteristics that may or may not evolve over time.

For example, with this definition in mind it should be clear by now that *Italian industrial districts* and *Californian technology districts* are all special cases of clusters. Italian districts consist of a large number of socially embedded SMEs that serve similar product-markets, i.e. traditional manufacturing sectors, while the latter consist of small start-up, medium, and large firms that stem from various industry sectors, but depend on the same resource-base, i.e. high-technology and skilled labor. All industrial districts are therefore clusters, but not all clusters are industrial districts.

2.4 The Effect of Clusters on Firm Performance

All of the reviewed Schools of Thought argue that firms in clusters should be better off than isolated firms. Yet, given the many different concepts and levels of observation it is becoming increasingly difficult to directly compare findings of different studies with each other. Although authors often claim to capture the effect of clusters, the methods they employ do not. To arrive at a realistic picture of the influence of clusters on firm performance and competitive advantage, it is therefore important to first identify what is really being studied before any conclusion can be reached. To this end, the following two sections discuss:

(1) Studies that investigate the effect of pure agglomerations on firm performance.

(2) Studies that investigate clusters of related and linked industries on firm performance.

The review provides valuable insights on the relationship between clusters and firm performance. It leads to a baseline model and the first set of research hypotheses.

2.4.1 Pure Agglomerations and Firm Performance

Table 6 provides an overview of well-known studies that investigate the relationship between pure agglomerations and firm performance. It shows in detail the methods that are being employed, the samples that are being studied, and the reported results. This section will review those studies that have the most relevance to the underlying research question.

The first one is Shaver and Flyer's work on how agglomeration affects the survival of foreign entrants in the USA. Their main thesis is that "*agglomeration will be characterized by adverse selection.*"[200] This means that firms, which have superior technology and resources, will not locate their activities in agglomerations and instead deliberately avoid them. The authors build their arguments on two assumptions. First, firms in agglomerations are heterogeneous when it comes to their resources and performance. There are superior firms and there are poor firms. Second, agglomeration causes technology spillovers from one firm to another and firms are not able to prevent them. Therefore, their superior technology or resource will inevitably diffuse over time and sooner or later be available to all competitors. While poorer firms benefit from these spillovers, superior firms lose their competitive edge.[201]

To prove their point, the authors choose to examine the long-term survival rate of foreign greenfield entrants from Canada, France, Germany, Japan, and the UK into US manufacturing industries between 1987 and 1995. As an indicator of agglomeration, the authors measure the proportion of own manufacturing industry activities that are present in the state in which a foreign plant locates. Their first results confirm the widely accepted assumption that firms agglomerate when choosing new locations. Firms are also more likely to locate their new plants in states where there is already a high level of own industry activity. Yet, they also find that the survival rate of these firms is significantly lower than of firms that locate their activities in states with lower levels of own industry activity.

To examine why firms in own industry agglomerations are more likely to fail the authors test their thesis of adverse selection, which predicts that superior firms will not locate in agglomerations, while poorer firms will. To do so, the authors equalize size with superiority. They justify their measure by arguing that size will increase the contribution of a firm to Marshall's sources of externalities. Their findings reveal that small firms are very likely to agglomerate, while large firms are less likely to do so. Taking their combined results into account, the authors then conclude that "*under these conditions [...] firms possessing superior technologies, human capital, training programs, suppliers, and distributors have the incentive to locate distant from other firms.*"[202]

200 Shaver/Flyer (2000), p. 1178.

201 See Shaver/Flyer (2000), pp. 1176ff.

202 Shaver/Flyer (2000), p. 1191.

Table 6 - Empirical studies of agglomerations and firm performance

Author(s)	Method of measurement	Sample			Dependent variable	Results
		Industry	Time	Country		
Baptista/Swann (1998)	Regional employment in two-digit industries	Ten two-digit manufacturing industries	1975-1982	UK	Innovation performance	Firms in regional agglomerations of own industry employment are more likely to innovate.
Shaver/Flyer (2000)	Proportion of firm's own industry activity in states	Foreign entrants from four-digit manufacturing industries	1987-1995	USA	Firm survival	Foreign direct invested firms are more likely to fail in states with a higher degree of own industry agglomeration.
Sternberg/Arndt (2001)	Eleven predefined European regions of varying sizes	Manufacturing	1995-1999	Europe	Innovation performance	Firms are more likely to innovate in regions where: 1) manufacturing employment is agglomerated. 2) R&D expenditure to GDP ratio is high. 3) regional and cross-regional firm networks are strong.
Beaudry (2001)	County-level employment in five-digit industries	Aerospace	1988-1994	UK	Firm performance (growth and patenting)	1) Firms in own industry agglomerations are growing faster than the average. 2) Firms in other industry agglomerations are growing slower than the average. 3) Firms in agglomerations of innovative firms are more likely to innovate themselves.

Table 6 (continued)

Author(s)	Method of measurement	Sample			Dependent variable	Results
		Industry	Time	Country		
Stuart/Sorenson (2003)	Distance based measure and links among firm-university patents	Biotechnology	1978-1995	USA	Firm performance (time-to-IPO)	Proximity to agglomerations of: 1) specialized labor positively influences firm performance. 2) competitors reduces firm performance.
Canina/Enz/Harrison (2005)	Zip code counts of hotels	Hotel services	2000	USA	Firm Performance (room revenue and rooms sold)	Locating in agglomerations of 1) high-end competitors increases a hotel's performance. 2) low-end competitors decreases a hotel's performance. 3) high strategic differentiation amplifies the effects.
Folta/Cooper/Baik (2006)	MSA Counts of firms	Biotechnology	1973-1998	USA	Firm performance (patenting, firm alliances, private equity offerings)	Inverse U-shaped relationship between agglomeration size and firm performance: When agglomerations get too large firm performance starts to decrease.
McCann/Folta (2011)	MSA Counts of firms	Biotechnology	1973-1998	USA	Patenting performance	Firms in agglomerations that: 1) have higher stocks of patents generate more patents. 2) are younger generate more patents.

While Shaver and Flyer's study has been the starting point to a fruitful discussion about the economies and diseconomies of clusters, a closer look reveals several methodological flaws. First, by equalizing agglomerations with clusters the authors implicitly assume that agglomerations provide firms with the opportunity to profit from Marshall's externalities, a quality which is inherent to industrial districts, i.e. a special case of clusters. To be explicit, agglomerations are geographical concentrations of firms that are not linked and also not necessarily related to each other. Therefore, it is safe to assume that the level of competition in agglomerations is as high as in clusters, but without the benefits of e.g. a shared culture that fosters mutual trust and cooperation. This would partly explain why firms in agglomerations are more likely to fail. Second, Shaver and Flyer chose US states as unit of observation. This is a particular problem which, was already discussed in the previous section.[203] Consequently, there is no understanding about what is going between the firms in these states and to what extent they share resources with each other or whether or not they have established relationships with each other. Third, as a bi-product of their investigation, the authors find that firms in agglomerations are more likely to survive, if they already have existing operations in the US and if they belong to industries where US firms have greater international operations. Given that no further information is available, it could be assumed that foreign entrants chose these particular locations to be close to their customers and/or suppliers. Internationalization scholars have long shown that this is particularly true for SMEs, who often enter new markets because of existing relationships and inter-firm networks.[204] While this would explain Shaver and Flyer's main finding that smaller firms are more likely to agglomerate than larger ones, it would also hint to the existence of clusters and thus be an indicator that agglomerations tend to harm the survival rate of firms, while clusters benefit them.

Next, Stuart and Sorenson set out to explain how agglomerations affect the performance of young biotechnology firms in the USA. More precisely, the authors examine how geographic proximity to experts in biotechnology, incumbent biotechnology firms, and venture capitalists affects founding rates and the performance of startups. To measure geographic proximity the authors use distance-weighted measures of the local concentration of the three factors relative to the focal firm.[205] Agglomerations are calculated according to the geographical distribution of biotechnology firms, while firm performance is being measured as the time between the founding of a startup and its initial public offering (IPO).

Examining new venture creation first, the authors find that proximity to experts, venture capitalists, and other biotechnology firms significantly and positively increases founding rates. Regarding firm performance, the results are not quite as clear. While proximity to biotechnology experts increases firm performance, firms located near to many competitors and

203 See section 2.3.1.1.

204 See Bell (1995), p. 71 and Chetty/Agndal (2007), p. 24.

205 For a more detailed explanation about the employed algorithm see Stuart/Sorenson (2003), pp. 236ff.

those in proximity to many venture capital firms have lower firm performance.[206] The harmful effect of being close to competitors coincides with the previously discussed study and seems to capture competition and congestion costs. As the number of firms in agglomerations grows and the industry matures, firms tend to become structurally and strategically similar[207], implying that they compete in similar supply and demand markets. The harmful effect of being close to venture capital firms on the other hand suggests that the availability of funding reflects the attractiveness of an agglomeration to potential entrepreneurs and a firm's competitors, two factors which over time also increase the level of competition. Interestingly, these harmful effects seem to affect poorly funded firms most severely, while financially strong firms perform exceptionally well.[208]

Building explicitly on the previous studies, which found that agglomeration economies seem to affect firms differently, McCann and Folta investigate which firms are most likely to profit from them. The authors draw from the knowledge-based view of the firm and theorize that firms with higher abilities to generate knowledge from external resources will benefit disproportionally from agglomeration externalities.[209] To test their hypothesis the authors use a sample of US biotechnology firms and data about their patenting activities from 1978 to 1998. To measure agglomerations, the authors count the presence of firms in MSAs. Firm performance is measured as a firm's patenting activity. By equalizing a firm's current patent stock with its ability to learn and absorb knowledge from external sources, the authors find that young firms and firms with larger patent stocks benefit more from being located in agglomerations. While there is again no understanding about the mechanisms at work, the findings tend to confirm Stuart and Sorenson in that it is the superior and resource dependent firms that profit the most from agglomeration externalities.[210]

2.4.2 Clusters of Related Industries and Firm Performance

Although the previous studies have produced valuable insights on the agglomeration phenomenon, their results are not directly transferable to clusters. In response to this situation, a series of studies emerged recently in which researchers have adapted their methodologies to be able to identify clusters - as opposed to agglomerations - and study their influence on firm performance. They are summarized in table 7 and show the concept under investigation and the methods that are being employed. This section reviews those studies that carry the greatest relevance to the underlying research question.

---

206 See Stuart/Sorenson (2003), pp. 242ff.

207 See DiMaggio/Powell (1991), pp. 66f.

208 See Stuart/Sorenson (2003), pp. 250f.

209 See McCann/Folta (2011), pp. 108ff.

210 See McCann/Folta (2011), pp. 120f.

Table 7 - Empirical studies of clusters and firm performance

Author(s)	Cluster Concept	Method of measurement	Sample			Dependent variable	Results
			Industry	Time	Country		
Visser (1999)	Industrial district	Expert opinion on a pre-selected district in Lima	Clothing	1994	Peru	Firm performance (including employment size and growth, sales and wage per worker)	Firms in districts have stronger performance than firms outside districts.
Staber (2001)	Industrial district	Distance based on 10km around focal firm	Knitwear	1960-1998	Germany (Albstadt)	Firm survival	Locating in: 1) high-density districts raises firm failure. 2) diversified districts increases firm survival.
Zhang/Li (2008)	Cluster	Two pre-selected clusters	Textile and ICT	2005	China	Firm Performance (sales growth)	Business ties within clusters positively influence firm performance.
Gilbert/ McDougall/ Audretsch (2008)	Cluster	MSA; *LQ* of employment, input-output data	ICT services	1990-2000	USA	Firm Performance (sales growth and product innovation)	1) Firms in clusters perform better than isolated firms. 2) Technological knowledge transfer through patents does not explain why firms cluster.

Table 7 (continued)

Author(s)	Cluster Concept	Method of measurement	Sample			Dependent variable	Results
			Industry	Time	Country		
Wennberg/ Lindqvist (2010)	Cluster	Regions and counties; *LQ* and counts of employees and plants, input-output data	23 service and manufacturing industries from five different clusters	1993-2002	Sweden	Firm Performance (firm survival, tax payments, wages per employee)	Firms in clusters: 1) have higher survival rates 2) create more jobs 3) pay more taxes 4) pay higher wages
Kukalis (2010)	Cluster	Region; *LQ* of employees, input-output data, expert opinion	Pharmaceutical and semiconductor	1976-2006	USA	Firm Performance (ROA, ROS)	Early in the industry lifecycle clustered and isolated firms performed equally. Late in the industry lifecycle: 1) isolated firms performed better than clustered firms, 2) and in recessionary times isolated firms performed better than clustered firms.
Liao (2010)	Cluster	Survey	Taiwanese manufacturing	2006	China	Production performance	1) Clusters alone have no impact on performance. 2) Manufacturing resources facilitate positive impact of clusters on performance.

Gilbert, McDougall, and Audretsch for example combine LQs of regional employment and input-output data to identify ICT clusters at the MSA level.[211] The authors examine whether technological spillovers, which they define as the direct or indirect transfer of technological knowledge from one party to another, explain the performance of new ventures in clusters.[212] To capture spillovers the authors use firms' patenting activities, a method that became prominent through the Geography of Innovation School. It examines the extent to which a given patent is cited by other patents. A high citation number serves as indicator for the strength of spillovers from one patent to another. Using sales growth and the number of new products that have been introduced between 1990 and 2000 as performance indicators, the authors find that firms in clusters perform better than isolated firms, but that technological spillovers as measured by patent cross-citations are not able to explain why firms locate in clusters.[213]

Although their findings confirm that clusters are beneficial to firms, their insights regarding technology spillovers are heavily restricted by the fact that the authors use patenting activities to measure knowledge transfer. Other mechanisms such as formal and informal communication channels, inter-firm mobility of employees, and cooperation remain unexamined. Due to their chosen methodology, the authors also fail to investigate the process by which external knowledge is integrated into a firm's existing knowledge stock and eventually ends up in contributing to produce a patent.

Given that innovation is a complex social process, it is not unusual that inventors are not completely aware of all the knowledge sources they utilized and where that knowledge came from. For example, it is very likely that an inventor will cite a prominent patent A or research study B on which his innovation C is based. Yet, the same does not necessarily hold true if a vital hint for the development of innovation C came from a conference speaker, who during his presentation referred to study B and by doing so alerted the inventor to take a look at it. In this case, it would be highly unlikely that the inventor would cite the conference speaker in his patent application, although in their earlier cited study Dahl and Pedersen have shown that this event is (a) not uncommon and (b) presents the maybe most obvious case of a technology spillover.[214]

Referring to the contradiction between cluster scholars' belief that firms should benefit from being in a cluster and findings of agglomeration studies, which seem to suggest the opposite, Kukalis investigates whether or not firms located in clusters outperform isolated firms. The author draws from an extensive database of firms from the semiconductor and pharmaceuti-

211 This methodology is based on Porter's Cluster Mapping Project (see Porter (2003), pp. 549ff. and section 2.3.1.1).

212 See Gilbert/McDougall/Audretsch (2008), p. 408.

213 See Gilbert/McDougall/Audretsch (2008), pp. 414ff.

214 See section 2.3.1.3.

cal industry that covers the time between 1976 and 2006. These firms consist of the 100 largest US headquartered semiconductor and pharmaceutical firms, respectively.

To identify clusters the author uses quantitative and qualitative methodologies. First, clusters are identified using a similar methodology as Gilbert and colleagues. These findings are then complemented by a qualitative analysis in which 15 industry experts of firms and industry associations within each of the two industries were interviewed. Finally, a firm is assigned to a given cluster, if its primary R&D facility is physically located within the boundaries of one of the previously identified industry clusters. Firm performance is measured in terms of return on assets (ROA) and return on sales (ROS). Only those firms remained in the sample whose data were publicly available.

Using these variables, Kukalis then examines the effect of clusters on firm performance over the lifecycle of both industries. The author's key findings reveal that early in the industry lifecycle clustered and isolated firms perform equally, while late in the industry lifecycle isolated firms outperform clustered firms. Thus, the author does not find support for the proposition that clusters benefit firm performance. Kukalis' findings therefore complement Shaver and Flyer's results that large companies outside of own industry agglomerations perform equally or better than agglomerated firms.[215]

In an attempt to reconcile earlier findings, Wennberg and Lindqvist study the effect of clusters on the survival and performance of newly founded firms. Their starting point is the explicit notion that "*one reason of the inconsistent results of these studies is the variation in methodologies applied*"[216], because "*none of the empirical studies of cluster effects on new firms has aggregated multiple groups of related industries.*"[217] Using the same method as Gilbert and colleagues and Kukalis, the authors' sample is derived from all Swedish firms that were started between 1993 and 2002 in knowledge intensive industries such as ICT, financial services, medical equipment, and biopharmacy. To assess the influence of clusters, firm performance is measured in terms of survival, tax payments, and wages paid per employee.

The authors' main findings indicate that new firms in strong clusters of own and related industries have higher survival rates and stronger financial performance.[218] This can be contrasted to earlier findings of agglomeration studies, which found that own industry concentrations have a harmful effect on firm performance. This may indicate that the existence of related industries in clusters is a key driver for the performance of new firms as opposed to the harmful homogeneity in own industry agglomerations.

What the presented studies have failed to provide, however, is an understanding of firm-level characteristics besides size and age that are responsible for the observed performance differentials. To address this issue, it is therefore helpful to turn to studies that explicitly ex-

---

[215] See Kukalis (2010), p. 22

[216] Wennberg/Lindqvist (2010), p. 225.

[217] Wennberg/Lindqvist (2010), p. 227.

[218] See Wennberg/Lindqvist (2010), pp. 235f.

amine how clusters and certain firm-level characteristics are related to firm performance. A look into the literature, however, reveals that at the time of writing to this author's knowledge only two studies briefly analyze this issue.

First, Zhang and Li examined how sales growth of Chinese firms in two pre-selected textile and ICT clusters is influenced by personal ties of managers to actors within and outside their cluster's boundaries. Drawing from a sample of 163 firms, the authors find that business ties with suppliers, buyers, and supporting institutions within clusters greatly enhance firm performance, while ties beyond a cluster are not as important.[219]

Second, Liao investigated how the production performance of Taiwanese manufacturing firms in China was influenced by clusters and firm-level characteristics. Drawing simultaneously from the resource- and knowledge-based view of the firm as well as the network perspective, the author hypothesizes that inter-organizational trust, a firm's manufacturing resources, and knowledge management system will be important moderators. Using a sample of 102 Taiwanese firms, the author finds that manufacturing resources indeed facilitate a positive relationship between clusters and manufacturing performance, while inter-organizational trust and knowledge management systems do not.[220]

2.5 Summary of Findings: The Baseline Model

The evidence so far points to the fact that clusters indeed benefit their member firms, but only if they comprise a diverse set of linked industries. Own industry agglomerations seem to impose heavy congestion costs on their member firms without the associated advantages of clusters. The latter on the other hand, positively influence firm performance by providing ample opportunities through the presence of specialized suppliers, access to knowledge and information, social networks, and improved productivity. This leads to the first hypothesis:

Hypothesis 1: *Clusters that comprise a diverse set of geographically concentrated and linked industries have a positive influence on firm performance.*

Yet, the previous findings also seem to suggest that there is a difference between large and established firms as well as new and small firms. Marshall noted early on that large, vertically integrated firms are able to benefit from internal returns to scale and are therefore less likely to be dependent on their local environment. Moreover, Kukalis' findings suggest that being in a cluster is harmful to large firms as they have to deal with increased congestion costs without the associated benefits. This leads to the second hypothesis:

Hypothesis 2: *The relationship between clusters and firm performance will be negatively moderated by firm size.*

---

219 See Zhang/Li (2008), p. 625.

220 See Liao (2010), pp. 166f.

New firms on the other hand, while more flexible and adaptable when it comes to environmental changes, usually suffer from a lack of resources and low market visibility. The work on California's technology districts has shown that small firms benefit disproportionally from their cluster location as they significantly lower their input and overhead costs, while providing them with access to a large market of potential customers. Older firms on the other hand, tend to be more rigid and hierarchical with already established supply chains and product-markets. The presented studies also suggest that they have more to lose than to gain when locating in clusters. This leads to the hypothesis that younger firms should benefit more from their cluster location than older firms:

Hypothesis 3: *The relationship between clusters and firm performance will be negatively moderated by firm age.*

Taken together, hypothesis one leads to the baseline model as depicted in figure 16 complemented by the first set of contingency factors "Age" and "Size" that are hypothesized to influence the relationship between clusters and firm performance.

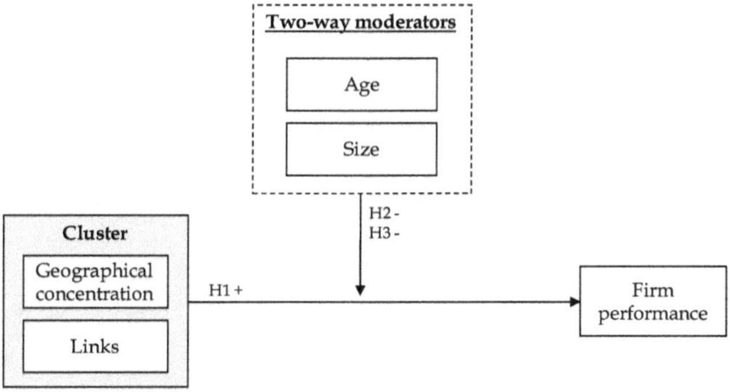

Figure 16 - Baseline model complemented by the first set of contingency factors

The **baseline model** addresses hypothesis H1 and the key assumption of the cluster literature that clusters of a diverse set of linked industries benefit their member firms. In this study, clusters are conceptualized as a higher-order construct that consists of only two dimensions: "Geographical concentration" and "Links" among cluster-firms. This reflects the notion that the interrelatedness dimension is not a means to its own end. Instead, interrelatedness is a precondition for links in clusters. Thus, measuring the extent to which firms in clusters form links among each other also reflects the extent to which they are interrelated. Additionally, the baseline model is complemented by the first set of contingency factors and their respective hypotheses H2 and H3.

Beyond these two factors, the results of Zhang and Li as well as Liao suggest that there are more firm-level characteristics besides size and age that are responsible for the observed performance differentials between cluster-firms. Yet, both studies fall short in capturing the full scale of the cluster phenomenon, for exploiting the full potential of clusters calls for more than just business ties or manufacturing resources. How, for example, can firms tap into pools of skilled labor and prevent their employees from being hired away by competitors? What internal processes are necessary to successfully integrate valuable knowledge and information from external cluster sources? What do firms need to successfully engage in inter-firm networks?

These open points are related to the research questions set forth in the introduction and are addressed in the next chapter. It develops the theoretical model that will guide the empirical analysis of the identified internal characteristics in the remainder of this study.

3 Theoretical Model of Internal Characteristics to Create Competitive Advantages through Clusters

The aim of this chapter is to develop a theoretical model of internal characteristics beyond size and age that enable firms to create competitive advantages through clusters. The underlying research process is illustrated in figure 17.

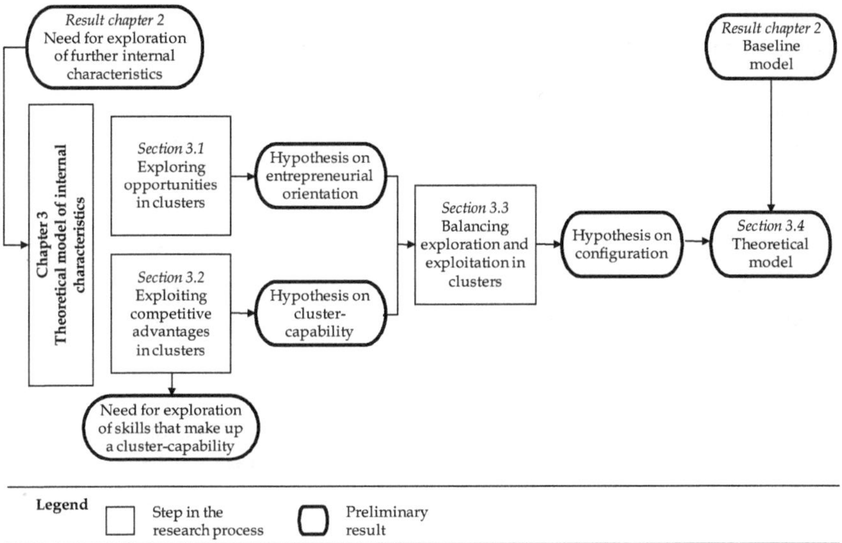

Figure 17 - Outline of chapter 3

To this end, management literature offers two complementary theories: entrepreneurship and strategic management.[221] Traditionally, both fields have existed independently of one another. Applied to the cluster context in section 3.1, the field of entrepreneurship provides an explanation of how firms explore short-term economic opportunities through clusters. Strategic management on the other hand is discussed in section 3.2. It explains how firms utilize their capabilities to make use of the resources that are prevalent in clusters to exploit already existing competitive advantages.

This traditional view subscribes to a contingency perspective[222] and suggests that it is sufficient for firms to act either entrepreneurial or strategic in clusters to be successful. Recent

221 See for an overview of both fields Meyer/Neck/Meeks (2006), pp. 19ff.

222 According to Schoonhoven, the Contingency School argues that the effectiveness of internal organizational variables depends on contextual conditions. They should therefore be aligned to other aspects of the organization such as its external environment or specific task requirements (see Schoonhoven (1981), p. 350). The Contingency School is characterized by the fact, that it only examines bivariate relationships between two variables and thereby ignores the effect of other potentially influential variables (see Wolf (2008), p. 452).

research, however, suggests that entrepreneurial firms are often unable to turn opportunities into competitive advantages due to a lack of strategic resources and capabilities. Similarly, firms that lack entrepreneurship see their competitive advantages erode over time as they are unable to renew their resources and capabilities.[223] Strategic entrepreneurship is the concept that has arisen from this insight. It takes a holistic, configurational perspective[224] and highlights that firms need to simultaneously seek short-term economic opportunities and turn them into a series of long-term competitive advantages.[225] It is discussed in section 3.3.

Because both views are to some extent mutually exclusive, the discussion leads to competing hypotheses about how the identified characteristics enable firms to create and defend competitive advantages through clusters. The chapter concludes in section 3.4 with a summary of the findings in the theoretical model that will guide the remainder of this research study. As an additional outcome, it also exposes the need to further explore actual skills that are relevant in clusters. This serves as input for an explorative case study in chapter 4.

3.1 Opportunity Exploration through Entrepreneurship in Clusters

Within the field of entrepreneurship economic or "*entrepreneurial (Schumpeterian) rents may be achieved by risk-taking and entrepreneurial insights in an uncertain/complex environment.*"[226] The dominant logic within entrepreneurship theory is the Austrian School of Economics[227], which rests on two fundamental assumptions:

(1) The market is seen as being in a constant state of motion swinging between equilibrium and disequilibrium as supply and demand are subjects to permanent change.

(2) Firms earn rents through the entrepreneurial discovery and exploitation of economic opportunities.[228]

The following section 3.1.1 discusses the Austrian School's basic premises of the market being in motion and the role of the entrepreneur in exploring opportunities. In section 3.1.2 follows a discussion on the concept of entrepreneurial orientation, which explains how firms explore opportunities. In section 3.1.3 it is then applied to the cluster context to derive a hypothesis about how it enables firms to profit from their cluster location.

---

223 See for example, Hitt et al. (2001), p. 480; Wiklund/Shepherd (2003), pp. 1312f.; Wiklund/Shepherd (2005), p. 85.; Walter/Auer/Ritter (2006), pp. 558f.; Stam/Elfring (2008), pp. 104ff.

224 The Configurational School to strategy suggests that firms should align their strategy, internal capabilities, and organizational structure in consideration of their environment, simultaneously. A firm that achieves a "good fit" among these variables is then able to outperform other firms. In contrast to the Contingency School, the Configurational School examines complex patterns of multiple independent variables and thereby arrives at more meaningful insights (see Wolf (2008), pp. 454ff.).

225 See Hitt et al. (2006), p. 2.

226 Mahoney/Pandian (1992), p. 364.

227 The most important representatives to the Austrian School of Economics are Joseph Schumpeter and Israel Kirzner. Further representatives are Carl Menger, Friedrich Hayek, Ludwig Mises, and Ludwig Lachmann (see Jacobson (1992), pp. 783f.).

228 See Jacobson (1992), p. 785.

3.1.1 Basic Premises of the Austrian School of Economics

3.1.1.1 A Market in Motion

The market in the Austrian School of Economics is seen as being in a constant state of motion.[229] Superior profits are the result of a process of discovery and exploitation of market imperfections or inefficiencies. In this respect, **the Austrian School offers two alternative perspectives** regarding the way in which markets operate. While the mainstream theorizes that markets are always in a state of disequilibrium, Schumpeter argues that markets are subject to business cycle fluctuations that move from equilibrium to disequilibrium and vice versa.

For Schumpeter, competitive advantages are the result of market disruptions that he sees as an act of creative destruction *"that incessantly revolutionizes the economic structure [...] incessantly destroying the old one, incessantly creating a new one."*[230] It is a process of revolution, because it disrupts the market equilibrium and alters industry structure in a way that once held competitive positions erode and become obsolete over time.[231] It is a creative process, because its essence is innovation.[232] *Creative destruction* takes place in cycles, which are separated from each other by phases of equilibrium. The process itself, however, is ongoing in that the economy is either in a state of revolution or in a phase in which the effects of past shocks get absorbed by the economy. Both together, i.e. revolution and absorption, constitute the economic cycle and keep the market in motion.[233] The process of economic development starts when innovative agents introduce "new combinations", such as new products, production processes, and organizational structures.[234] When new combinations are introduced in the market, the innovator temporarily outcompetes his rivals and earns economic rents. These rents provide incentives for other economic actors to imitate the innovator and appropriate some of his profits. Increased competition gradually reduces the profits that can be generated until they finally disappear, at which point the market enters a new state of equilibrium. According to Schumpeter, the profit generated through innovations only provides the means to pursue new innovations and thereby restarts the cycle of creative destruction. Superior economic rents are therefore temporary phenomena that eventually get competed away.[235]

Opposite to Schumpeter, **the Austrian School's mainstream** argues that the market is constantly in disequilibrium due to *"entrepreneurial errors which have resulted in shortages, surplus,*

---

229 See for a discussion on the Austrian School also Millonig (2002), pp. 117ff.

230 Schumpeter (1975), p. 83.

231 See Schumpeter (1993), p. 138.

232 See Stevenson/Jarillo (2007), p. 157.

233 See Schumpeter (1993), p. 137.

234 See Schumpeter (1934), p. 66.

235 See Jacobson (1992), p. 787.

and misallocated resources."[236] Entrepreneurial errors happen, because the market process requires the participants to meet each others' needs based on expectations, hunches, intuitions, and heuristics causing their decisions to be incorrect some of the time. These errors leave space for improvements as customer needs are not fully met by new and existing products or because some resources are priced too high and others too low. Entrepreneurs, that are alert to these opportunities, act as arbitrageurs and purchase resources where prices are too low, recombine them, and sell them in markets where prices are too high. Entrepreneurship in this sense is seen as an equilibrating action that drives the use of resources towards the fulfillment of customer needs. Once all customer needs are fulfilled and the inefficiencies eliminated, the market moves towards equilibrium.[237] The setback, however, is that "*many potentially advantageous opportunities go unnoticed. [...] An enormous amount of ignorance stands in the way of the complete coordination of actions and decisions of the many market participants.*"[238] Therefore, an immense number of inefficiencies is likely to exist unperceived that keeps the market in constant disequilibrium.[239]

The differing ability to discover and exploit previously unexploited opportunities is based on asymmetries in information and beliefs. Firms that are alerted to available opportunities constantly scan the environment and thereby gather more information than others, and they can use this information to their advantage to find and assess the value of opportunities. Hence, entrepreneurial profits depend on the possession of superior information. In this context, firms can employ two strategies. They can either imitate their rivals or they can innovate and introduce new combinations to the market. The process of competition is in both cases interpreted as a "*discovery procedure*"[240]. It moves towards better mutual awareness among market participants and the reduction of information asymmetries through which profits are competed away.[241] The market, however, never reaches equilibrium, because innovations are interpreted as a continuous process; inefficiencies remain and the possibility of earning superior profits keeps the entrepreneur in a sustained state of alertness.[242]

Summing up, in both perspectives firms can employ two alternative strategies: **imitation and innovation**. Imitation moves the market towards a stabilizing equilibrium, while innovation disrupts the status quo and moves the economy forward. Both strategies take place in the same context of economic progress. The difference lies in the strategic intention of the firm, which can reduce a performance gap by imitating a successful rival or create a temporary

236 Kirzner (1997), p. 70.

237 See Kirzner (1997), pp. 70f.

238 Jacobson (1992), p. 787.

239 The reader should note, that equilibrium means precisely that all inefficiencies are eliminated, i.e. that supply is perfectly in balance with demand and that prices reflect the true value of any resource, product, or piece of information. In equilibrium models market participants are not able to e.g. bid higher prices or undersell competitors, etc. (see Hayek (1948), pp. 92ff).

240 Hayek (1978), p. 179.

241 See Kirzner (1997), p. 72.

242 See Jacobson (1992), pp. 787ff.

competitive advantage through innovation. The strategic objective in both cases, however, remains the same: the improvement of the individual competitive position in a dynamic environment.[243]

3.1.1.2 The Entrepreneur as discoverer of economic opportunities

Entrepreneurship fulfills a central function within the Austrian School of Economics, because firms create competitive advantages through discovering market inefficiencies or through the process of creative destruction. The prospect of superior economic profits serves as the driving force behind these actions.

Schumpeter differentiates between entrepreneurs and managers. An **entrepreneur** is defined as an individual that introduces new combinations, i.e. the introduction of innovative products, processes, and organizational structures. He is a principal agent of change whose actions disrupt the status quo and move the economy forward. For Schumpeter, an entrepreneur is someone who starts the process of creative destruction and leads the economy to disequilibrium. As soon as he routinely administers what has been created, he loses his status as entrepreneur and turns into a manager.[244] The **manager** lacks the ability to create and carry out new combinations, because his actions are based on routines and safety thinking. He adapts to radical changes in the external environment through imitation of the entrepreneur's innovation and thereby diffuses relevant information to other members of society, which leads to a new equilibrium.[245] In Schumpeter's view imitators are not entrepreneurs.[246]

What Schumpeter's conceptualization lacks, however, is an explanation about the process through which the entrepreneur gains insights on the feasibility of new combinations. Kirzner's view differs herein. He stresses the informational aspect of entrepreneurship that stems from the perception of previously unexploited opportunities. Asymmetries of belief and information are preconditions for the discovery of opportunities and not all opportunities are always obvious to everybody. To recognize an opportunity, an entrepreneur has to have previous knowledge that is related to the new information which triggers its discovery. Acquiring this information is difficult, because modern societies emphasize specialization and different cohorts in society are defined by their unique fields of expertise, lifestyles, education, and social status. The result is a variety of interdependent roles in which individuals know only a small segment of each other's personal circumstances.[247]

Information and insights about entrepreneurial errors, inefficiently used resources, unmet needs, and the effects of political and technological shifts are therefore unevenly distributed

---

243 See Millonig (2002), p. 119.

244 See Schumpeter (1934), p. 74. In Schumpeter's view entrepreneurship varies across the life of an individual and is only a temporary phenomenon.

245 See Schumpeter (1964), pp. 116ff.

246 See Millonig (2002), p. 120; Smith/Di Gregorio (2006), p. 135.

247 See Simmel (1950), pp. 317ff.

among the overall population.[248] Consequently, opportunities come most frequently to individuals or firms that are located at advantageous positions within networks of different members of society. This argument stems directly from Granovetter's important work on *"the strengths of weak ties"*[249] between individuals and their acquaintances. He argues that *"acquaintances, as compared to close friends, are more prone to move in different circles than oneself. Those to whom one is closest are likely to have the greatest overlap in contact with those one already knows, so that the information to which they are privy is likely to be much the same as that which one already has."*[250]

Empirical studies confirm the assertion that weak ties, as they are characteristic for social networks, provide aspiring entrepreneurs with access to information and resources beyond those available in their own social circle.[251] Aldrich and Zimmer showed that opportunities are the result of relationships and exchanges that take place within networks. Furthermore, exploiting opportunities (i.e. entrepreneurship) requires the skills to mobilize resources. The same types of networks and contacts required to identify opportunities are also necessary to acquire the resources needed to exploit them. Being embedded in such networks facilitates *"linkages between aspiring entrepreneurs, resources and opportunities."*[252] Networks assist in the acquisition of resources and enhance the likelihood of discovery and exploitation.[253] Kirzner therefore views *"the entrepreneur not as a source of innovative ideas ex nihilo"*[254], but as being able to mobilize resources and to know how to combine them to exploit opportunities once they are discovered.

Summing up, there exist important differences between Schumpeter's position and that of Kirzner, which are depicted in figure 18.

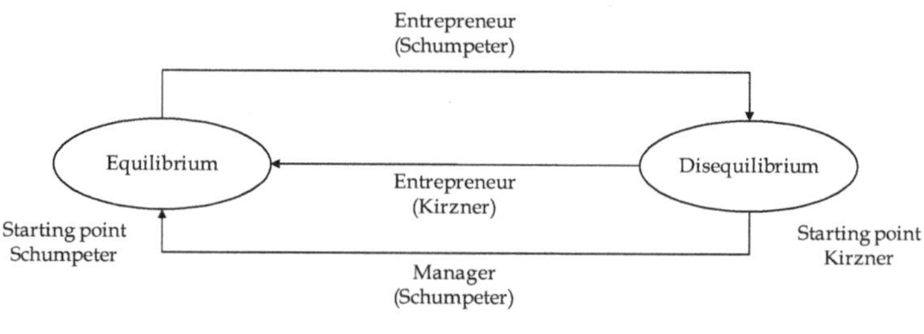

Figure 18 - The entrepreneurial process seen from Schumpeter's and Kirzner's position
(Source: translated from Millonig (2002), p. 121)

248 See Shane/Venkataraman (2000), p. 222.
249 Granovetter (1973).
250 Granovetter (1974), pp. 52f.
251 See Granovetter (1983), p. 209.
252 Aldrich/Zimmer (1986), pp. 8f.
253 See Low/MacMillan (2007), p. 148.
254 Kirzner (1973), p. 134.

For Schumpeter, entrepreneurial actions create and destroy markets, whereas for Kirzner, entrepreneurs act within the structure of the market and move it towards equilibrium. Furthermore, in Schumpeter's view only innovators are entrepreneurs. For Kirzner, entrepreneurship also encompasses the improvement upon existing combinations and/or the imitation of innovations as long as it is based on an information advantage.[255] It is important to note that in both perspectives markets *"are neither eroding into sheer chaos nor stabilizing to a final equilibrium."*[256] The common element of both types is that entrepreneurial actions are new types of behavior designed to exploit opportunities that others have not noticed.[257] Noticing opportunities requires the possession of superior information. The strategic imperative for entrepreneurs is therefore to constantly diversify their information base by establishing weakly tied social networks to gather, evaluate, and utilize information.[258]

3.1.2 Exploring Opportunities through Entrepreneurial Orientation

After this introduction into the basic premises of the Austrian School of Economics, this section explains the set of processes, methods, and styles by which firms explore new opportunities, experiment with existing resources, and undertake risky ventures and resource acquisitions to create new combinations. Within the literature on entrepreneurship this is reflected by the concept of entrepreneurial orientation (EO).[259] The key dimensions that characterize a firm's EO include a willingness to act proactively towards opportunities, innovate, and take well-calculated risks in their response.[260]

Proactiveness involves taking initiative by identifying and seeking new opportunities to exploit first-mover advantages.[261] It suggests a forward-looking perspective to act in anticipation of future needs and shape the environment to influence trends or even create demands.[262] According to Venkatraman, proactiveness comprises *"seeking new opportunities which may or may not be related to the present line of operations, introduction of new products and brands ahead of competition, strategically eliminating operations which are in the mature or declining stages of life cycle."*[263] What is striking in this definition is the assumption that proactive firms actively scan the environment to seek new opportunities that go *beyond* their present line of activities. This is noteworthy insofar as the discussion in section 3.1.1.2 has shown that to

---

255 See Kirzner (1978), p. 59.

256 Smith/Di Gregorio (2006), p. 136.

257 See Hitt et al. (2001), p. 50.

258 See Millonig (2002), pp. 121f.

259 See Lumpkin/Dess (1996), p. 162. In the literature, EO is alternatively also discussed under the "Corporate Entrepreneurship" label, which is defined by Zahra (1991, p. 260) as the *"formal or informal activity aimed at creating new business in established firms through product and process innovations and market developments."*

260 See Rauch et al. (2009), p. 763.

261 First-mover advantages usually describe the profits that firms can reap by being first-to-market. This study, however, follows the conceptualization of Lumpkin and Dess (1996, p. 146) that *"the second firm to enter a new market [is] as pioneering as the first entrant and just as likely to achieve success via proactiveness."*

262 See Lumpkin/Dess (1996), pp. 146f.

263 Venkatraman (1989), p. 949.

discover an opportunity an entrepreneurial firm has to possess prior knowledge that is in some sense related to the new information that triggers its discovery. This implies that proactive firms have to engage in efforts to diversify their information and knowledge base by e.g. building an extensive network of weak ties with other firms.

Innovativeness reflects the Schumpeterian notion that entrepreneurial firms introduce new combinations as an act of creative destruction and thereby shift resources from existing firms to new ones. It shows a firm's tendency to experiment with new and existing resources by promoting new ideas, creativity, and novelty to introduce new products, processes, or technologies. Innovative firms are willing to depart from existing technologies and commit a considerable amount of resources to venture into the unknown and develop new capabilities. As such, innovativeness is central when it comes to pursuing new opportunities.[264]

Risk-taking refers to the uncertainty of decision makers about the outcome of future situations due to a lack of information. Baird and Thomas separate risk in venturing into the unknown, committing a large amount of resources, or borrowing heavily without certainties about future outcomes.[265] Risk-taking, however, does not mean "*reckless decision making, but rather, a reasonable awareness of the risks involved, and an attempt to manage these risks.*"[266] It refers to decisions made in situations where the probability of future gains or losses is objectively or subjectively given. In the managerial context, risk refers to the well-known risk-return trade-off and represents the degree to which "*managers are willing to make large and risky resource commitments – i.e., those which have a reasonable chance of costly failures.*"[267]

The discussion shows that there is a close relationship between the dimensions of proactiveness, innovation, and risk-taking. Proactively pursuing opportunities and experimenting with innovative resource combinations are both resource consuming postures that carry with them the inherent risk of failure; yet, the more the firm's entrepreneurial actions depart from its traditional line of operations and venture into unexplored market niches, the higher is its chance to get a head start and realize superior economic profits.[268] Proactiveness and innovativeness therefore crucially depend on the firm's willingness to take well calculated and managed risks. Thus, EO provides firms with the ability to find opportunities that others have overlooked, thereby differentiating them from their competitors and enabling them to create competitive advantage.[269]

The relationship between a firm's EO and its performance has received extensive empirical attention. Rauch and colleagues reviewed 51 published studies in a meta-analysis that cut across different industrial and cultural settings and that together represent 14,259 companies.

264 See Lumpkin/Dess (1996), p. 142; Rauch et al. (2009), p. 763.

265 See Baird/Thomas (1985), pp. 231f.

266 Morris/Trotter (1990), p. 22.

267 Miller/Friesen (1978), p. 923.

268 See Lee/Lee/Pennings (2001), p. 618.

269 See Wiklund/Shepherd (2005), p. 86.

They found that there is a positive and moderately large relationship between EO and firm performance. This suggests that firms are indeed likely to benefit from an entrepreneurial strategic posture and these results have been found to be robust across different contextual settings.[270]

Despite its importance, EO has so far not attracted any attention in the cluster context. There exist, however, several studies that examine the effect of EO on firm performance in different environmental settings and its impact on networks and relationships. Their results provide important implications about how firms explore opportunities in clusters.

3.1.3 Hypothesis on Entrepreneurship in Clusters

This section aims to derive a hypothesis about how firms use their EO to explore opportunities that abound in clusters. To this end, it first reviews selected studies on EO under different environmental settings, before examining its impact on networks and relationships.

In a longitudinal analysis over a seven year period Zahra and Covin examined the influence of EO on the performance of firms in hostile versus benign environments. Hostile environments are characterized by high levels of competitive intensity, a large amount of uncertainty with regards to market developments, and a high influence of competitive forces beyond the firm's sphere of influence. Their results show that firms in hostile environments that have adopted an EO had higher performance than their non-entrepreneurial peers. Due to the longitudinal design of their study, Zahra and Covin also demonstrated, that a firm's EO *"may take many years to fully pay off."*[271] Managers should therefore adopt a long-term perspective in developing and maintaining an EO.[272]

Using a sample of small firms and a longitudinal design over a two year period, Wiklund and Shepherd explored the effect of a firm's EO under different external contingencies. The authors revealed several findings. First, regardless of possible contingencies, firms with an EO always perform better than peers that act less entrepreneurial. Second, businesses acting in opportunity and resource constrained environments benefit the most from having an EO. In fact, EO can be used to overcome severe external constraints, as it provides a strategic mechanism for firms to differentiate themselves from their competitors. Third, an EO allows firms to create disequilibrium by "shaking-up" their industry and thereby generating a stream of opportunities. Subsequently, those same firms can then profit the most from the changing competitive landscape as they proactively seek out attractive but risky niches and innovate in response to newly perceived needs.[273]

---

270 The calculated corrected correlation across all studies was $r = 0.242$, revealing a substantial effect of EO on firm performance (see Rauch et al. (2009), p. 778).

271 Zahra/Covin (1995), p. 55.

272 See Zahra/Covin (1995), p. 55.

273 See Wiklund/Shepherd (2005), pp. 85f.

Two studies have also examined the effect of EO in the international context. Zahra and Garvis for example, used data from US American companies to examine the effect of hostility of the international environment on the relationship between EO and firm performance. They defined environmental hostility similar to the previous studies as the result of industry changes, uncertainties with regards to demand conditions, radical innovations, and rivalry among competitors. Their results show that in hostile international environments EO can enhance firm performance. This implies that managers in such environments should pursue a proactive approach to their environment and abandon conservative risk-averse options. The authors furthermore revealed that high performing firms in benign environments also pursue an EO. They do this in anticipation of future changes to safeguard against strategic surprises, to further widen their growth opportunities, and to extend their strategic alternatives.[274]

Dimitros and colleagues on the other hand, surveyed Greek firms that showed strong international activities in different industrial sectors. The authors drew a distinction between uncertain and hostile environments. Uncertainty refers to environmental instability and reflects the difficulty to predict the outcome of change. Hostility on the other hand deals with scarce environments and a high degree of competition. While hostility presents external forces that go beyond management's immediate control, uncertainty can be managed through experience and organizational learning. This implies that entrepreneurial firms that are able to operate in an uncertain home environment can transfer their experience to other uncertain international markets.[275] The authors are able to confirm this assumption as firms assign priority to uncertain environmental conditions in their home base as opposed to uncertainty in their foreign host countries. This finding indirectly supports Porter's notion of domestic clusters as key driver for a firm's international success.[276] Domestic uncertainty reinforces the positive effects of an EO and thereby prevents organizational inertia, which then serves as source of competitive advantage abroad.[277]

Taken together, the studies reveal that firms in environments where rivalry and uncertainty is high and change frequent are far better off when they purse an EO, that is when they proactively seek attractive but risky new opportunities and innovate in their response.

With regards to the impact of EO on networks and relationships, the discussion in section 3.1.1.2 shows that entrepreneurial firms rely heavily on networks and relationships to explore opportunities and mobilize resources in their response. To address this issue, Sarkar and colleagues examined the effect of alliance entrepreneurship on firm market performance. The authors argue that entrepreneurial strategies facilitate access relationships to mobilize those resources and capabilities that are "*commonly found in the interstices between firms, uni-*

274 See Zahra/Garvis (2000), pp. 485f.

275 See Dimitratos/Lioukas/Carter (2004), pp. 24f.

276 See section 2.2.5 and Porter (1990), pp. 71ff.

277 See Dimitratos/Lioukas/Carter (2004), pp. 34f.

versities, research laboratories, suppliers, and customers."[278] Firms that can mobilize resources that are owned or controlled by partners may profit from their value-creating potential by exploiting previously identified opportunities. Since the number of potential alliance partners that possess a suitable resource profile is limited, it is likely that alliance entrepreneurship will result in first-mover advantages. Firms that are better informed about the future value of a potential alliance partnership may reap its advantages ahead of competitors.[279] Using a sample of US American technology companies with alliance experience, the authors find strong evidence that alliance entrepreneurship positively influences firm performance. It enables firms to learn new skills and get access to complementary resources of their partners thereby leading to competitive advantage. These effects are even enhanced in dynamic environments where market profiles and customer preferences are subject to permanent change. In such environments, access relationships allow firms to earn a premium by facilitating the speedy development of new resource combinations that can serve upcoming market trends.[280]

In a similar study, Marino and colleagues examine the influence of EO on strategic alliance formation by using a diverse sample of firms located in Finland, Greece, Indonesia, Mexico, the Netherlands, and Sweden. The authors argue that a firm's tendency to enter into alliances will be directly influenced by its EO as alliances enable firms to pursue an entrepreneurial strategy. For example, innovative firms can use cooperative agreements to mobilize a diverse set of resources and thereby maintain high levels of innovation. In the same way, they can also hedge against risk by forming multiple alliances and thereby reduce their dependence on a few resource providers. Finally, entrepreneurial firms can proactively engage in strategic alliances with critical resource providers to exploit upcoming opportunities; a fact that was already confirmed by Sarkar and colleagues. The authors' results confirm their hypothesis and show that firms with an EO indeed form multiple strategic alliances with partner firms.[281]

Thus, both studies find that an EO enables firms to mobilize resources by forming alliances with partners in their external environment. They also provide several competitive advantages including uncertainty reduction, the exploitation of opportunities through complementary resources, risk and cost sharing, and access to diverse knowledge and skills.

Similarly, firms that adopt an **EO in clusters** should be able to profit from ample opportunities as clusters are a key source of information and a stock of valuable resources. In clusters, entrepreneurial firms can tap into different opportunity sources. Along the *horizontal and vertical dimensions* proactive firms can diversify their information and knowledge base through their informal networks that go beyond their immediate social circle. These net-

278 Powell/Koput/Smith-Doerr (1996), p. 118.

279 See Sarkar/Echambadi/Harrison (2001), pp. 702f.

280 See Sarkar/Echambadi/Harrison (2001), pp. 708f.

281 See Marino et al. (2002), pp. 147ff.

works can provide valuable information about upcoming market trends, changing customer needs, and new combinations that could potentially disrupt industry structure and lead to new market niches. In this context, *"actors are not deliberately 'scanning' their environment in search of a specific piece of information but rather are surrounded by a concoction of rumors, impressions, recommendations, trade folklore, and strategic information."*[282] In the *horizontal dimension,* firms target similar markets. This creates rivalry and serves as an incentive for firms to constantly innovate and differentiate each other from their competitors. Consequently, firms adopting an EO should be better off as they are able to observe their competitors and act appropriately in response to emerging opportunities by introducing new combinations. Along the *vertical dimension* on the other hand, suppliers, buyers, and service providers engage with each other in close relationships. For these networks, clusters provide opportunities to close information gaps that emerged due to vertical industry specialization. By engaging in joint cooperation, firms become aware of each other's needs and discover existing but previously unexploited opportunities.

Summing up, firms that adopt an EO should be better able to explore emerging opportunities in clusters and mobilize the necessary resources in their response. They should therefore have higher levels of performance than their peers that act less entrepreneurial:

Hypothesis 4: *The relationship between clusters and firm performance will be positively moderated by a firm's entrepreneurial orientation.*

3.2 Advantage Exploitation through Strategic Management in Clusters

Strategic management is concerned with setting the direction of the firm and ensuring its long-term survival by enabling it to achieve and defend competitive advantages.[283] A firm is said to have a **competitive advantage** when it implements a strategy that generates above-average returns[284] and that its competitors are unable to duplicate or find too costly to imitate. It can be confident that it has achieved one or more competitive advantages only after competitor's efforts to imitate its strategy have failed or ceased. The durability of a competitive advantage, however, is strongly dependent on the firm's ability to erect barriers to imitation that limit the speed with which its competitors are able to acquire new skills and competence to challenge its market position.[285] A firm's competitive advantage is therefore always a comparative advantage that is valued relative to other firms.

---

282 Grabher (2002), p. 38 (emphasis added in the original).

283 See Teece/Pisano/Shuen (1997), p. 509.

284 Above-average returns are returns that are higher than what an investor can expect to earn from any other investment with a similar amount of risk (see Hitt/Ireland/Hoskisson (2009), p. 5).

285 See Hitt/Ireland/Hoskisson (2009), p. 5.

Within the strategy field, the resource-based view of the firm[286] (RBV) emerged as *the* dominant paradigm during the 1990s that firms use to achieve competitive advantages. It suggests that a firm's unique resources and capabilities are the critical link to above-average performance. In the following, section 3.2.1 first discusses the basic premises of the RBV and the value generating potential of strategic resources. Section 3.2.2 then shows how firms utilize organizational capabilities to turn this potential into actual competitive advantages. In section 3.2.3, these insights are then applied to the cluster context to derive a hypothesis about how a distinct cluster-capability enables firms to make use of the resources that are prevalent in clusters.

3.2.1 Basic Premises of the Resource-Based View of the Firm

3.2.1.1 Resource Heterogeneity and Imperfect Factor Markets

The RBV emerged in the late 1980s and early 1990s as direct critique to Porter's competitive strategy framework.[287] While Porter views firms as bundles of value activities, resource-based scholars view it as a bundle of resources and capabilities, which determine its strengths and weaknesses. Resources are assets that are controlled or owned by a firm, whereas capabilities refer to its distinctive and superior abilities of exploiting and combining resources in order to accomplish its targets.[288] Unlike RBV scholars, Porter places little emphasis on the impact of firm specific characteristics on performance. The underlying assumption is that factor markets are perfectly competitive and that firms can easily acquire all the resources they need to implement a viable product-market strategy based on a unique configuration of their value activities. Resources are therefore highly mobile, which over time makes competing firms identical in terms of their resource endowment.[289]

For RBV scholars however, the assumption of perfect factor markets does not hold true. A perfectly competitive factor market would require that the price of any given resource perfectly reflects the economic value that can be created by putting the resource to use. In that case, the (hyper-rational) seller of the resource would ex-ante be able to anticipate every possible way in which the resource can be used and simply price the resource according to the highest achievable value: "*If strategic factor markets are perfect, then the cost of acquiring stra-*

[286] All approaches that view a firm's superior economic performance as a result of its unique internal resources and capabilities are summarized in the following under the "resource-based view" label (see for example Amit/Schoemaker (1993); Barney (1986); Barney (1991); Prahalad/Hamel (1990); Wernerfelt (1984)). Contemporary approaches such as the dynamic capability approach (Teece/Pisano/Shuen (1997)) and the knowledge-based view of the firm (Kogut/Zander (1992)) will not be discussed separately as they represent only slight modifications of the RBV and are based on the same core logic (see Barney/Clark (2007), pp. 22ff).

[287] See section 2.2.5.

[288] In the early contributions, there was no explicit distinction between resources and capabilities. Barney (1991, p. 367) for example, defined firm resources as including "*all assets, capabilities, organizational processes, firm attributes, information, knowledge etc. controlled by a firm.*" In the interest of readability, the following discussion will therefore use the term resources until the distinction becomes theoretically relevant in section 3.2.2.

[289] See Porter (1991), pp. 107ff.

tegic resources will approximately equal the economic value of those resources once they are used to implement product market strategies."[290] This suggests that no matter what strategies a firm implements with the help of its resources, those strategies will not be a source of economic rents.[291] This contradicts Porter's central assumption that the ability of firms to enter an attractive industry and achieve a favorable product-market position is an explanation for superior economic performance.

In contrast, the RBV builds on the notion of imperfect or not existent strategic factor markets, which leads to two alternative assumptions:

(1) Resources are heterogeneously distributed among firms and

(2) imperfectly mobile, allowing resource differences to persist over time.

The main reasons for imperfect factor markets are information asymmetries between buyers and sellers of resources. Only when the buying firm possesses superior expectations about the economic value of a resource compared to the selling firm, the purchase becomes viable as the resource remains underpriced. In this case, the buyer can exploit its (Ricardian[292]) rent generating potential, because the costs of acquiring the resource are lower than the economic value that can be created by using it in a superior way.[293]

In addition to imperfect factor markets, Dierickx and Cool suggest that some resources cannot be purchased at all, because they lack an appropriate factor market. They refer to resources that are so deeply embedded in a firm's organizational environment that they would lose significant economic value when used in an alternative setting. Instead, this type of highly specific resources has to be built internally and upgraded over time. In this case, economic rents stem less from information asymmetries and imperfect factor markets than from a firm's property rights that allow the control of resources that are not available to its competitors.[294]

Hence according to the resource-based logic, a firm's performance stems ultimately from its controlled or owned unique resources producing Ricardian efficiency rents as opposed to monopolistic rents in Porter's market-based framework.

3.2.1.2 Competitive Forces and Isolating Mechanisms

Although resource heterogeneity and immobility represent the two central assumptions of the RBV, it does not mean that a strategy that is build on any given resource holds the poten-

290 Barney (1986), p. 1231.

291 See Barney/Clark (2007), pp. 16f.

292 Ricardian rents are returns on the efficient use of an existing stock of resources, which is superior to resources held by other firms. From this perspective, profits are ultimately a return to the unique assets owned and controlled by the firm (see Spanos/Lioukas (2001), p. 911).

293 See Barney (1986), p. 1234. Additionally, firms can also be lucky or have good fortune and acquire resources whose actual value is greater than what was originally expected. This resource was ex-ante similarly underpriced.

294 See Dierickx/Cool (1989), p. 1505.

tial to contribute to a firm's competitive advantage. In order to add to a firm's superiority, resources furthermore have to be valuable, rare, not substitutable, and not imitable (so called VRIN). These isolating mechanisms can be seen as indicators of how heterogeneous and immobile a given resource is and consequently how useful it is to limit the competitive forces that threaten to erode a firm's competitive advantage.

To be a source of competitive advantages it is essential that resources are **valuable**, in that they allow a firm to develop and implement a strategy that improves its efficiency and effectiveness. In addition, the product or service that results from this strategy has to be valued by the market, i.e. the customer. Only when resources contribute to the development of products that are perceived and valued as being superior to other similar products do they qualify as sources of competitive advantage.[295] It is important to note that it is ultimately the market that determines the value of a resource-driven strategy. By ignoring the market firms run the risk that they acquire strategic resources that do not contribute to value creation. A firm might allocate resources to create a superior and highly sophisticated product, but this very same product will fail to generate a competitive advantage, if it does not create the willingness of customers to pay for it. This means, that the value of a firm's resource base needs to be evaluated against the background of its specific market environment.[296]

Furthermore, resources that contribute to competitive advantage have also to be **rare**. This ensures that the firm that is controlling a valuable and rare resource can implement a strategy that differentiates it from its competitors and creates a unique competitive advantage. On the other hand, valuable resources that are not rare can be held by a large number of firms which can all put that resource into a similar use. While this would create competitive parity in an industry and ensure firm survival, none would be able to achieve a competitive advantage over its competitors. As Barney notes, how rare a resource has to be in order to generate a competitive advantage is difficult to assess. He therefore defines a resource as rare as long as the number of firms that are in control of it is less than the number of firms necessary to create a perfectly competitive market.[297]

Another important requirement for resources to be a source of competitive advantage is that they are **imperfectly imitable**. A competitive advantage will be short-lived if it is based on easily imitable resources. To be able to imitate a critical resource a firm has first to identify the underlying sources of a competitor's advantage and second be able to retrace the steps that have been necessary to acquire and/or develop that resource. Yet, obtaining the necessary information or achieving the imitation of a critical resource can be difficult, if that resource is subject to barriers to imitation. Resources can be imperfectly imitable due to the unique historical conditions of their creation, a causally ambiguous link with a firm's competitive advantage, or their social complexity.

---

[295] See Barney (1991), p. 106.

[296] See Barney/Clark (2007), p. 58.

[297] See Barney (1991), p. 107.

Historical resources such as the knowledge of groups of experts and scientists or a firm's organizational culture develop through continuous accumulative learning processes, first-mover advantages, and sometimes even chance. They are the result of path dependent decisions, time consuming efforts, and costly investments. A firm that would want to imitate such a historical resource would have to replicate the exact same historical development process that its competitor had to pass.[298] Therefore, the more historically unique a resource's development process was the less imitable that resource becomes.

Causal ambiguity means that the way in which a resource contributes to competitive advantage is not understood or understood poorly by a firm's managers. This happens especially in the case of complex synergetic resource bundles where numerous plausible explanations exist about the way in which each resource contributes to competitive advantage. As a result, imitating firms cannot state explicitly which resource represents the underlying cause of a competitor's advantage and are therefore unable to initiate an appropriate response.[299]

Social complexity further supports the non-imitability of resources and refers to the fact that they can only unfold their true potential in a combinatory mix of tangible and intangible resources. Such complementary resource bundles may consist of tangible assets such as machines and tools and intangible assets such as an organizational culture that promotes team work and the knowledge of experts on how to exploit those machines and tools to produce superior craft work. In these cases, barriers to imitation do not rest on causal ambiguity, but on the underlying complex social pattern of interaction between the complementary resource types.[300]

The final characteristic of strategic resources is their **non-substitutability**. This means that there must be no other resource that in itself is valuable, rare, and not imitable and that when it is put to use contributes to the implementation of an equivalent strategy. If such a resource or bundle of resources exists, firms can imitate or even outpace other leading firms by implementing similar strategies based on their own unique resource configuration. The higher the number of firms that can imitate a successful strategy by acquiring or developing substitutable resources, the closer the industry gets to competitive parity. In general, substitutability can take two forms. A resource can be substituted by a similar or by a very different resource. The latter is a particularly big threat amidst globalization and rapid technological change. In this new competitive landscape it is more than likely that a firm outpaces its com-

---

298 See Dierickx/Cool (1989), p. 1507.

299 See Barney (1991), p. 109; Starbuck (1992), p. 724. Although causal ambiguity remains an often cited requirement of strategic resources, it has not been without critics of which Collis stands out. Contrary to Barney and others, he states that "*causal ambiguity ultimately cannot be a source of sustainable competitive advantage because it contains the seeds of its own self-destruction*" (Collis (1994), p. 147). If an organization is not able to identify the sources of its own competitive advantage, then it is equally not able to manage or adapt to environmental change, in which case its competitive advantage erodes over time. On the other hand, if a firm takes action and changes the configuration of its resources, it runs the risk to unintentionally destroy its competitive advantage.

300 Barney (1991), p. 110.

petitors that previously held a competitive advantage by replacing a critical technology with e.g. a disruptive technology and thereby implement the same strategy more efficiently. Therefore, Collis concludes that the substitutability of a resource poses the biggest threat to a firm's competitive advantage.[301]

3.2.2 Utilizing Resources through Organizational Capabilities

So far, the discussion about the basic premises of the RBV has not differentiated between resources and capabilities. It has assumed that resources are valuable in and of themselves and has said nothing about how these resources are coordinated and put to use in order to create value for the firm. To this point, the process of value creation remains in a black-box. To resolve this issue, the RBV offers the concept of **organizational capabilities**. While resources refer to tangible and intangible assets and production inputs that are tied semi-permanently to the firm, organizational capabilities refer "*to an organizational ability to perform a coordinated task, utilizing organizational resources, for the purpose of achieving a particular end result.*"[302] Winter offers a precise definition of organizational capabilities and their constituting characteristics by conceptualizing them as "*a high level routine (or collection of routines) that, together with its implementing input flows, confers upon an organization's management a set of decision options for producing significant outputs of a particular type.*"[303] This definition rests upon the work of Cyert and March who define organizational capabilities as a firm's internal procedures.[304]

The notion of capabilities fundamentally rests on organizational routines and resources, which serve as their basic building blocks. **Routines** are concerned with the fulfillment of specific tasks and problems of low-complexity and represent "*forms, rules, procedures, conventions, strategies, and technologies around which organizations are constructed and through which they operate.*"[305] They develop over time when organizations are repeatedly faced with similar problems that allow developing a standard operating procedure. Examples include human resources hiring procedures or formal Total Quality Management rules. They formalize the way in which recurring tasks are approached and by doing so serve as coordination mechanism to effectively leverage and utilize a firm's resource base. This creates a sense of stability among the individuals of the firm so that over time routines become socially embedded and can be executed sub-consciously, which ultimately increases their efficiency.[306]

So, both capabilities and routines are conceptualized in the context of problem-solving and utilize resources to accomplish specific tasks. The main difference between them lies in their complexity. In contrast to routines, organizational capabilities can span departments and

---

301 See Collis (1994), p. 147; Barney (1991), p. 111.

302 Helfat (2003), p. 1; see also Amit/Schoemaker (1993), p. 35.

303 Winter (2000), p. 983; Winter (2003), p. 991.

304 See Cyert/March (1963), p. 179.

305 Levitt/March (1988), p. 320.

306 See Becker (2004), p. 662.

functions to solve complex tasks, which require the coordination of several resources and routines at the same time. Examples include complex processes such as product development, customer relationship management, controlling, or supply chain management. It is important to note that a collection of routines and resources does not represent an organizational capability unless it has proven to be reliable and applicable across various situations.[307] In addition, for a routine to qualify as a capability it has to be substantial in scale and significance, enable the production of output that significantly influences a firm's survival and prosperity, and management's awareness of its required inputs and intended effects.[308]

This requires time as firms use their experience and feedback to transform a singular problem-solving success into a reliable organizational capability.[309] It also means that it is difficult for competitors to imitate a firm's superior capability without gaining similar experiences and retracing the same development process by e.g. using time compressing activities such as learning through crash-courses.[310] In fact, it is exactly this time-consuming characteristic that makes organizational capabilities difficult to imitate and therefore strategically relevant to a firm's competitive advantage. Due to their composition and social embeddedness, capabilities are complex and therefore difficult to transfer from one organizational context to another.

Summing up, capabilities bundle a firm's resources by utilizing a set of complex routines and that is how they contribute to competitive advantage. For many RBV scholars they are the most important factor to distinguish firms from their competitors, because their complexity and social embeddedness makes them difficult to imitate. After all, if a firm dissolves, its capabilities vanish with it.[311] Consequently, RBV scholars agree that the strategic imperative for firms is not to focus on resources, but rather on the set of capabilities behind their appropriate building up.

To integrate this core logic into an organizing framework for a resource-based approach to strategy making, Grant developed a model that is centered on its key variables and propositions. It is illustrated in figure 19. Resource-based strategy making requires that the firm takes a deep look into its internal structure to (1) identify the existing resource base; (2) identify its capabilities; (3) appraise their rent-generating potential; (4) select an appropriate strategy; and if necessary (5) extend and upgrade the firm's stock of resources and capabilities.[312]

---

307 See Helfat/Peteraf (2003), p. 999.

308 See Winter (2000), p. 983.

309 See Schreyögg/Kliesch-Eberl (2007), pp. 915f.

310 See Dierickx/Cool (1989), p. 1507.

311 See Korhonen/Niemela (2005), p. 17.

312 See Grant (1991). Similarly, Teece summarizes the RBV's approach to strategy as "*(1) identify your firm's unique resources; (2) decide in which markets those resources can earn the highest rents; and (3) decide whether the rents from those assets are most effectively utilized by (a) integrating into related market(s), (b) selling the relevant intermediate output to related firms, or (c) selling the assets themselves to a firm in related businesses*"

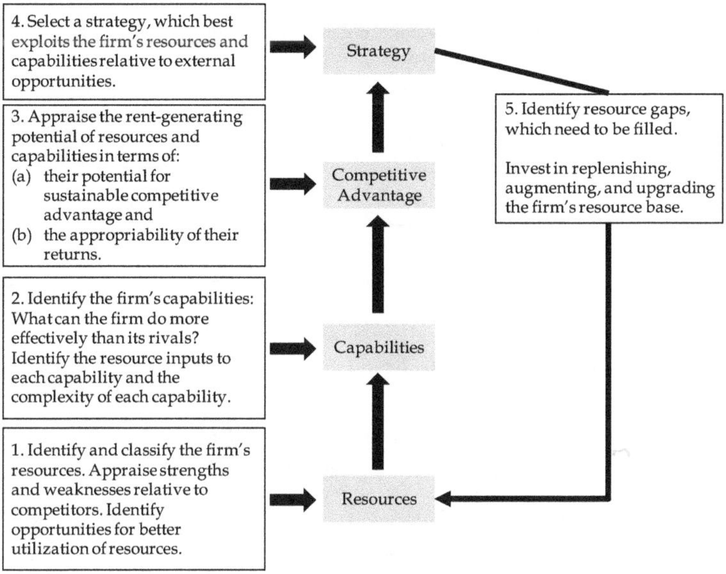

Figure 19 - A resource-based approach to strategy development
(Source: Grant (1991), p. 115)

The framework emphasizes that resources and capabilities always have to be appraised relative to a firm's competitors, which reflects the nature of competitive advantages as relative constructs. Therefore, every capability-driven strategy has to consider the competitive positions of the firm's rivals. The framework also hints to the fact that capabilities evolve within a hierarchy; an issue that is discussed in the following.

Hierarchies of Capabilities

The discussion so far suggests that capabilities evolve within a hierarchy (see figure 20). The base of the hierarchy includes the know-how of individuals, resources, and routines and combines to create skills designed to perform certain tasks, which can be highly product and process-specific. On the second level, task-specific capabilities are integrated within company functions such as marketing, human resources, or finance. On the highest level of aggregation, broad and general capabilities such as networking and cost controls, are formed and maintained from the integration of more specialized capabilities. These higher-level capabilities can span many functions and departments.[313]

(Teece/Pisano/Shuen (1997), p. 514). According to the RBV's basic assumption of imperfect factor markets, however, selling the firm's VRIN resources could prove difficult. The last point could therefore be restated as: (3) enter the particular market and generate Ricardian efficiency rents.

313 See Hoopes/Madsen (2008), pp. 397f.

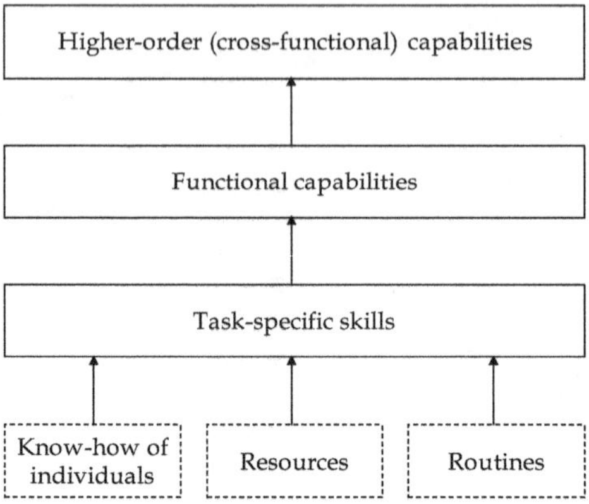

Figure 20 - A hierarchy of capabilities
(Source: adapted from Korhonen/Niemela (2005), p. 17)

Integration, however, is not easy. Performing specialized capabilities requires knowledge of specially trained experts. This knowledge is partly explicit and partly taken-for-granted, tacit, and deeply embedded in the firm's routines. It is therefore not enough to directly integrate specialized capabilities into a higher-order, cross-functional capability. For example, the creation of a higher order supply chain management capability requires more than just the sequential execution of purchasing, manufacturing, logistics, distribution, and strategic planning routines. There needs to be a coordinating authority that plans, directs, and controls the interaction of the different departments and functions, because higher-order capabilities cannot be directly linked to any individual in the firm. One common solution is the creation of cross-functional teams, composed of experts from different departments that have access to the functions' specialized knowledge and problem-solving routines and that directly report to top management.[314]

Furthermore, there are several important features about the hierarchy depicted in figure 20. First, each capability level builds on the level below, so that no higher-order capability can exist without its constituting lower-order capabilities and skills. Second, each level adds greater value to the firm. *Resources* on their own add little value to the firm, while *task-specific skills* deploy resources and routines to solve problems of low complexity and thereby add more value. *Functional capabilities* add even greater value, because they span their functional unit and integrate several task-specific skills to create synergy and a higher-level problem solving ability. Finally, *higher-order, cross-functional capabilities* add the greatest value, because they leverage resources and capabilities at the corporate strategy level, thus having a broader scope and maximizing synergy potentials across the firm.[315]

314 See Grant (2005), p. 150.

315 See Javidan (1998), pp. 62f.

Properly executed, **higher-order capabilities** carry the greatest potential to generate value. The higher the capability is in hierarchy, the more socially embedded it is in the organization. Its complex dependence on skilled individuals, resources, and proven problem-solving routines also means that it cannot simply be transferred across organizations or firms without also transferring its constituting components. Their complex architecture makes them therefore rare, difficult to substitute by other capabilities, and almost impossible to imitate. They are rare, because their complexity requires specific ingredients, which only a small number of firms are likely to have. They are also difficult to substitute, because the domains of higher-order capabilities are broad and general corporate tasks. Finally, they are hard to imitate, because their creation is subject to a causal ambiguous, time consuming, and socially complex learning process. It is therefore nearly impossible for an outsider to analytically break down what exactly it is about the higher-order capability of a competitor that adds to its competitive advantage. It is due to these characteristics that higher-order capabilities are especially important to the competitive advantage of the firm.

Summing up, the discussion on strategic management shows that resources are not valuable in and of themselves, but that firms rely on their organizational capabilities to turn their value-generating potential into actual competitive advantages. This core logic of the strategic management field mandates that firms in clusters also have to make use of a distinct cluster-capability to access the resources that are prevalent in clusters and turn them into competitive advantages. Therefore, the next section applies this logic to the cluster context to derive a hypothesis about how firms can make use of a distinct cluster-capability to create competitive advantages through clusters.

3.2.3 Hypothesis on Strategic Management in Clusters

In contrast to entrepreneurship theory, where EO is a well established construct that is readily applicable to explain how firms explore opportunities in clusters, neither the literature on clusters nor the literature on strategic management has so far produced insights on a distinct cluster-capability that explains how firms make use of the resources that are prevalent in clusters.

By combining the insights from the previous discussions on clusters and organizational capabilities, however, it is possible to explicate a **set of tasks** that a firm's distinct cluster-capability has to fulfill:

(1) Due to the importance of information asymmetries, the firm has to be able to utilize information sources that are prevalent in clusters.

(2) To access and mobilize resources in the long-run, firms also have to be able to maintain and nurture access relationships.

(3) Once the resources become accessible to the firm, they have to be strategically upgraded and augmented.

A cluster-capability that fulfills these tasks resembles in part but also goes far beyond what is known as *absorptive capacity* and *combinative capability*.[316] It allows firms to recognize the value of a given piece of information, assimilate it, and transfer it across departments to those units that can make the best use out of it. To achieve this task, the firm depends on individuals within its boundaries that are aware of where useful experts reside. These individuals translate knowledge that was produced externally in the cluster into a form that can be understood and used by the departments and individuals within the firm.[317] Once a firm has developed this ability, a self-reinforcing process emerges that increases its sensitivity towards other firms' and individuals' knowledge and information. That in turn enhances its awareness to emerging technological opportunities and thereby also increases its aspiration level to proactively exploit opportunities.[318] In contrast, firms, which are unable to relate external information and knowledge to their internal repertoire, may treat it as not applicable in their unique context or simply ignore it and thereby overlook potentially valuable opportunities.[319] Thus, a cluster-capability that resembles these qualities allows firms to make sense of the scattered information and knowledge that resides within clusters, assimilate it, and then utilize it towards their own ends.

Another set of capabilities that is not explicitly mentioned in the cluster literature, but that fulfill parts of a cluster-capability's tasks are network and alliance capabilities. *Network capabilities* express the ability to simultaneously manage a variety of relationships, while *alliance capabilities* refer to the ability of managing single relationships and alliances between two firms.[320]

Both capabilities draw on several theoretical perspectives[321], but research on their underlying components is mainly based on the insights provided by Kale and colleagues about the contributions of a firm's dedicated alliance function. The main responsibility of an alliance function is to act as a centralized coordination unit that facilitates the establishment of new alliances with external partners. Externally, it does so by being a visible point of contact for potential partners that want to establish new alliances. Internally, it is supposed to facilitate learning about current and past alliance experiences, improve the allocation of strategic resources to critical alliances, and monitor and evaluate alliance performance.[322]

Firms with a distinct cluster-capability that resembles traits of network and alliance capabilities can also enhance their access to critical resources by forming multiple cooperative alliances with other cluster-firms. It enables firms to create innovative resource bundles that

---

316 See Cohen/Levinthal (1990), p. 128 and Kogut/Zander (1992), p. 384.

317 See Bathelt/Malmberg/Maskell (2004), p. 44.

318 See Cohen/Levinthal (1990), p. 128.

319 See Bathelt/Malmberg/Maskell (2004), p. 44.

320 See Walter/Auer/Ritter (2006), p. 546.

321 These include the RBV, the dynamic capability approach, the knowledge-based view, and evolutionary economics (see Kale/Dyer/Singh (2002), p. 749 and Walter/Auer/Ritter (2006), p. 546).

322 See Kale/Dyer/Singh (2002), p. 752.

one firm cannot create on its own. Such a resource bundle might include the combination of an advanced technology held by one firm with another firm's access to and knowledge of specific markets.[323] Hence, firms can use clusters to upgrade and augment their resources and thereby maximize their value relative to other possible internal combinations.

In doing so, firms search for alliance partners with specialized resource profiles, depending on the types of resources needed.[324] *Similar resources,* such as those that can be found along the horizontal dimension, allow firms to primarily exploit already existing competitive advantages. They provide the opportunity to profit from the alliance partner's relative market position (e.g. brand reputation), to share market information in order to optimize the timing for investment choices, and to significantly reduce the time-to-market. Furthermore, horizontal alliances enable firms to optimize their capacity utilization, generate economies of scale, and profit from learning effects. The means are mainly formal and include JVs, strategic alliances, and the acquisition of competitors. *Complementary resources* instead, such as those that can typically be found along the vertical dimension of clusters, provide the opportunity to gain economies of scope, create synergies, and explore novel resource bundles that lead to the creation of new combinations.[325]

Yet, firms in clusters can usually choose from a larger pool of potential network and alliance partners than firms outside of clusters. This richness, however, also adds complexity to the selection process since the number of partners with a suitable resource profile and compatible strategic goals and objectives may be limited. Firms in clusters should therefore be able to separate those firms that can add value to their existing partner portfolio from those that may turn out to be potentially harmful. A distinct cluster-capability assists firms in this process by enabling them to make informed decisions about the future value of a potential partnership that may be available in clusters.

Summing up, the cited tasks and capabilities provide an initial understanding of how a cluster-capability enables firms to generate competitive advantages through clusters. Although it is not clear what elements actually define a distinct cluster-capability, it can still be hypothesized that it enables firms to make better use of the resources that are prevalent in clusters. They should therefore have higher levels of performance:

Hypothesis 5: *The relationship between clusters and firm performance will be positively moderated by a firm's cluster-capability.*

The identification of skills that actually define a cluster-capability is the subject of a fieldwork that was conducted in China and which is presented in chapter 4. At first, however, the next section discusses the emerging theory of Strategic Entrepreneurship, which emphasizes

323 See Stuart/Sorenson (2007), p. 214.

324 See Gulati/Nohria/Zaheer (2000), p. 207.

325 See Ireland/Hitt/Vaidyanath (2002), p. 430.

the need for a configurational approach to strategy that balances the exploration of new opportunities with the creation of strategic defenses to exploit what has been created.

3.3 Balancing Opportunity Exploration and Advantage Exploitation through Strategic Entrepreneurship in Clusters

The theory of Strategic Entrepreneurship is a newly emerging concept that combines elements from the fields of strategic management and entrepreneurship as both are concerned with how firms create and defend competitive advantages. It has emerged in response to the new competitive landscape of globalization and technological change. In this new competitive reality firms are increasingly less able to sustain a strategic advantage over a long period of time. Instead, firms need to (1) continuously identify structural changes in their environment that give rise to new short-term opportunities, (2) create and mobilize the resources necessary to exploit these opportunities, and (3) act in response to renew their competitive advantage.[326]

This holistic, configurational perspective to strategy integrates the entrepreneurial exploration of short-term opportunities with the establishment of strategic defenses to exploit the value that has been created.[327] Central to Strategic Entrepreneurship is the focus on heterogeneity, firm performance, and the acknowledgment of the emergence and far reaching consequences of the new competitive landscape (see figure 21).[328]

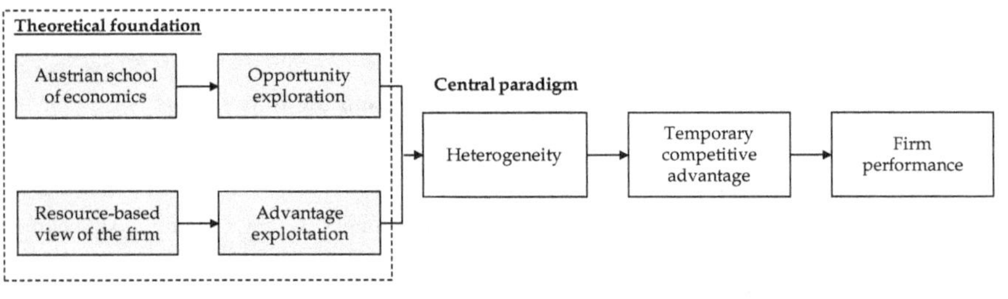

Figure 21 - Core logic of Strategic Entrepreneurship

The following section 3.3.1 first discusses the basic premises of Strategic Entrepreneurship. It emphasizes the need for a balance between the exploration of new opportunities and exploitation of already existing advantages, before integrating both perspectives into a unifying process model to strategy making. In section 3.3.2, this perspective is then applied to the

326 See Bettis/Hitt (1995), p. 16; Hitt et al. (2001), p. 480.

327 See Hitt et al. (2006), p. 2.

328 Meyer and colleagues (2006, pp. 29f) for example found that in the Strategic Management Journal and the Journal of Business Venturing (both are leading journals in the strategic management and entrepreneurship field) 86 % and 46 % of all articles that have been published between 1980 and 2000, respectively, used firm performance as the dependent variable.

cluster context to derive a configurational hypothesis about how firms generate competitive advantages through clusters.

3.3.1 Basic Premises of the Strategic Entrepreneurship Theory

3.3.1.1 The Need for a Balance between Exploration and Exploitation

According to entrepreneurship theory, competition is dynamic and generates a continuous stream of opportunities. It demands that firms continuously perceive these opportunities and introduce new combinations in their response in order to generate above-average returns. Thus, dynamic competition emphasizes the process of exploration. "*Exploration includes things captured by terms such as search, variation, risk taking, experimentation, play, flexibility, discovery, innovation.*"[329] In a fast changing environment it allows firms to pursue opportunities that have gone unnoticed by competitors.[330] Yet, it is an uncertain, chaotic, and unpredictable process where excessive exploration can turn into a frenzy of experimentation, search, and innovation (see figure 22). It can lead firms into a series of failures without rewarding benefits, because firms suffer the costs of experimentation and devote too few resources to develop and exploit the opportunities that have been discovered.[331]

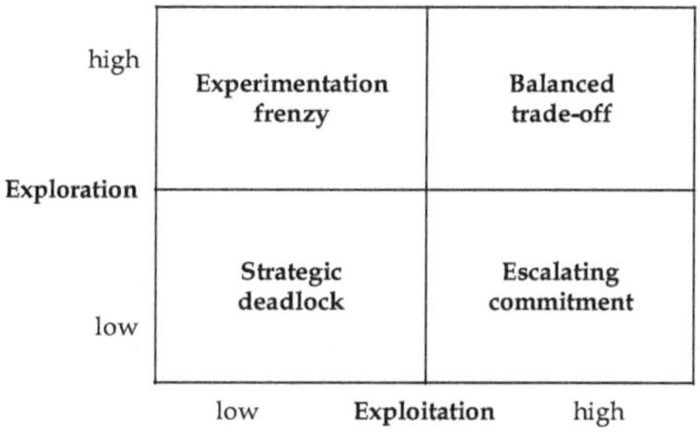

Figure 22 - The tension between exploration and exploitation

On the other hand, the field of strategic management and with it the RBV assume that competition takes place under static market conditions. Once a firm has achieved a sustainable competitive advantage, the environment surrounding it turns into an equilibrium in which prices, qualities, and resources are given as objective, all times governing data. Consequently, the resource configurations that have led to any firm's competitive advantage must be perfect in the sense that there is no other next best resource configuration that can be achieved.[332] Thus, static competition places a premium on the process of exploitation. "*Exploitation includes such things as refinement, choice, production, efficiency, selection, implementation,*

[329] March (1991), p. 71.

[330] See Michael/Storey/Howard (2006), pp. 57f.

[331] See Liu (2006), pp. 147f.

[332] See Kirzner (1997), p. 65.

execution."[333] It refers to the process of retrieving, applying, and nurturing current resources and capabilities that have proven to generate above-average returns. In its positive form it can lead to the further building up towards a long-term competitive advantage. In its negative form, however, it can lead to escalating commitment towards resources and capabilities that have become obsolete due to structural shifts in the external environment (see figure 22). In this case, the firm continues to invest time and effort and eventually becomes entrapped in a self-reinforcing negative cycle in which it starts "throwing good money after bad money". In the worst case, the firm becomes locked in a certain strategic orientation and unable to perceive strategic alternatives. Such a destructive behavior can even lead a once successful pattern to turn into a pattern of failure.[334]

To avoid falling into this trap, the literature on Strategic Entrepreneurship emphasizes the need to balance the processes of exploitation and exploration in a continuous trade-off as an excess in either dimension inhibits the risk of failure (see figure 22). As the dominant logics of the fields of entrepreneurship and strategic management, the next section therefore discusses the Austrian School of Economic and the RBV in terms of their arguments and assumptions most relevant to firm performance. This then serves as common ground for their integration into a process model of Strategic Entrepreneurship.

3.3.1.2 Strategizing in a General Process Model of Strategic Entrepreneurship

Derived from the need for a holistic, configurational perspective on strategy, this section integrates the Austrian School and the RBV into a process model of Strategic Entrepreneurship based on a discussion about their similarities, differences, and complementarities most relevant to firm performance (see table 8).

Regarding their **similarities**, both the RBV and the Austrian School of Economics and Entrepreneurship share the same objective of explaining how firms earn superior economic rents. They emphasize that the source of competitive advantages lies in the possession of heterogeneous resources that are bundled together in firms. These acquire resources in imperfect factor markets in which agents share different expectations and information about the true value of a given resource. Due to these information asymmetries regarding the net present value (NPV) of a given resource and its expected future value if it is put in a different use, firms can purchase resources where prices are too low, recombine them with their existing resource bundles, and sell the outcome where prices are too high. Gathering superior information and acquiring underpriced strategic resources that lend heterogeneity to the firm are of strategic importance. For both the RBV and the Austrian School loosing heterogeneity implies that superior economic rents (competitive advantages) diffuse and eventually get competed away: "*Regardless of the rent, [...] competitive advantage requires that the condition of hete-*

333 March (1991), p. 71.

334 See Schreyögg/Kliesch-Eberl (2007), pp. 916ff; Zander/Kogut (1995), p. 87; Kraatz/Zajac (2001), p. 634.

rogeneity be preserved. If the heterogeneity is a short-lived phenomenon, the rents will likewise be fleeting."[335]

	Austrian School of Economics	Resource-Based View
Similarities	• Focus on firm performance • Resource heterogeneity as source of competitive advantage • Importance of information asymmetries	
Differences	• Competitive disequilibrium model • Temporary competitive advantages	• Competitive equilibrium model • Sustainable competitive advantages
Complementarities	• Role of the individual • Subjective resource appraisal • Entrepreneurial alertness	• Emphasis on managing resources strategically • Establishment of isolating mechanisms

Table 8 - Characteristics of the Austrian School of Economics and the RBV

However, a **distinct difference** also separates the RBV from the Austrian School. In its original form, the RBV does not focus on the market being in motion or on dynamic competition and instead relies heavily on competitive equilibrium models. The RBV emphasizes sustainability of competitive advantage and views imitable strategies as not being able to create value. For the Austrian School on the other hand, strategies that can be duplicated have value, because lags between the time new combinations are introduced to the market and the time they are imitated by rivals allow the firm to earn superior economic profits. Competitive advantages are therefore seen as a temporary phenomenon, rather than being sustained indefinitely. Yet, in recent times the assumption of dynamic competition and temporary competitive advantages has become accepted in much of the literature on strategic management. Evidence can be found in the concepts of the new competitive landscape, hypercompetition, and the dynamic capabilities approach.[336] It is therefore safe to assume, that there is a wide consensus within the field of strategic management to view competition as being dynamic.

Besides their similarities and differences, a set of **complementarities** exists that promotes an integration of both fields into a unifying process model. Integrating the entrepreneurial role allows to open up the black-box of the RBV and to explain how resources contribute to competitive advantages. According to Foss and Ishikawa, the RBV suppresses the way how resources are appraised and deployed to new uses, treats all knowledge and information about

335 Peteraf (1993), p. 182.

336 See Bettis/Hitt (1995); D'Aveni (1994); Eisenhardt (2000); Foss/Ishikawa (2007); Porter (1991); Teece/Pisano/Shuen (1997); Winter (2003).

the future value of a given resource as objectively given data, and neglects the creation of new combinations out of existing resources. It is here that the Austrian School has shown that the future contribution of resources to value creation is not objectively given data, but a subjective appraisal that depends on the entrepreneur's related knowledge, accumulated experience, and alerted mind. Expectations about the NPV of a given resource therefore differ widely across agents. Some agents can realize rents by purchasing resources where prices are below their NPV and selling them where prices are too high or combining them with their existing resource stock and selling the outcome in appropriate product markets. In contrast, if the NPV of resources is given as objective data, agents will hold the same expectation about their future value and all rents will be priced away. Different expectations and entrepreneurial appraisals are therefore important pre-conditions of competitive advantages.[337]

On the other hand, the RBV contributes to entrepreneurship theory an understanding of the importance of the firm to manage resources strategically to exploit existing advantages and extend their duration. Because factor markets are imperfect, the RBV emphasizes the need to upgrade homogenous input into heterogeneous output by combining externally acquired resources with complementary resources held by the firm. To maintain the value that has been created, firms have to continuously nurture, develop, and extend their existing resource stock.[338] In addition, establishing isolating mechanisms creates information asymmetries between innovators and imitators that impede profits being instantaneously competed away before the firm can appropriate sufficient rents. Eventually, rivals will understand the underlying sources of the entrepreneurial firm's competitive advantage, but it is time consuming. The RBV therefore "*suggests that firms wishing to obtain expected above normal returns from implementing product market strategies must be consistently better informed about the future value of those strategies than other firms in the same market.*"[339] The strategic imperative for firms is therefore to constantly increase their information advantage and identify the value creating potential of externally and internally available resources.

With this discussion in mind, it is now possible to formulate a process model about the way in which firms explore new opportunities and exploit existing advantages to create wealth as illustrated in figure 23.

337 See Foss/Ishikawa (2007), pp. 754ff.

338 See Ireland/Hitt/Sirmon (2003), p. 978; Alvarez/Barney (2006), p. 102.

339 Alvarez/Barney (2006), p. 99.

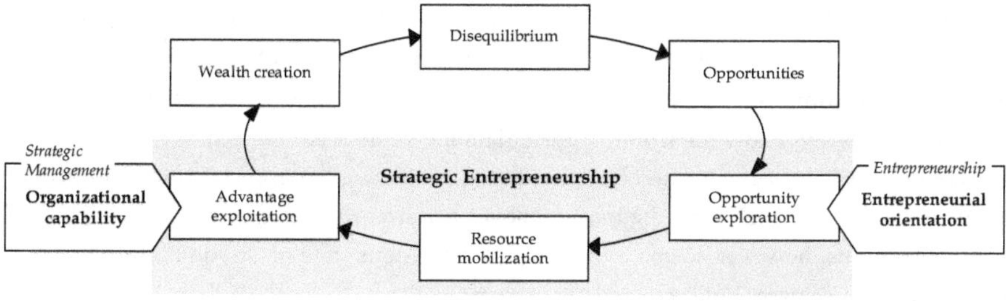

Figure 23 - Process model of Strategic Entrepreneurship

It includes a firm's EO as means to explore opportunities and its organizational capabilities by which it turns the potential of its resources into actual competitive advantages. The concept of Strategic Entrepreneurship combines both through a balanced trade-off. It is based on three fundamental assumptions: (1) Resources are heterogeneously distributed among firms, (2) resource markets are imperfect, and (3) the market is seen as being in motion. Central to this model is the notion of imperfect resource markets in which entrepreneurs bid for resources based on current prices and anticipated future outcomes.[340] This assumption is central to the RBV and can also be found in the Austrian School. Although Schumpeter did not explicitly use the term "resources", his thoughts can easily be translated into the notion that ultimately, competition takes place in imperfect resource markets[341]: "*In capitalist reality as distinguished from its textbook picture, it is not [price-guided] competition which counts but the competition from the new commodity, the new technology, the new source of supply, the new type of organization (the largest-scale unit of control for instance) – competition which commands a decisive cost or quality advantage and which strikes not at the margins of the profits and the outputs of the existing firms but at their foundations and their very lives.*"[342]

At the outset of competition, a market in disequilibrium generates a stream of economic opportunities. In response to their perception, the entrepreneur tries to mobilize simple resources and combine them into a firm of complex resource bundles that is aligned to its external environment. Yet, the existing resource stock sets limits to the firm's strategic alternatives and the opportunities it can explore. To increase its options the firm has to continuously gather superior information about underpriced resources, acquire them, and deploy them through its capabilities in response to the opportunities it wants to pursue. Acquiring resources, however, is costly and their value depends entirely on the entrepreneur's strategic judgment. In this context, the entrepreneur's task is to find resources that are priced in such a way that the firm can create more value by combining them with its existing resource stock than the market at that price.[343]

340 See Foss/Ishikawa (2007), p. 759.
341 See Mathews (2002), p. 38.
342 Schumpeter (1975), p. 84.
343 See Mathews (2010), p. 238.

Once resources become part of the firm, it is management's task to strategically upgrade and augment the acquired resource stock and to produce new goods and services in response to explored opportunities.[344] Effective isolating mechanisms increase the duration of competitive advantages and allow the firm to appropriate the value it has created.[345] Eventually, the entrepreneurial firm's rivals succeed in imitating its innovation and over time profits get competed away at which state the market moves towards equilibrium. The introduction of new innovations, however, keeps the market in a constant state of disequilibrium through which it continues to provide economic opportunities.[346]

Summing up, the strategic imperative of firms is to continuously renew their competitive advantages by exploring new opportunities to acquire and manage superior resources to successfully compete in today's dynamic environment. Using these theoretical insights, it is now possible to derive a configurational hypothesis about how firms create and defend competitive advantages through clusters. The next section discusses a newly emerging but limited set of research studies, which suggest that firms have to combine their EO with strategic resources and capabilities in order to increase their performance.

3.3.2 Hypothesis on Strategic Entrepreneurship in Clusters

The aim of this section is to derive a hypothesis about how firms create and defend competitive advantages through clusters using the configurational perspective of Strategic Entrepreneurship. Therefore, this section first reviews a newly emerging set of research studies that is in line with the configurational perspective and that suggests a need to combine a firm's EO with its strategic resources and capabilities to increase performance. These arguments are then applied to the cluster context and used to formulate a hypothesis based on a configurational perspective.

The first study was conducted by Wiklund and Shepherd. Using a sample of Swedish SMEs, the authors find that firms endowed with knowledge-based resources such as market and technology knowledge perform better when they pursue an EO. They argue that such firms are better able to capitalize on their knowledge-based resources by engaging in entrepreneurial activities as they enhance their awareness about where to look for opportunities. On the other hand, firms that lack an EO are unwilling to enthusiastically exploit the opportunities they have identified through their knowledge-based resources, leaving their potential severely underutilized.[347]

In their subsequent study that was already discussed in section 3.1.3, Wiklund and Shepherd also explicitly examined a configurational model consisting of a firm's EO, financial re-

---

344 See Mathews (2002), p. 35.

345 See Ireland/Hitt/Sirmon (2003), p. 978.

346 A market in equilibrium would imply that entrepreneurial firms would have discovered optimal resource combinations where everything is put to its optimal use. At this point, competition would inevitably come to a halt as there would be no need for further innovation (see Mathews (2010), p. 239).

347 See Wiklund/Shepherd (2003), pp. 1312f.

sources, and environmental characteristics. The authors find that a configurational model is more relevant than contingency models for studying the relationship between entrepreneurial strategy making and firm performance.[348]

Similarly, Walter, Auer, and Ritter examined the effect of network capabilities and EO on firm performance. Their findings stemming from 149 university spin-offs also suggest that network capabilities strengthen the relationship between EO and firm performance. According to the authors, entrepreneurial ambitions alone, as exhibited in high levels of EO, do not create lasting value. Instead, both characteristics impact one another and only together result in high levels of performance.[349]

Finally, in the most recent study Stam and Elfring investigate how a new venture's intra- and extraindustry social capital influence its EO. Using data from 90 new ventures in the open source software industry, the authors also find support for a configurational approach. More precisely, the authors find that the combination of a firm's EO and network centrality, i.e. social capital, significantly strengthens firm performance.[350]

To conclude, the configurational perspective to strategy suggests that in order to continuously renew their competitive advantages firms have to combine short-term opportunity seeking with long-term advantage-seeking behavior. In clusters then, firms can profit from the existence of diverse industries, highly skilled employees, sophisticated demand for their products, and superior infrastructure. Due to these structural characteristics, clusters are a key source of competitive advantage for the firm as they provide a continuous stream of opportunities along their horizontal and vertical dimensions. To avoid being distracted by this abundance of opportunities and risk falling into a frenzy of experimentation and excessive exploration, firms have to apply a strong cluster-capability in order to exploit the advantages they create. Similarly, firms that are already in existence of a strategic advantage need to explore new avenues of wealth creation within their cluster as excessive exploitation can lead to escalating commitment. This leads to the final hypothesis that a firm's EO and its cluster-capability *together* moderate the relationship between clusters and firm performance:

Hypothesis 6: *The relationship between clusters and firm performance will be positively moderated by a firm's entrepreneurial orientation together with its cluster-capability.*

With this final hypothesis in mind, the next section integrates the generated insights into the theoretical model that will guide the remainder of this research study.

348 See Wiklund/Shepherd (2005), p. 85.

349 See Walter/Auer/Ritter (2006), pp. 558f.

350 See Stam/Elfring (2008), pp. 104ff.

3.4 Summary of Findings: The Theoretical Model

The identified constructs and their hypothesized relationships are summarized in the theoretical model depicted in figure 24. Note that while the EO construct is completely defined by its underlying elements of proactiveness, innovativeness, and risk-taking, the elements that define a firm's cluster-capability are still unknown. This will be addressed by the fieldwork presented in chapter 4.

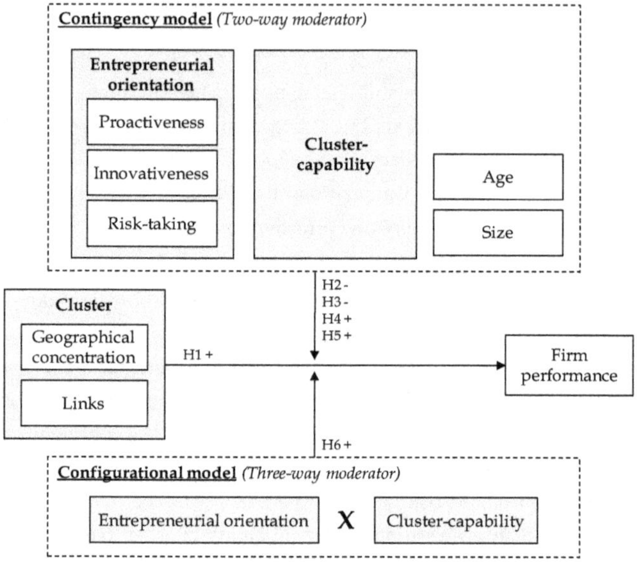

Figure 24 - The theoretical model

In addition to the baseline model, the **two-way moderator model** represents hypotheses two to five, which suggest that a contingency model underlines the relationship between clusters and firm performance. According to this model, EO and cluster-capability are seen as being independent from one another. Thus, firms can choose to be either entrepreneurial or develop a cluster-capability as both characteristics are hypothesized to lead to higher performance.

The **three-way moderator model** represents hypothesis six and suggests that a configurational model is best suited to reflect the way in which clusters influence firm performance. Here, EO and cluster-capability *together* increase the positive effect of clusters on firm performance. Thus, firms that have the ability to simultaneously perceive the arising opportunities in clusters and turn them into actual competitive advantages are assumed to enjoy high levels of performance. Table 9 provides a summarized overview of the research hypotheses that underline the combined theoretical model.

No.	Hypotheses
Baseline model	
1	Clusters that comprise a diverse set of geographically concentrated and linked industries have a positive influence on firm performance.
Contingency model	
2	The relationship between clusters and firm performance will be negatively moderated by firm size.
3	The relationship between clusters and firm performance will be negatively moderated by firm age.
4	The relationship between clusters and firm performance will be positively moderated by a firm's entrepreneurial orientation.
5	The relationship between clusters and firm performance will be positively moderated by a firm's cluster-capability.
Configurational model	
6	The relationship between clusters and firm performance will be positively moderated by a firm's entrepreneurial orientation together with its cluster-capability.

Table 9 - Summary of research hypotheses

Due to their underlying theoretical perspective, the contingency and configurational models are to some extent mutually exclusive. To resolve the question, which of the two models is best suited to explain the relationship between clusters and firm performance, chapter 5 addresses an empirical survey-based study that was carried out in China.

Before that, the next chapter discusses a fieldwork that is based on formal in-depth interviews with executives from 14 German manufacturing companies located in China's industrial clusters. Its aim is to identify the set of skills that defines a firm's cluster-capability as the ones reviewed in section 3.2.3 do not sufficiently cover all of the tasks that would enable a firm to fully exploit its cluster location.

4 Case Study to Identify Skills that make up a Firm's Cluster-Capability

As shown by the literature review in the previous chapters, up until now research has not been able to establish a well-defined set of skills that explains how firms create and defend competitive advantages through clusters. Accordingly, appropriate measures and their empirical tests in the cluster context are still missing. This chapter addresses this issue with a fieldwork that was conducted among 14 German manufacturing companies in China's industrial clusters. It is outlined in figure 25.

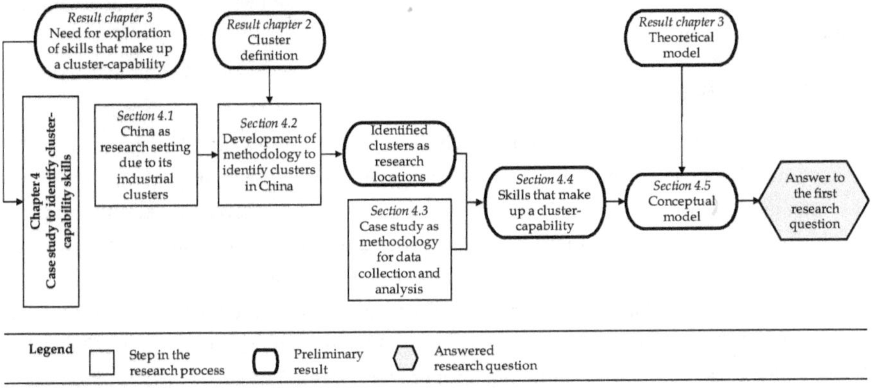

Figure 25 - Outline of chapter 4

The fieldwork has two key objectives:

(1) To *explore* skills and their measures that help firms succeed in clusters.

(2) To explain *how* these skills assist firms in creating and defending competitive advantages through clusters.

Because of its intangible and difficult to observe nature, the first objective seeks to **explore** the content and the more tangible and observable measures of a firm's actual cluster-capability. In doing so, this study follows the suggestion of Barney, Wright, and Ketchen to use an explorative study of an intangible capability to elicit a set of skills and tangible measures.[351] The construct and its measures can then be tested in a large-scale investigation, which will be the subject of chapter 5.

The second objective builds on the first one and follows the **explanatory** design of the present fieldwork. It seeks to explain how and why these skills allow firms to outperform their peers.

351 See Barney/Wright/Ketchen (2001), p. 637.

To this end, section 4.1 establishes China as the research setting and section 4.2 discusses the first step in the fieldwork. Based on the cluster definition that was developed in chapter 2, it identifies clusters in selected cities and municipalities that serve two main purposes. First, they represent the research locations. The firms studied are either located or operate to a large degree in these clusters. Second, they serve as evidence to corroborate the empirical findings against additional data points. Section 4.3 then describes the general case study methodology and analytical process that was followed during the fieldwork. Section 4.4 presents the data analysis and discuses the identified skills that make up a cluster-capability. In order to increase their robustness, it also enfolds a set of relevant literature to ground the identified skills and their measures to existing theory. The chapter concludes in section 4.5 by consolidating the findings in the conceptual research model of this study and providing an answer to the first research question.

4.1 Research Setting: China

This section establishes China as the research setting of the case study. Due to its centrally planned development model, China's industrial organization centers around a vast number of economic development zones. Firms in these regions enjoy preferential tax rates and import-export tariffs as well as sophisticated infrastructure among other things that encourage geographical concentration of foreign and domestic firms alike. An internet-based desktop research conducted by this author at the time of writing revealed the existence of 54 National Economic and Technological Development Zones, 54 High-Tech Industrial Zones, 13 Bonded Areas, 14 National Border and Economic Cooperation Zones, 59 National Export Processing Zones, twelve National Tourist and Holiday Resorts, four Taiwanese Investment Zones, nine Bonded Logistic Parks, ten Bonded Port/Free Trade Port Areas, and five Special Economic Zones (SEZ). Over time, many of these zones, which were originally designed on the drawing board, evolved into leading edge clusters of their particular industry. This makes China particularly suitable to study the competitive behavior of firms in clusters.

Therefore, section 4.1.1 provides an overview of China's economic development since the start of the reform era and section 4.1.2 discusses the country's current economic performance. Section 4.1.3 concludes with China's regional development policy that is responsible for the establishment of these economic development zones and their gradual evolution into industrial clusters.

4.1.1 A Brief History of China's Economic Development

At the time of China's political opening up, the Chinese Communist Party spearheaded by Deng Xiaoping initiated a widespread reform policy aimed at modernizing the country's economy. After the state planned pre-reform era, the years that followed were characterized by rapid economic development. Today, China reemerged as global player with a strengthened and internationally competitive economy. To understand this transformation, this section will provide a brief description of economic development in China.

The state planned economy that dominated the time between 1949 and 1978 was characterized by the central government's attempt to discredit and abolish individual commerce. Following socialist principles, production factors were allocated to the people and provinces were urged to rely on their own resources. Private enterprises were replaced by state controlled entities and the State Plan governed the economy.[352] As a result, factories were under strict control of the government. Manufacturers were expected to follow the State Plan producing the items and quantities specified, providing no incentives to exceed expectations. Market-economy like mechanisms such as efficiency, meeting demand, and competition were abolished altogether.[353] Instead, the focus shifted to providing employment for the entire population in what came to be known as the "iron rice bowl". The system guaranteed each worker a job until retirement. They were selected based on occupational inheritance, rather than for actual competencies or skills. Once in the system, there were limited incentives to improve performance creating several sources of operational inefficiency and waste.[354]

The era between 1978 and 2001 of **economic reform and rapid development** opened China to market competition and made it less reliant on central planning. What followed were far reaching reforms involving the restructuring of state owned enterprises (SOE), establishing privately owned enterprises, and encouraging FDI under the open door policy. This led to two-digit growth that continues until today.[355] During the 1990s, SOEs were gradually faced with market competition and held responsible for profit and losses. Due to structural inefficiencies, many were even allowed to go into bankruptcy creating huge unemployment, particularly in rural areas.[356] Yet despite ongoing reforms, the central government still interferes regularly in operations of both state- and privately owned enterprises.[357]

The current stage of **ongoing economic development and reemergence as global player** has come along with the country's accession into the World Trade Organization (WTO) in December 2001. Since then, market access for foreign companies entering China has been improved, export rates have further increased, and a fierce competition in the domestic market emerged forcing Chinese companies to become more competitive.[358]

---

352 See Choosin/Kwan/Cheung (1996), pp. 115ff.

353 See Handfield/Withers (1993), p. 86; Zhou/Chuah (2002), p. 281.

354 See Zhao/Flynn/Roth (2006), pp. 456f.

355 See Ramaseshan/Yip/Pae (2006), p. 63.

356 See Zhao/Flynn/Roth (2006), p. 459.

357 See Xu/Jayaram/Xu (2006), p. 370. According to the OECD, the line between government and SOEs is still vague as decisions made by SOEs sometimes reflect the government's objectives, rather than purely commercial goals (see Herd (2010), p. 115).

358 See Zhao/Flynn/Roth (2006), pp. 460f.

4.1.2 The Economic Performance of Contemporary China

Today, China's economic development policy remains growth oriented. Between 2003 and 2008 the economy grew by more than 10 % on average, largely fueled by ongoing productivity improvements, high saving rates, ongoing deregulation, and a favorable global economic environment.[359] Despite the economic crisis of 2008 and 2009, the country's economy grew by 8.7 percent in 2009 hitting a year on year growth of 11.9 percent in the first quarter of 2010. This was largely due to China's 589 billion US$[360] stimulus package that was launched in 2009 to boost domestic demand and infrastructure investment in particular.[361]

As a result, in the second quarter of 2010 China overtook Japan as the second largest economy. Japan's nominal gross domestic product (GDP) totaled 1.288 trillion US$, while China's totaled 1.377 US$. Yet, on a yearly basis China still remains the world third largest economy with more than 4.9 trillion US$, but is poised to overtake Japan in the long-term.

This sustained level of economic growth has strengthened China's share of world production and the value of traded goods. According to the OECD, the share of China in world GDP accounted for 7.2 % in 2008.[362] At the same time, China's manufacturing sector became highly integrated with the world economy. Between 1978 and 2008, China's export volume grew yearly by 17.5 % to 1.43 trillion US$ in 2008. Today, the export sector is an important pillar of the Chinese economy and accounts for 33.4 % of GDP.[363]

As a result, China is becoming ever more attractive for foreign companies, due to its growing market potential and the improving business environment. Yet, by far China's most important competitive advantage when compared to other manufacturing nations is its low-cost labor. Hourly wages for manufacturing labor in 2009 accounted for only 1.93 US$ compared to 9.3 US$ in Hungary, 26.29 US$ in the USA, and 40.36 US$ in Germany. However, due to the rapid economic development and economic upgrading, wages are rising continuously on an average year on year basis of 14 % since 2000.[364] Using growth projections by the Worldbank, China's GDP per capita will reach 4.800 US$ in 2020. In comparison, this is almost as much as the 2008 level of Turkey and Malaysia.[365] Even so, China will stay the preferred low-cost country thanks to its scale and ongoing economic development.

---

359 See Kuijs (2009), p. 3.

360 Exchange rate US$ to RMB = 6.94912.

361 See Worldbank (2010), p. 2; Kuijs (2009), p. 4.

362 See Herd (2010), p. 24.

363 See China National Bureau of Statistics (2011).

364 See China Statistics Press (2010).

365 See Kuijs (2009), p. 14.

4.1.3 Reasons for Choosing China as Research Setting

The previous sections show that China's strong economic growth was driven by the continuous open door policy, ongoing liberalization, and low cost labor. However, the economic development benefitted mostly the urban population in China's coastal provinces.[366] Although FDI in China summed up to almost one quarter of the worldwide investment for developing countries in the second half of the 1990s, these investments almost exclusively took place in the coastal provinces with Guangdong, Fujian, and Jiangsu receiving the lion's share. The cause of this unbalanced inflow of FDI can be found in China's regional economic policy during the 1980s and 1990s.

To implement its open door policy, the government established SEZs in the four southern coastal cities of Xiamen, Shantou, Shenzhen, and Zhuhai. In these laboratories of economic reform foreign firms received investment incentives such as tax holidays, reduced tax rates, and duty free import and export of production factors. Due to their success, the government then opened 14 further coastal cities to FDI. As a result, these zones evolved into strong industrial clusters that set the basis for the following economic development.[367]

Today, China's economic landscape is characterized by a steep east-west slope with higher levels of economic development and highly competitive industrial clusters along the coast.[368] This unequal distribution is illustrated in figure 26. It caused strong migration from rural areas to the economically well developed centers in the east.[369] In response to the rising levels of social inequality, the central government initiated gradual reforms to harmonize the distribution of economic welfare.[370]

At the heart of this attempt lies the **Great Western Development Strategy** that was implemented by the 10th and 11th five-year plans. Central to both five-year plans are policies that intend to trigger a structural change of the Chinese economy to reverse some of the negative developments caused by the open door policy. The aim is to stop the migration of young skilled and entrepreneurial talents to the coastal areas. Between 2001 and 2005 the total investments under the Western Development Plan amounted to 1.4 % of GDP. These funds were largely used to establish new growth clusters in China's hinterland by promoting favorable economic policies, improvements in infrastructure, and openness to attract investments from domestic and international companies.[371]

---

366 See Lam (2006a), p. 7.

367 See Zhao/Flynn/Roth (2006), p. 457.

368 See Taube/Ögütcü (2002), pp. 3ff.

369 See EIU (2008), p. 6.

370 See BMI (2008), p. 24. The term "harmonious" is an allusion to the economic policy implemented under President Hu Jintao. He advocates building a "harmonious society" to solve worsening social tensions. The concept originates from Confucian ideology that views harmony as the most precious thing (see Wo-Lap Lam (2006), p. 280).

371 See Herd (2010), p. 131.

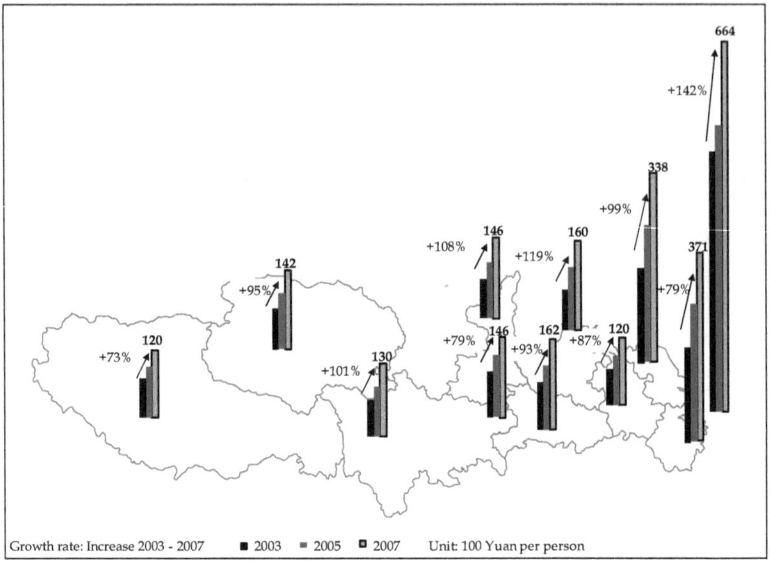

Figure 26 - Development of GDP per capita across central and western China
(Source: Own illustration with data based on China National Bureau of Statistics (2011))

According to these policies, provincial governments in less developed regions are granted the right to attract domestic and foreign firms from preferred industries such as logistics, high-tech/electronics, and automotive by busing SEZs as investment vehicles.[372] These industries benefit in terms of preferential tax, land and housing rates, registration and visa fees, and easy access to credit. Furthermore, special policies such as the "*Directory of Dominant Industries in the Middle and Western Regio*n" of the state council offer preferred tax rates and long-term subsidies to foreign firms and encourage JVs with domestic entities.[373]

As a result, the FDI rates of China's western provinces have seen steady growth since 2003 with the municipality Chongqing experiencing growth rates of 147 % in the years between 2005 and 2007. In comparison, over the same time period the whole province of Sichuan experienced a growth in FDI of 62 %. By promoting these regions, the government attempts to create new industry clusters, increase employment prospects, and thereby expand inland markets in order to boost sustainable economic growth and lessen the country's dependence on exports.[374]

---

372 See Taube/Ögütcü (2002), p. 33. The priority target for foreign investments include agriculture, industrial construction related to energy, communications and raw materials, high technology, environmental protection, and development projects in central and west China. Furthermore, the government is especially focusing on export-oriented companies and companies with long-term investment plans (see EIU (2008), p. 50).

373 For further details concerning the new *Corporate Income Tax Law* that took effect at January 1st of 2008 see EIU (2008), pp. 47ff.

374 See Taube/Ögütcü (2002), p. 2; EIU (2008), p. 8.

As can be seen from this discussion, China's planned economy model relies largely on the concept of SEZs and industrial clusters as main vehicle for its regional development policy. In the beginning of the 1990's, investments were first concentrated in the southern Perl-river delta, the Yangtze-river delta in the east, and the Bohai-rim delta in the north. The development was then spread to further cities along the coast. The final stage was reached in the late 1990's when the country launched its "GoWest" program. Over time, these zones evolved into strong industrial clusters.[375] This makes China most appropriate to study the competitive behavior of firms in clusters.

4.2 Research Location: China's Industrial Clusters

After explaining why China was chosen as the research setting of this study, section 4.2.1 discusses the methodology that was employed to identify regional industrial clusters that would eventually serve as research locations. The detailed approach and the resulting cluster configurations are presented in the sections 4.2.2 to 4.2.5.

4.2.1 Cluster Identification Methodology

In section 2.4 some of the methods that are usually used to identify clusters have already been discussed in terms of their advantages and shortcomings. Simple analytical techniques use counts of employment or firm plants on the regional or ZIP code level as indicators for the presence of clusters, while more sophisticated ones use distance based measures in predefined geographical areas. However, they are only able to identify simple agglomerations of firms and ignore further constituent cluster characteristics such as the degree of interrelatedness with respect to multiple dimensions and formal and informal links among firms. More contemporary approaches are based on Porter's Cluster Mapping Project. This approach or variations of it have been used in various countries including Gilbert and colleagues' and Kukalis' studies on ICT and pharmaceutical clusters in the USA, respectively, Wennberg and Lindqvist's study on new entrepreneurial firms in Sweden, Blasio and Addario's study on industrial districts in Italy, and Miller and colleagues' Cluster Mapping Project in the United Kingdom.[376]

Despite its advantages, one major and important drawback is the methodology's reliance on a single quantitative measure for links among industries, since input-output data only capture formal buyer-seller relations. Further measures such as the reliance on a common resource base are excluded from the analysis. Consequently, Porter remarks "*that input-output links are just one of many forms of externalities or linkages between industries within a cluster, but have the advantage that systematic data is available.*"[377] Thus, although the Harvard approach

375 See Lam (2006a), p. 7.

376 See de Blasio/Di Addario (2005), pp. 9f; Gilbert/McDougall/Audretsch (2008), p. 412; Wennberg/Lindqvist (2010), p. 228; Kukalis (2010), p. 463; Miller et al. (2001), pp. 21ff.

377 Porter (2003), p. 563.

represents an important step towards a comprehensive identification of clusters, it still falls short on capturing their multidimensional characteristics. To counter this shortcoming, this study extends the Harvard approach by incorporating multiple facets of industry interrelatedness. The methodology and data used are illustrated in figure 27.

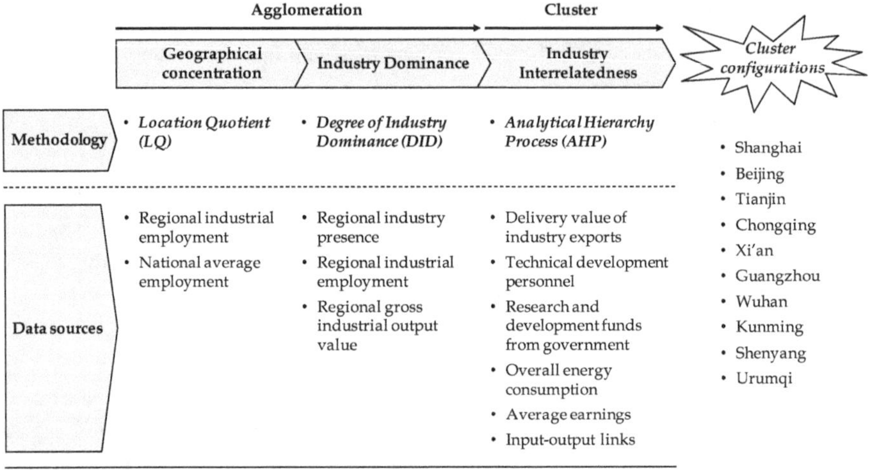

Figure 27 - Cluster identification methodology

The process starts by identifying regional agglomerations of manufacturing industries. This is performed by first determining the degree of geographical concentration of all industries located in a given region in terms of their regional employment figures. All industries that have been found to be geographically concentrated are then analyzed with regards to their degree of dominance, a measure that indicates the absolute economic performance of a particular industry. To identify the actual presence of clusters, these industries are then subjected to a quantitative technique to compute their degree of interrelatedness. These steps and the data used are discussed in greater detail in the following sections.

A particular challenge in applying this methodology is unique to the Chinese context as data availability varies greatly between provinces and municipalities. In China, industries are classified according to the Industrial Classification for National Activities of China-Code (CSIC). It is based on the widely used International Standard Industrial Classification of All Economic Activities-Code (ISIC-Code). It groups together manufacturing enterprises into categories, if they produce the same type of goods or if they use similar raw materials, production processes, technologies, or skills.[378] The CSIC is organized hierarchically with each level containing more details. It comprises 20 sections (1-letter code), 95 divisions (2-digit

378 See for example Porter (2003), p. 550; Feser/Bergman (2000), p. 2.

code), 396 groups (3-digit code), and 913 classes (4-digit code). Levels beyond 4 have been discontinued in the past.[379]

While some provinces provide very detailed data down to the 3- and 4-digit level, the majority limit their data to the 2-digit division level. Therefore, this study works with 2-digit data of manufacturing industries as they exhibit the greatest consistency across provinces and municipalities. In the CSIC these activities are classified in the "Industry" section. It comprises the subsections "Mining" (including coal, stone, and earths), "Manufacturing", and "Production and Supply of Power, Gas, and Water".

Furthermore, regional and local employment figures used to calculate the degree of geographical concentration and data used to calculate the degree of interrelatedness are only available for municipalities and a small number of large provincial capitals. Other Chinese cities do not provide consistent data across these categories. The identification of industrial cluster configurations is therefore confined to the municipalities Shanghai, Beijing, Tianjin, and Chongqing and the provincial capitals Xi'an, Guangzhou, Wuhan, Kunming, Shenyang, and Urumqi.

After this brief introduction, the next section discusses the methodologies that are used to identify clusters in China in greater detail.

4.2.2 Geographical Concentration

The first step involves measuring the degree of geographical concentration of firms in a particular location. One commonly used measure for the existence of geographical concentrations is the **location quotient**. A *LQ* is a relative measure that relates the number of people employed (or firms) in a certain location to a national reference distribution, usually the total national number of people employed (or total number of firms) in all industries outside the observed location.[380] The *LQ* as a measure for geographical concentration can be described by the equation:

$$LQ = \left(\frac{\frac{E_{ij}}{E_{in}}}{\frac{E_j}{E_n}} \right)$$

where

- E_{ij} indicates the number of people employed in industry i of region j,
- E_{in} indicates the national number of people employed in industry i,
- E_j indicates the total number of people employed in region j, and

[379] The latest version was introduced in 2002, i.e. revision 2 (CSIC Rev. 2). In its current version the code corresponds to revision 3 of the ISIC-Code, which was published in 1989 and updated to ISIC Rev. 3.1 in May 2002 (see UN Department of Economic and Social Affairs (2008), p. 1).

[380] See Krätke (2002), pp. 28f.; vom Hofe/Chen (2007), p. 3; Sölvell/Lindqvist/Ketels (2003), p. 109; Porter (2003), p. 559; Wennberg/Lindqvist (2010), p. 228.

- E_n indicates the total national number of people employed in all industries.[381]

A *LQ* higher than 1 indicates a regional concentration of employment in industry *i*, when compared to the national average rate of employment in industry *i*.

The present study calculates the *LQ* on the basis of relative employment figures. It compares employment on the municipality and provincial capital level to the national average rate of employment. Employment data for all variables E_{ij}, E_j, E_{in}, and E_n for the municipalities Shanghai, Beijing, Tianjin, and Chongqing are extracted from the 2007 edition of the China Labour Statistical Yearbook.[382] An important limitation concerns the data for the local variables E_{ij} and E_j. In its current version, the China Labour Statistical Yearbook provides these data only on the provincial and municipality level. While this poses no constraint for the data of Shanghai, Beijing, Tianjin, and Chongqing, data for the remaining provincial capitals had to be extracted directly from their respective city statistical yearbooks.

It is important to note that while the *LQ* measures the existence and strength of a geographical concentration of employment i.e. agglomeration, it does not provide final evidence for the existence of a cluster. To account for a cluster, agglomerations have to be related or linked to each other, a characteristic that is not captured by the *LQ*.[383]

Furthermore, the *LQ* captures the local importance of an industry for a specific region. It does so by measuring whether or not a region is host to a particularly large share of that industry when compared to the national average. Yet, it does not measure the absolute size of that industry in the observed region. When measured in absolute terms, it is possible to obtain high *LQ* values for an industry that is considered to be small on the national level, but that is heavily concentrated in one location. In addition, it is also possible that the *LQ* ignores a large local industry (when seen in absolute terms) whose geographical concentration in that particular region turns out to be too small when compared to the geographical concentration of that industry in other regions. Thus, the *LQ* tends to overstate the importance of small industries that are highly concentrated in one region, and understate the importance of large industries that are concentrated in several different regions across the country.

To counter this shortcoming, this study therefore employs the *degree of industry dominance* to capture the actual importance of an industry for a particular region as an additional absolute measure. It is introduced in the next section.[384]

Furthermore, since the *LQ* depends on the CSIC-Code, which classifies employment (or the number of firms) according to industry sectors, it is only possible to identify geographical concentrations of firms that tend to serve a common *product-market*. Agglomerations of firms

---

381 See Fingleton/Igliori/Moore (2005), p. 292.

382 See China Statistics Press (2007a).

383 See Krätke (2002), p. 30 and Rosenfeld (1997), p. 7f.

384 See Fingleton/Igliori/Moore (2005), pp. 292f. To avoid this problem, some studies measure geographical concentration in absolute terms and then introduce pre-defined (arbitrary) thresholds to identify agglomerations (see Brenner (2007), p. 556).

that are related to each other in terms of a common *resource-base* are ignored, if the geographical concentration of their respective industry sectors is low. In this case, the analysis depends on qualitative bottom-up approaches such as case studies and survey-based data to investigate the non-quantifiable foundation of resource-based clusters.[385] In contrast, a resource-based cluster can be identified for those regions that host several highly geographically concentrated industries that are small in absolute terms. In this case, it can be investigated whether or not these industries are interrelated to each other. If these industries are interrelated, it is likely that they form a cluster. In the final step then, it is possible to infer from the nature of the interrelatedness to the underlying resource base that serves as common ground for the formation of that cluster. This approach will be presented in section 4.2.4.

4.2.3 Industry Dominance

The next step involves the calculation of the **degree of industry dominance** (DID) for those industries that have been found to be geographically concentrated. The DID is calculated by (1) the number of firms operating in a particular industry compared to the number of companies operating in all other industries of that region and (2) the number of people employed in a particular industry compared to the number of people employed by all other industries in that region.[386]

Furthermore, dominant industries contribute exceptionally to the economic prosperity of a region. Therefore, this study also measures the Gross Industrial Output Value (GIOV) as an additional measure for DID. The GIOV is defined as "*the total volume of final industrial products produced and industrial services provided during a given period. It reflects the total achievements and overall scale of industrial production.*"[387]

In the graphical visualization the DID is indicated by the diameter of a circle that represents a particular industry. The higher the DID, the larger is the diameter of that industry. To graphically depict three equally weighted measures (an industry's number of firms, number of employees, and GIOV) as indicators of DID, this study employs a geometrical distance-based measure. For any given region, it calculates the circle-diameter as a vector in a three-dimensional space and is described by the following equation:

$$DID_i = \left(\sqrt[2]{\left(\frac{f_i}{F}\right)^2 + \left(\frac{e_i}{E}\right)^2 + \left(\frac{g_i}{G}\right)^2} \right) * 100$$

where

- f_i is the number of firms in industry i,
- F is the total number of firms,

385 See Krätke (2002), p. 35.

386 See Romanelli/Khessina (2005), p. 351.

387 China Statistics Press (2008), p. 547.

- e_i is the people employed in industry i,
- E is the total number of employees,
- g_i is the GIOV of industry i, and
- G is the total GIOV.

Similarly to the calculation of the *LQ*, the data for the six measures used to calculate the DID are extracted from the statistical yearbooks of the respective cities and municipalities.

4.2.4 Industry Interrelatedness

4.2.4.1 Measures of Industry Interrelatedness

In the absence of data that indicates the extent to which firms form links among each other, the degree of interrelatedness is used as next-best proxy to determine the existence of clusters. As shown in section 2.3, besides serving a common product-market, firms also frequently co-locate in clusters to access a common resource base such as infrastructure, technology, skills, labor, and natural resources. Therefore, industry interrelatedness is a complex construct that is reflected by multiple indicators.

Methodologies to measure the degree of industry interrelatedness have long been dominated by Rumelt's and Montgomery's approaches introduced in 1974 and 1982, respectively. Rumelt classified firms into industries according to similarities in terms of products, markets, and technologies.[388] This conceptualization of relatedness was later picked up and further developed by Montgomery, who discovered that Rumelt's classification was highly correlated with measures of relatedness based on SIC-codes.[389]

Despite their wide use, both methodologies also received intensive criticism for their low explanatory power in empirical research about industry diversification. Traditional SIC-code based methods are therefore increasingly being seen as inappropriate to measure the degree of industry interrelatedness. Keats for example argued that researchers' "*reliance on readily obtainable SIC participation data should be replaced by a quest for a richer conceptualization that can incorporate consideration of managerial issues and treatment of various forms of diversification as potential solutions to a multivariate set of problems.*"[390]

To identify additional measures for the interrelatedness construct, Stimpert and Duhaim as well as Pehrsson surveyed managers of large diversified firms to evaluate how they perceive the relatedness of their firms' businesses. Using a behavioral perspective, the authors confirm the perception of relatedness as similarity in products and markets. Yet, both studies

388 See Rumelt (1974), pp. 11ff.

389 See Montgomery (1982), pp. 302ff.

390 Keats (1990), p. 69.

also find that managers hold additional conceptualizations of relatedness including similarities in the use of common resources and value chain activities.[391]

Therefore, in this study industry interrelatedness is measured in terms of **product-market attributes** (similarities in product technologies, product value, customers, product lifecycles), **resource attributes** (similarities in general management skills, technological skills, market knowledge, capital availability), and **value chain attributes** (similarities in supplier-buyer and vertical transaction relationships). The actual measures are summarized in table 10.

Product-Market	Resources	Value Chain
Delivery Value of Industry Exports	• Technical Development Personnel • R&D Funds from Government • Overall Energy Consumption • Average Earnings	Input-Output Links

Table 10 - Measures to calculate the degree of industry interrelatedness

Product-Market Interrelatedness

Product-market attributes are captured by the measure "Delivery Value of Industry Exports". It is provided in Renminbi and comprises the value of all goods exported to foreign countries by a particular industry. It is an indicator of an industry's engagement in exporting activities.[392] Firms that are engaged in exporting activities depend on common resources such as sophisticated infrastructure (e.g. sea- and airports) and highly skilled employees. Additionally, they have to master similar challenges including currency fluctuations, customs, or trade and export barriers. In contrast, industries that show low degrees of exporting activities are dominated by firms that focus primarily on the domestic product-market. These firms are also likely to depend on e.g. similar production technologies and end customers. Therefore, the "Delivery Value of Industry Exports" measure represents a good proxy for the product-market dimension.

Resource Interrelatedness

Resource attributes are captured by the measures "Technical Development Personnel", "R&D Funds from Government", "Overall Energy Consumption", and "Average Earnings". The measure "Technical Development Personnel" reflects the dependence of a particular industry on technological skills and innovation capacity.[393] The measure "R&D Funds from Government" comprises funds for R&D activities that are made available by the Chinese government to particular industries. It is a measure of the availability of capital through go-

[391] See Stimpert/Duhaime (1997), pp. 119f. and Pehrsson (2006), pp. 272ff.

[392] See China Statistics Press (2002), p. 278.

[393] See China Statistics Press (2007b), p. 401; Lumpkin/Dess (1996), p. 143.

vernmental subsidies.[394] The measure "Overall Energy Consumption" refers to the total energy consumption (coal, petroleum, gas, electricity) of a particular industry and is provided in standard tons equivalents.[395]

While the data for these measures can be extracted from the statistical yearbooks of the respective cities and municipalities, the data for the measure "Average Earnings" has to be extracted from the China Statistical Yearbook, which is only available at the provincial and municipality level.[396] "Average Earnings" refers to the average earnings of a person that is employed in a particular industry and is provided in Renminbi. It is a measure of the dependence of a particular industry on skilled and semi-skilled employees.[397]

Value Chain Interrelatedness

Value chain attributes are captured by the measure "Input-Output Links". It represents buyer-supplier transactions between industries. Due to its complexity, it will be discussed in greater detail.

Methods to analyze links between industries date back to the 17th century and were first introduced in the form of Quesnay's "Tableu Economique". But it was not until 1953 when Leontief picked up and further refined Quesnay's approach that analytical techniques based on economic **input-output tables** became used in national accounting systems worldwide in general and in cluster research in particular.[398] The analysis is based on the grouping of firms according to their main economic activity as reflected in the SIC-code. So called *commodity-based methods* use symmetrical transaction matrices, in which any cell t_{ij} captures the monetary value of a transaction that has taken place between industry i and industry j over a given period of time.[399] Input-output tables are commonly used as an initial step to identify clusters. The basic idea is to identify linkages between industries based on vertical transaction relationships or similarities in resource and product-markets.[400]

While input-output tables are commonly used on the national level due to data availability, their use on the regional level is restricted by the fact that most countries do not offer comprehensive data on the regional and provincial level. A common approach is therefore to use qualitative methodologies such as survey based data or to deduct regional input-output tables from national tables (non-survey methods).[401] Feser and Bergman, for example, suggest applying national input-output tables as "*templates for developing a strategic view of a re-*

394 See China Statistics Press (2007b), pp. 402f.
395 See China Statistics Press (2007c), pp. 149ff.
396 See China Statistics Press (2007a), pp. 187 ff.
397 See China Statistics Press (2008), p. 182.
398 See Hewings/Jensen (2000), pp. 295ff.
399 See Feser/Bergman (2000), p. 5.
400 See vom Hofe/Chen (2007), p. 4; Feser/Bergman (2000), p. 3; Krätke (2002), p. 35.
401 See Hewings/Jensen (2000), pp. 307ff.; Krätke (2002), p. 35.

gional manufacturing economy."[402] This approach is particularly helpful when data availability is high on the national level, but low at the sub-national level such as in the case of China.[403]

One major setback of input-output tables is their **aspatial nature**. They contain no information on how geographically close firms in identified clusters are to each other.[404] Geographic proximity, however, is a key dimension of clusters. The present study counters this limitation by incorporating the *LQ*. By doing so, this study follows the suggestion made in section 2.3 to make use of several variables and measures to truly identify a cluster in all its dimensions, as neither the *LQ* nor input-output tables alone are able to do so.[405]

Another limitation of using input-output tables is their inability to account for interregional or even international trade and transactions.[406] By accounting exclusively for one region instead of interregional transactions, the analysis overlooks important patterns that are not confined to artificially drawn boundaries. As a result, interregional clusters might not be identified to their fullest extent.

With regards to data availability, China's input-output data are only available for the year 2002, while the remaining measures are based on data from the year 2006. Collecting and analyzing input-output data is resource and time-consuming so that this process is conducted only every eight years.[407] Exceptions are the input-output data for Shanghai that were obtained for the year 2005 through personal request at the Shanghai Municipal Statistics Bureau.

Similar to the calculation of the *LQ*, the input-output data is only available at the provincial level. While this poses no restriction on the analysis of the municipalities Beijing, Shanghai, Tianjin, and Chongqing, the analysis of the remaining cities has to be conducted according to the non-survey methods suggested by Feser and Bergman. Thus, the provincial input-output tables serve as templates for the input-output tables at the provincial capital level.

4.2.4.2 Mathematical Calculation of Industry Interrelatedness

The aggregated industry interrelatedness construct is calculated as the weighted average of its six measures. Due to data consistency, a higher weight is assigned to the measure "Input-Output Links". The calculation of the degree of industry interrelatedness proceeds in five steps and is based on the **Analytical Hierarchy Process** (AHP) introduced by Saaty.[408] The

---

402 Feser/Bergman (2000), p. 2.

403 See vom Hofe/Chen (2007), p. 7, 24; Krätke (2002), p. 35.

404 See vom Hofe/Chen (2007), p. 2.

405 Similar to this study, Czamanski and Czamanski in their study first identified 16 industrial clusters, which they describe as purely aspatial. The *LQ* is then introduced to calculate whether or not the firms in those clusters show a satisfactory level of geographical proximity to each other (see Czamanski/Czamanski (1976), pp. 27ff.).

406 See vom Hofe/Chen (2007), p. 2 and Feser/Bergman (2000), p. 4.

407 See National Bureau of Statistics (2005), pp. 3ff.

408 See for an example Saaty/Vargas (2001), pp. 13ff.

AHP is a technique that systematically evaluates various elements by comparing them to a reference value using a *pairwise comparison*. A numerical value is derived from that process and imported into a lower triangular matrix, allowing diverse elements to be processed and compared in a structured way. In the final step, each element is assigned to a value on a pre-defined scale, which in this case represents the degree of industry interrelatedness. For a pairwise comparison of industries *i* and *j* the AHP proceeds according to the following steps:

(1) Conduct a pairwise comparison of all industries *i* and *j* by dividing their values in such a way that the result takes values between 0 and 1.

(2) Import the resulting values in a lower triangular matrix.

(3) Assign each value to a 4-point scale indicating the partial degree of interrelatedness between industry *i* and *j*.

(4) Calculate the aggregated degree of industry interrelatedness based on the assigned values of the partial measures.

(5) Assign the resulting value to a 4-point scale indicating the aggregated degree of interrelatedness between industry *i* and *j*.

Step 1 represents the actual pairwise comparison between two industries with regards to a particular measure. Suppose that the industries "Metals" and "Electronics" are pairwise compared with regards to the measure "Technical Development Personnel". Suppose further, that "Metals" employs more "Technical Development Personnel" than "Electronics". To arrive at values between 0 and 1, step 1 therefore divides the value of "Electronics" by the value of "Metals". The result indicates the degree of dependence of both industries on the "Technical Development Personnel" resource. A high value indicates that both industries rely heavily on that resource and are therefore interrelated with respect to that resource (i.e. measure). In contrast, a low value indicates that both industries do not share that resource and are therefore also not significantly related to each other.

Step 3 then assigns each of these values to a 4-point scale that indicates to what degree two industries *i* and *j* are interrelated in terms of a particular measure. In the above example, a high value would correspond to a high value on the 4-point scale and indicate that the two industries "Electronics" and "Metals" are both strongly dependent on "Technical Development Personnel", while a low value would indicate that they are not interrelated in terms of that resource.

Step 1 to 3 are conducted for each partial measure of the interrelatedness construct, while Step 4 calculates the aggregated degree of interrelatedness between two industries *i* and *j* and step 5 then assigns the resulting value to a 4-point scale.

This approach will be explained in greater detail in the following sections.

Pairwise Comparison of the "Input-Output Links" Measure

The starting point for the pairwise comparison are the input-output tables for a total of N industries i and j whereby $i, j = 1,\ldots, N$. The data for the measure "Input-Output Links" is captured in input-output tables. Each cell t_{ij} represents the monetary value of goods that has been exchanged between industry i and j. In order to arrive at the degree of interrelatedness between these industries, the comparison needs to be based on a reference value. In this case, the reference value is the total monetary value of goods that industry i sold to all other industries except itself. Putting cell t_{ij} in relation to this value indicates the share of the total monetary value of goods that industry i # sold to industry j. The higher that share is, the higher is the degree of interrelatedness between these two industries.

Therefore:

- t_{ij} is the monetary value of goods that industry i (row) has sold to industry j (column),
- t_{ii} is the monetary value of goods that was sold within industry i, and
- z_i is the total monetary value of goods that industry i has sold to all other industries except itself.

$$z_i = \sum_{j=1}^{N} t_{ij} - t_{ii} \qquad \text{with } i = 1, \ldots, N$$

Thus, z_i is the reference value that is used for the pairwise comparison of any two industries i and j. It is used to calculate b_{ij}, which represents the share that industry i has sold to industry j in relation to the total amount of goods z_i:

$$b_{ij} = \frac{t_{ij}}{z_i} \qquad \text{with } i = 1, \ldots, N$$

In contrast to the absolute values t_{ij}, the entries b_{ij} represent the share of the total monetary value of goods that industry i sold to industry j. Suppose that industry i sold goods to industry j and vice versa. b_{ij} then represents the flow of goods from i to j, while b_{ji} represents the flow of goods from j to i. Consequently, b_{ij} indicates the degree to which industry i depends on industry j as product-market and the degree to which industry j depends on industry i as resource market. Similarly, b_{ji} indicates the degree of dependence in the opposite direction.

In the next step, the entries b_{ij} are transformed and imported into a lower triangular matrix with entries c_{ij} by calculating the arithmetic mean of the two-way transactions b_{ij} and b_{ji}.

$$c_{ij} = \frac{b_{ij} + b_{ji}}{2} \qquad \text{with } i = 1, \ldots, N$$

c_{ij} shows how dependent industries i and j are on each other in both product *and* resource-markets. Similar to the initial step, each entry c_{ij} is then compared to the maximum value c_{max} of the resulting triangular matrix in order to assign it to a 4-point scale with values between 0 and 3:

$$c_{max} = Max\left\{ c_{ij} \middle|_{j = 1, \ldots, N-1}^{i = 2, \ldots, N} \right\}$$

The values for the "Input-Output Links" measure T_{ij} are then assigned to a 4-point scale between 0 and 3 according to the following equation:

$$T_{ij} = \begin{cases} 0, & \text{if} \quad c_{ij} \leq 0.25 * c_{max} \\ 1, & \text{if} \quad 0.5 * c_{max} \geq c_{ij} > 0.25 * c_{max} \\ 2, & \text{if} \quad 0.75 * c_{max} \geq c_{ij} > 0.5 * c_{max} \\ 3, & \text{if} \quad c_{ij} > 0.75 * c_{max} \end{cases}$$

One limitation of this approach is that the value of T_{ij} for two industries i and j cannot be directly compared with the value of T_{ij} between the same two industries in another region. This is because the underlying values for c_{max} differ across regions as the present input-output tables do not contain interregional trade data. Thus, what would be considered a strong degree of interrelatedness in one region could be considered a medium degree of interrelatedness in another.

Pairwise Comparison of the Remaining Measures

In contrast to the measure "Input-Output Links", which already represents a pairwise comparison of two industries in terms of the exchanged monetary value of goods, the initial step for the remaining indicators consists of performing the pairwise comparison first.

Thus, there is a high degree of interrelatedness between industries, if the values for their respective indicators:

- p_i: Technical Development Personnel for industry i,
- f_i: R&D Funds from Government for industry i,
- o_i: Overall Energy Consumption for industry i,
- a_i: Average Earnings for industry i, and
- d_i: Delivery Value of Industry Exports for industry i

are similar to each other. Because all measures follow the same method of construction, the following discussion is limited to the calculation of the "Technical Development Personnel" measure for all industries $i = 1, \ldots, N$. In contrast to the input-output link measure, the first step involves the creation of a lower triangular matrix with g_{ij} as the pairwise comparison of industry i and j for the measure "Technical Development Personnel":

$$g_{ij} = \frac{Min\,\{p_i, p_j\}}{Max\{p_i, p_j\}} \qquad \text{with} \quad i = 1, \ldots, N$$

More precisely, the pairwise comparison transforms the values of the "Technical Development Personnel" measure into values between 0 and 1. These values are then imported into a lower triangular matrix. In contrast to the measure "Input-Output Links", these values can be directly assigned to a value between 0 and 3 on a 4-point scale, indicating the degree of interrelatedness between the industries i and j with respect to the "Technical Development Personnel" resource.

$$P_{ij} = \begin{cases} 0, & \text{if} \quad p_{ij} \leq 0.25 \\ 1, & \text{if} \quad 0.5 \geq p_{ij} > 0.25 \\ 2, & \text{if} \quad 0.75 \geq p_{ij} > 0.5 \\ 3, & \text{if} \quad p_{ij} > 0.75 \end{cases}$$

For all industries i and j with $i, j, = 1, \ldots, N$:

- P_{ij} indicates the degree of interrelatedness between industries i and j with respect to the "Technical Development Personnel" resource,
- F_{ij} the degree of interrelatedness between industries i and j with respect to the "R&D Funds from Government" resource,
- O_{ij} the degree of interrelatedness between industries i and j with respect to the "Overall Energy Consumption" resource,
- A_{ij} the degree of interrelatedness between industries i and j with respect to the "Average Earnings" resource, and
- D_{ij} the degree of interrelatedness between industries i and j with respect to the "Delivery Value of Industry Exports" measure.

After all partial measures have been assigned to a 4-point scale, the final step involves the calculation of the aggregated degree of interrelatedness for all industries i and j.

Calculation of the Aggregated Interrelatedness Variable

As previously stated, the measure "Input-Output Links" carries a greater significance for the industry interrelatedness variable and therefore enters the equation with a greater weight:

$$m_{ij} = \left(\frac{P_{ij} + F_{ij} + O_{ij} + A_{ij} + D_{ij}}{5}\right) * 0.5 + T_{ij} * 0.5 \qquad \text{with} \quad i = 1, \ldots, N$$

The resulting values are then assigned to a 4-point scale indicating the aggregated degree of industry interrelatedness for all industries i and j with $i, j = 1, \ldots, N$"

$$Interrelatedness\ I_{ij} = \begin{cases} \text{no,} & \text{if } m_{ij} \leq 0.75 \\ \text{weak,} & \text{if } 1.5 \geq m_{ij} > 0.75 \\ \text{medium,} & \text{if } 2.25 \geq m_{ij} > 1.5 \\ \text{strong,} & \text{if } m_{ij} > 2.25 \end{cases}$$

4.2.5 Empirical Landscapes of Regional Cluster Configurations

After the completion of all calculations, the final step includes the graphical visualization of the regional cluster configurations. The DID is depicted by the size of the respective circle, while the degree of interrelatedness is depicted by the type of lines between related industries: a *dotted line* represents a weak, a *dashed line* a medium, and a *solid line* indicates a strong degree of interrelatedness. Industries with no link between each other are not interrelated (see figure 28).

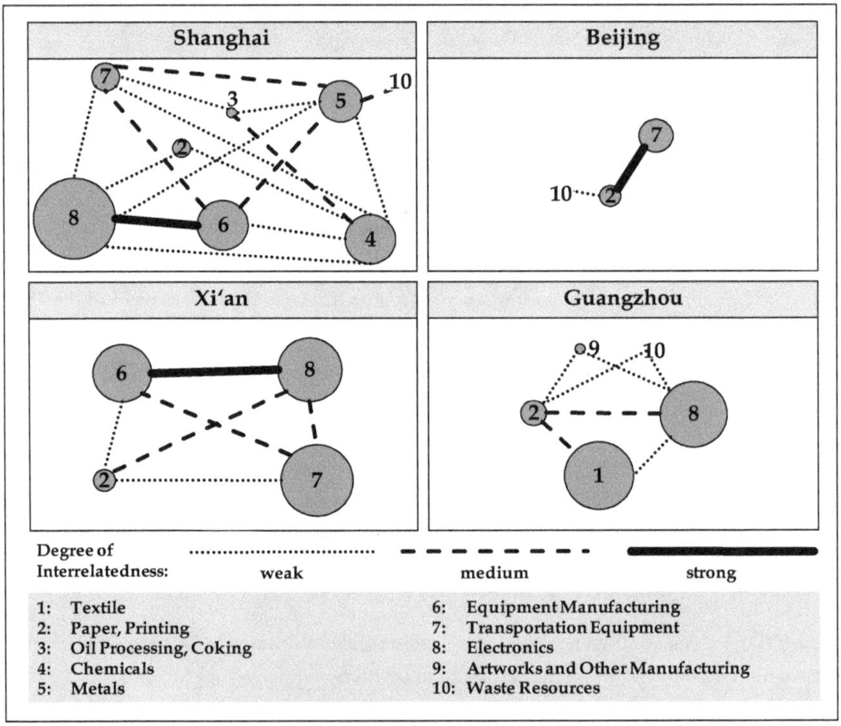

Figure 28 - Regional cluster configurations for case study locations in China

As mentioned before, the configurations also distinguish agglomeration from clusters. For example, a set of geographically concentrated industries that are not related to each other indicate an agglomeration of firms. In contrast, interrelated industries indicate the presence of a cluster.

The charts depicted in figure 28 represent the cluster configurations for Shanghai, Beijing, Xi'an, and Guangzhou as the firms that have participated in this study are either located or operate there to a large degree. The charts for the remaining cities and municipalities of Tianjin, Chongqing, Wuhan, Kunming, Shenyang, and Urumqi are provided in appendix 2.

So far, the identified cluster configurations have not been put in relation to each other. To allow for a true to scale comparison, all values have to undergo an additional transformation according to the economically strongest region, i.e. Shanghai. It serves as reference value for the remaining cities. The transformation is calculated according to the following equation:

$$s_k = \frac{\sqrt[2]{\left(\frac{F_k}{F_S}\right)^2 + \left(\frac{E_k}{E_S}\right)^2 + \left(\frac{G_k}{G_S}\right)^2}}{\sqrt{3}}$$

where

- F_k is the total number of firms in region k,
- F_S is the total number of firms in Shanghai,
- E_k is the total number of people employed in region k,
- E_S is the total number of people employed in Shanghai,
- G_k: Gross Industrial Output Value for region k. and
- G_S: Gross Industrial Output Value for Shanghai.

The value s_k is then multiplied with the diameters of all circles. The result indicates the industry dominance of all identified clusters in relation to Shanghai's clusters. Figure 29 provides a comprehensive overview of the ten identified landscapes of regional cluster configuration.[409]

[409] The reader should note that the layout of the identified clusters landscapes was altered for the sake of visualization. The degree of dominance and interrelatedness remain true to scale.

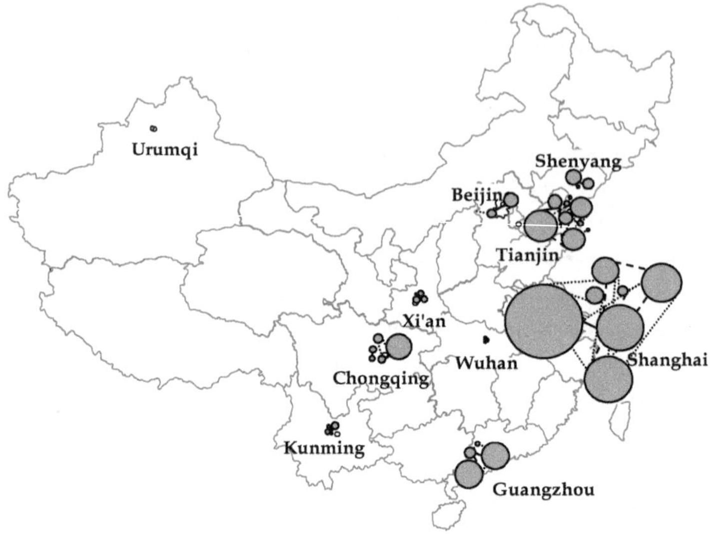

Figure 29 - Overview of regional cluster configurations in China

Shanghai

Figure 29 shows that Shanghai remains by far the most important economic and urban industrial region of China, while the remaining cities and municipalities lag considerably behind. The city's landscape is dominated by competitive, export-oriented manufacturing industries that are the main engine of its economic performance.[410] As illustrated in figure 28, Shanghai boasts high-performing clusters that form around complex capital goods and associated high-tech component industries. These industries make up the lion's share of its GIOV and also employ the largest number of people (see table 11).

Shanghai's strengths lie in its size and highly diversified manufacturing sector that underwent major structural changes and industry shakeouts. Over the past decade, light industries such as textile, footwear, and garments have lost shares and made way to high-value industries such as transport, engineering, electronics, and metals.[411] Thus, Shanghai will for the foreseeable future remain China's economic gravity point and further increase its innovation capacity.[412]

---

410 According to estimates by the Worldbank, in the aggregate Shanghai's dominant manufacturing industries export more than 60 % of their output (see Yusuf/Nabeshima (2009), p. 72).

411 See Yusuf/Nabeshima (2009), p. 66.

412 See Wu (2007), pp. 549ff.

ID	Industry	Firms	Employees	GIOV (in 100m US$)
8	Electronics	2119	590900	790.78
5	Metals	1687	261900	364.38
4	Chemicals	2443	342700	312.55
6	Equipment Manufacturing	2443	371600	286.1
7	Transportation Equipment	716	201800	272.65
3	Oil Processing, Coking	48	24500	132.25
2	Paper, Printing	948	142800	64.65
10	Waste Resources	37	2500	2.89

Table 11 - Shanghai's industry composition according to economic indicators
(Source: Data based on China Statistics Press (2007b))

Beijing

Beijing is widely seen as China's first post-industrial city, its political and cultural center. The city has seen the retreat of more and less labor-intensive manufacturing industries. As a result of this deindustrialization, the city hosts only two dominant and geographically concentrated industries, namely automotive and paper and printing. When compared to the economic performance of Shanghai's major industries, Beijing's automotive industry comes in only sixth in terms of its key economic indicators (see table 12).

ID	Industry	Firms	Employees	GIOV (in 100m US$)
7	Transportation Equipment	404	109550	144.42
2	Paper, Printing	528	68120	22.72
10	Waste Resources	9	540	0.43

Table 12 - Beijing's industry composition according to economic indicators
(Source: Data based on China Statistics Press (2007d))

Though Beijing lacks a strong manufacturing cluster of related industries, the city hosts a large number of science and technology-oriented high-tech start-ups, research institutes, and associated service industries. Today, Beijing ranks second only to Shanghai in terms of its innovation performance.[413] Together, these two cities account for almost 70 % of foreign R&D facilities in China giving rise to a growing number of multinational companies (MNCs) locating their regional headquarters there.[414]

---

413 See Guan et al. (2009), p. 805.

414 See Sun/Wen (2007), p. 406. In Beijing, the majority of R&D facilities and high-tech startups are located in the Zhongguancun Science Park. Due to its strong innovative capacity, over the years it has attracted much attention of researchers and policy makers alike (see for example Yu/Xin (2003); Dong/Tann (2005); Tan (2006) Tzeng (2010)).

Xi'an

Xi'an's industrial profile is largely influenced by its strong knowledge infrastructure, which has given it a considerable advantage in the high-tech sector. The city hosts more than 47 higher education institutions, 365 science research institutions, and various national laboratories and engineering centers producing a steady stream of skilled engineers. It is a heritage of its former history as important military equipment manufacturing and research center. After China's opening-up most facilities were switched to civilian use.[415]

Although considerably smaller in scale than Shanghai's industry, Xi'an hosts a strong electronics and information technology cluster that formed around its knowledge infrastructure. It is supplemented by an automotive industry that focuses on electrical vehicles (see table 13). With regards to service industries, Xi'an is also known as software and IT-development location.

ID	Industry	Firms	Employees	GIOV (in 100m US$)
7	Transportation Equipment	47	88442	43.06
8	Electronics	171	65164	30.43
6	Equipment Manufacturing	168	63830	22.32
2	Paper, Printing	73	22523	5.47

Table 13 - Xi'an's industry composition according to economic indicators
(Source: Data based on China Statistics Press (2007e))

One particular industry that is deeply embedded in Xi'an's resource-based cluster is the semiconductor industry. It has participants across the whole semiconductor supply chain from materials to design, production, and testing.[416]

Guangzhou

Guangzhou, the provincial capital of Guangdong, is an important regional export hub in southern China's Pearl River delta. The city is well-known for its light industries particularly textile, apparel, shoes, toys, gifts, replica arts, and furniture industry.[417] Due to industry restructuring and its proximity to Shenzhen and Hong Kong, Guangzhou moved towards high-tech electronics and heavy industries in recent years (see table 14).[418]

415 See Wang/Lin (2008), p. 166 and also Zhang (2009), p. 14.

416 See Wang/Lin (2008), p. 166.

417 Some of these export-oriented clusters have leading roles in global markets (see Schröder/Waibel/Altrock (2010), p. 4).

418 See Lam (2006b), p. 13.

ID	Industry	Firms	Employees	GIOV (in 100m US$)
8	Electronics	844	322386	180.47
1	Textile	977	385792	75.09
2	Paper, Printing	433	131832	27.96
9	Artworks	143	52789	11.52
10	Waste Resources	11	2392	2.09

Table 14 - Guangzhou's industry composition according to economic indicators
(Source: Data based on China Statistics Press (2007f))

In addition, in the late 1990s and early 2000s major Japanese automakers have entered China through operations in Guangzhou. In response, a large number of automotive suppliers and local parts manufactures have set up operations there to support the developing automotive industry.[419] As a result, an automotive cluster is slowly taking shape in Guangzhou, which at the time of data collection, is not concentrated enough to be reflected in figure 28.

After identifying and describing suitable industrial clusters that served as research locations, the next section introduces the methodology that was followed during the case study-based research.

4.3 Research Methodology: Case Study

Empirical research can broadly be differentiated in qualitative and quantitative research (see table 15).[420] **Quantitative research** can be further distinguished in experiments and surveys. Both depend on random samples to gather and analyze numerical data. In *experiments*, researchers observe contemporary events and social phenomena through comparison between groups, whereby various behavioral or contextual factors are controlled for. They are commonly used for research questions of the *"how"* and *"why"* type. *Surveys* on the other hand, move from the concept of discretely cut groups to samples drawn from broader populations in order to study the relationship between variables. The objective here is to test existing hypotheses and propositions that predict how the world should be and assign statistical probabilities to potential outcomes. Relevant research questions relate to the *"who"*, *"what"*, *"where"*, *"how many"*, and *"how much"* type.[421]

Qualitative research on the other hand, relies on a variety of empirical materials including interview transcripts, recordings and notes, observational records, documents, audiovisual files, personal experience, and statistical data. In contrast to quantitative research, where there is a wide agreement regarding legitimate methodologies, the field of qualitative re-

419 See Sasuga (2008), pp. 5f.
420 See Punch (2005), pp. 66ff.
421 See Yin (2009), pp. 8ff.

search is defined by a diverse set of methodologies and research practices.[422] The goal of qualitative research is to explore, describe, and explain contemporary phenomena in the context of their occurrence instead of quantitatively measuring them. One widely used approach to qualitative research is the **case study**, which is particularly helpful in answering research questions related to the how and why type such as "*how did they do it?*" and "*why did it work?*" The main difference to experiments is the extent of control over behavioral and contextual events. While in experiments key independent variables can be manipulated directly and precisely, the case study approach is conducted in the "field" where behavioral aspects cannot be manipulated.[423]

	Quantitative		**Qualitative**
Methodology	Experiment	Survey	Case Study
Research questions	How and why	Who, what, where, how many, how much	How and why
Objective	Observation of social phenomena	Study relationship between variables	Explore and explain phenomena in the context where they occur
Data Source	Random samples of discretely cut groups	Random samples from wider population	Interviews, transcripts, recording, notes, observations, statistical date, etc.

Table 15 - Overview of quantitative and qualitative research

Yin defines the case study as "*an empirical enquiry that investigates a contemporary phenomenon in depth and within its real-life context.*"[424] It is a research strategy that focuses on understanding the dynamics and decisive elements present within a given setting "*by recognizing patterns of relationships among constructs within and across cases and their underlying logical arguments.*"[425]

The case study approach is particularly helpful in exploratory research designs when little is known about a phenomenon and current understanding is insufficient.[426] The **strength of the case study** is its ability to describe and illustrate events, test existing theory, or generate new theory as it emphasis the inductive development of constructs, their content and measures, and testable theoretical propositions.[427] As Siggelkow puts it, "*getting closer to constructs and being able to illustrate causal relationships more directly are among the key advantages of case re-*

422 See Denzin/Lincoln (1994), p. ix.

423 See Yin (2009), pp. 11f.

424 Yin (2009), p. 18.

425 Eisenhardt/Graebner (2007), p. 25.

426 See Eisenhardt (1989a), p. 548.

427 See Eisenhardt (1989a), pp. 534f.

search vis-à-vis large-sample empirical work."[428] The case study is thus open to and to some degree also dependent on the use of theory to guide the research and analysis of data.[429]

A commonly mentioned **weakness of the case study** approach is its lack of a representative sample. In fact, case study samples are often chosen precisely because they are special and do not conform to previously held beliefs. Therefore, particular care needs to be taken to avoid arriving at narrow and highly context-specific insights that are difficult to generalize to a broader population.[430] To avoid this issue, it is most important to choose an appropriate case study design.

4.3.1 Case Study Design

In contrast to quantitative research, which draws a random sample from a pre-determined population to ensure statistical representativeness, qualitative research relies on **theoretical sampling**. That is, cases are chosen deliberately and for theoretical instead of statistical reasons. The research is guided and controlled by the emerging theory whereby data collection and analysis determine what to study next.[431] The cases may therefore be chosen to replicate previous cases or extend existing theory, or they may be chosen to represent extreme ends of a phenomenon to provide examples of polar types.[432]

As is already evident, the case study approach can involve single or multiple case studies. **Single case studies** can richly describe a single phenomenon and they are chosen because they are opportunities for unusual research access, unusually revelatory, represent an extreme example, or do not fit a theoretical proposition. **Multiple case studies** allow comparing findings across cases, add confidence to the final results, and provide a stronger base for theory building. In addition, constructs and measures are more precisely delineated, because it is easier to determine multiple construct dimensions to their fullest extent when using multiple cases.[433]

A central advantage of multiple case studies is that they resemble standalone quasi-experiments. Using **replication logic**, findings from one case can be contrasted with findings from other cases and then analytically generalized to an existing or emerging theory. For replication, cases are thus selected to predict either a similar or a contradictory result. If the

---

428 Siggelkow (2007), p. 22.

429 The case study differs herein from other qualitative designs such as grounded theory and ethnography. *Grounded theory* is a research strategy whose purpose it is to generate new theory that is grounded in fresh data. Theory is therefore inductively generated from data (see Strauss (1987), p. xi; Glaser/Strauss (1967)). *Ethnography* requires that the researcher participates overtly or covertly in its research subjects' way of life for an extended period of time. The primary objective is to observe and describe what happens in a naturally given setting (see Hammersley/Atkinson (1995), pp. 9f).

430 See Eisenhardt (1989a), p. 547.

431 See Glaser (1992), p. 101.

432 See Eisenhardt (1989a), p. 537.

433 See Eisenhardt/Graebner (2007), p. 27.

data supports the theory and the majority of findings turn out to be as predicted, successful replication may be claimed.[434]

Another important decision in the design stage of case studies relates to selecting the appropriate **unit of analysis**. That is, defining what the actual case is. The selection depends on the research question and the propositions that are to be tested.[435]

In the current study, the explicated tasks of a cluster-capability led the theoretical sampling of suitable cases. The unit of analysis is the competitive behavior of firms in clusters. The research itself is set in China and based on the population of German companies in China's industrial clusters. This population was chosen mainly for two reasons.

First, this setting is extensively used in research on clusters and agglomerations. It became popular through studies that investigated the location choice of foreign companies in the USA during the 1980s and 1990s.[436] Investigating foreign entrants allows treating the sample cases as *quasi-experiments*. It controls for the path dependent, socio-cultural, and non-economic factors that may impact the location decision and the competitive behavior of domestic firms. Thus, location decisions are less likely to be impacted by e.g. existing plant locations, personal living preferences, ethnic networks, or clan and family commitments. This makes it easier to control for variables that could invalidate conclusions regarding relevant firm-level characteristics.[437] To further prove external validity of the findings, in chapter 5 the identified characteristics will be subjected to a large-scale empirical study among domestic firms in China.

Second, with Eastern Europe in their backyard, the majority of German companies view China in terms of its huge market potential as opposed to only another low-cost sourcing or manufacturing base.[438] This view is also reflected in China's growing importance as location for German direct investment (see table 16).

In 2009, German net direct investment in China reached an all time high of 3.4 billion US$, increasing 21 % compared to the pre-financial crisis year 2007, a number which is expected to rise even further in the future. Given that FDI is the most advanced and complex market entry strategy and that it involves the establishment of a considerable physical presence in the host country[439], it is evident that German companies choose their China locations more carefully. This makes them most appropriate for this study.

434 See Yin (2009), pp. 54ff.

435 See Yin (2009), pp. 29ff.

436 Selected studies include Luger/Shetty (1985), Woodward (1992), Smith/Florida (1994), Head/Ries/Swenson (1995), and Shaver/Flyer (2000).

437 See Punch (2005), pp. 68ff. for an overview of experimental and quasi-experimental research designs.

438 See Heininger/Gehnen (2008), p. 19.

439 See Cavusgil/Knight/Riesenberger (2008), pp. 418f.

Rank	Country	2007	2008	Change (in %)	2009	Change (in %)
1	Luxembourg	16.9	5.1	-70	16.7	227
2	UK	11.1	9.3	-16	12.0	29
3	Italy	5.8	0.5	-91	8.5	1,600
4	France	3.2	-2.4	-175	5.4	325
5	Ireland	6.9	0.5	-93	4.0	700
6	USA	1.6	9.9	519	3.6	-64
7	Malta	1.9	-0.3	-116	3.5	1,267
8	China	2.8	1.8	-36	3.4	89
9	Denmark	0.8	0.9	13	2.7	200
10	Austria	-10.5	5.4	151	2.6	-52

Table 16 - Germany net FDI in billion US$[440]
(Source: Based on data provided by BMWi (2010))

4.3.2 Data Collection

The present case study combines various data collection techniques such as interviews, documents and archival records, publicly available information, and statistical data.

The **interview** is one of the main data sources, particularly when multiple cases are investigated. It is a guided conversation with a fluid and flexible stream of questions rather than a query with rigid structure. The most common type of interviewing is a face-to-face verbal and visual interchange between the researcher and the interviewee. Face-to-face interviews are often conducted as in-depth or focused interviews. In this special type of interviews **key informants** answer questions regarding the facts of a matter or their opinion on the investigated events.[441] According to Yin, *"well-informed interviewees can provide important insights into such affairs or events. The interviewees also can provide shortcuts to the prior history of such situations, helping [the researcher] to identify other relevant sources of evidence."*[442]

The interview process itself can be conducted in a structured or unstructured way. In **structured interviews** the respondent is asked a series of pre-defined questions that are targeted towards answering the investigated research question, while room for variation is limited. **Unstructured interviews** on the other hand, are useful in understanding the complex behavior and emotional reactions of individuals. They impose no a-priori determined structure that could limit the range of potential insights. They are particularly helpful in generating

440 Exchange rate EUR to US$ = 1.3495.

441 See Fontana/Frey (1994), p. 361.

442 Yin (2009), p. 108.

rich and unexpected data.[443] A mixed approach is the **semi-structured interview**. It is conducted in a structured way but with open-ended questions. The major advantage is that findings are comparable across interviews, while respondents are still allowed to come up with unexpected insights.

In line with its explorative character, this study made use of semi-structured in-depth interviews. The goal of the interviews was to investigate the research topic from the perspective of the interviewees and to compare findings across cases. The informants have been selected from a database compiled by the German Chamber of Commerce in Shanghai. It is the largest German organization in China with an extensive list of contacts. The database holds various information including company name and type, industry, contact information of senior personnel, major products, and a short company profile.[444] For the final sample, the contact persons that were provided by the database were contacted first and then asked to help identify the key informants.

The *key informants* were selected based on two main criteria. First, they had to hold key positions during the decision-making process that led to the current firm-location in China. This offered the opportunity to understand the motives that led to that decision and treat the informants as observers and interpreters of the long-term activities of their firm. Second, the informants had to be powerful enough to understand and influence the competitive behavior of their firm in China's clusters. This allowed inferring from the underlying firm characteristics that led to that behavior to performance related outcomes. Therefore, the final sample of informants consists of people that participated in the decisions that led to the entry of their company into China, and which at the time of study obtained influential top-management positions. The interviewees and their companies are shown in table 17. To ensure anonymity the names of the companies are disguised.

Each but one has its headquarters either in Shanghai or Beijing with Semiconductor being the only exception, which is located in Xi'an. Four companies moved their headquarters within the last seven years to Shanghai with Sharp-Ring being the most recent in 2008. The companies entered China between 1991 and most recently 2005. They have been chosen based on their industry affiliation to correspond to the industries that are located in the clusters of Shanghai, Beijing, Guangzhou, and Xi'an.

One particular **weakness of interviews**, however, is that they are subject to bias, as interviewees may poorly recall past events or imprecisely articulate their thoughts and insights. This risk can be mitigated by using multiple, highly knowledgeable informants who view the phenomenon under investigation from diverse perspectives. They can include organizational individuals from different hierarchical levels or departments, or knowledgeable individuals

443 See Punch (2005), pp. 170ff.

444 See www.german-company-directory.com. At the time of writing, the database held more than 3,700 profiles of German companies in storage.

from other organizations and outside observers.[445] Additionally, interview data can be corroborated with information from other data sources.[446]

Company	Year of market entry	China headquarters before	China headquarters today	Industry	Informant
Cart	1998	-	Shanghai	Commercial equipment	General Manager
Flavor	1996	Shenyang	Shanghai	Beverages	General Manager
Frontgate	1999	-	Beijing	Construction	General Manager
Image	2004	Beijing	Shanghai	Medical devices	General Manager
Importer	2005	-	Beijing	Automotive	VP (China)
Interior	2005	-	Shanghai	Customized furniture	Managing Director
Material	1997	-	Shanghai	Raw material processing	CEO (China)
Pigment	1994	-	Shanghai	Chemicals	Director
Pioneer	1995	-	Shanghai	Energy	CEO (China)
Semiconductor	2003	-	Xi'an	Semiconductor	Director
Sensor	1996	-	Shanghai	Construction	CEO Asia Pacific
Sharp-Ring	1994	Taicang	Shanghai	Machine tools	General Manager
Tire	2001	-	Shanghai	Automotive	CEO (China)
Topgear	1991	Wuhan	Shanghai	Automotive	President Asia

Table 17 - Description of the companies studied

Therefore, upon selection each informant received an introductory email presenting the team of researchers and the purpose of the interviews. In order to prepare, the interviewee also received a brief overview of the topics to be raised in the interview and information about additional data requirements such as internal documents and archival records.[447] In the present study, information was gathered through self-report at the companies' internet ho-

445 See Eisenhardt/Graebner (2007), p. 28.

446 This process is also known as *triangulation*. The logic implies that findings from one type of data source are checked against the findings derived from other types with the aim to enhance their validity. Punch (2005, p. 214) cites an example in which the results of a qualitative investigation are checked against a quantitative study.

447 Documents and archival records for instance, are particularly helpful in corroborating data obtained from other sources and they can also be used to make inferences to new leads. They include diaries, letters, e-mails, notes, reports, proposals, presentations, meeting minutes, and news clippings of various sorts (see Yin (2009), p. 103).

mepage and publicly accessible business reports and used as input to the interview guide. Where possible, some statements of the interviewees have been further verified through additional research in the companies' historical material and recent public statements in newspapers and practitioner journals.

To further counteract the biases of the interviewees and ensure that everything is checked from multiple perspectives, this study also made extensive use of publicly available information and **official statistics**. They were used to identify suitable clusters in China that served as research locations and additional data points during the data analysis.

4.3.3 Data Analysis

There is a variety and diversity of approaches when it comes to qualitative data analysis. This poses a serious problem as it does not protect the researcher "*against self-delusion, let alone the presentation of unreliable or invalid conclusions to scientific or policy-making audiences.*"[448] In the field of business sciences, however, there has been much recent progress in the way qualitative data is analyzed and displayed. One approach that stands out and that is also followed in this study is that of Yin, Eisenhardt, and Graebner (see figure 30).

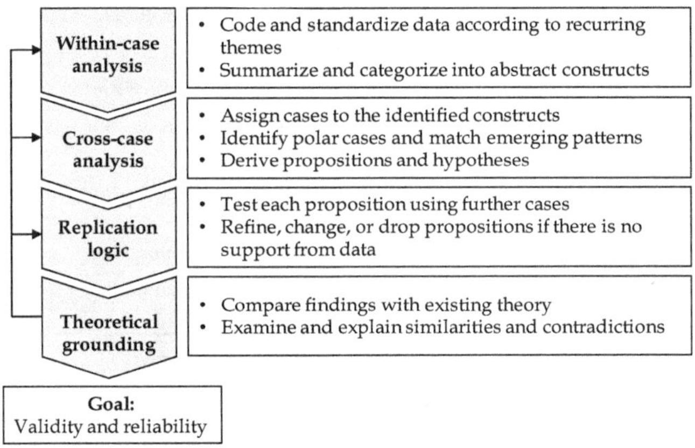

Figure 30 - Process of analyzing case study data

The process is based on **analytic induction.**[449] Constructs and their measures are developed from data and raised to higher levels of abstraction, while relationships are traced out subsequently. Findings are then verified by using existing theory. Thus, the analytical process alternates between data-driven proposition development and theory-driven verification. It is conducted in four steps:

448 Miles (1979), p. 591.

449 See Yin (2009); Eisenhardt (1989a), and Eisenhardt/Graebner (2007). Exemplary studies include Gilbert (2005), Eisenhardt (1989b), and Maurer/Ebers (2006).

(1) After each case study has been compiled from different data sources, the first key step is **within-case analysis**. The aim is to significantly reduce the volume of data to find unique patterns of each case without loss of relevant information. One common approach in this stage is coding.[450] Codes can be tags, names, or labels that are put against pieces of data in order to assign meanings to it. Codes can then be used on different levels of abstraction to summarize and categorize data into smaller and more meaningful units such as measures or higher-order constructs.[451]

(2) **Cross-case analysis** and pattern matching further support the process of coding. The aim is to use the higher-order constructs and measures that have been identified in the within-case analysis step and to look for similarities and differences across multiple cases. The cases are assigned to the identified measures to find polar cases with most and least assignments per construct. Based on these matched pairs, polar cases are compared with one another as they represent extreme examples of the same phenomenon. Hypothetical explanations and relationships are then framed on the basis of the analysis of the data.[452]

(3) The aim of the previous two steps is to arrive at distinct propositions about causal relationships between measures and higher-order constructs in such a way that each is supported by most of the data. In this stage, **replication logic** is used and the analysis alternates between theory and data. Further cases are investigated to test each proposition. If the data fails to support the proposition, then either the proposition is reformulated or the phenomenon under investigation is redefined so that the negatives cases are excluded from further analysis. This step is repeated until each proposition has been examined for each case.[453]

(4) To increase the confidence in the findings, the next step involves comparison with **existing literature** to examine and explain similarities and contradictions. This is particularly important as the findings often rest on a limited number of cases. Thus, any further corroboration, for example with contradicting or rival explanations, is likely to increase the robustness of the obtained results as the chance of neglecting conflicting findings is reduced.[454]

The ultimate aim of these steps is to increase the robustness of the findings and the general validity and reliability of the study.

450 See Eisenhardt (1989a), p. 540.

451 See Miles/Huberman (1994), pp. 55ff.

452 See Eisenhardt (1989a), pp. 540f. and Punch (2005), p. 197.

453 See Yin (2009), pp. 141ff; Hammersley/Atkinson (1995), pp. 234f.

454 See Eisenhardt (1989a), pp. 544f; Yin (2009), pp. 139f.

4.3.4 Case Study Validity and Reliability

Validity and reliability are important criteria to ensure high-qualitative case studies as researchers often work alone in the field, are limited in their information processing abilities, and focus on the findings rather than retracing how they reached their results.[455] To counter these biases, Yin developed the most prominent set of tests and several related tactics to ensure the quality of the research design. Table 18 provides a comprehensive overview of these tests and tactics.

Tests	Case Study Tactic	Stage of Research
Construct Validity	• Use multiple sources of evidence • Have key informants review draft case study report • Link constructs and measures to data	Data collection Data analysis
Internal Validity	• Do within-case analysis • Do cross-case analysis • Develop explanations • Address rival explanations	Data analysis
External Validity	• Use replication logic in multiple case studies • Use theory	Case study design Data analysis
Reliability	• Use case study protocol • Keep data storage	Data collection

Table 18 - Quality tests and case study tactics

Construct validity refers to the identification of correct operational measures for the concepts that are being studied by ensuring that there is substantial evidence in the data. The tactics apply mostly in the data collection and analysis and have been discussed extensively. **Internal validity** seeks to establish a causal relationship between constructs and is ensured by the second and third step of the data analysis stage. **External validity** defines the extent to which the findings can be generalized to a wider population. The main tactics involve a multiple case design and the use of replication logic in the third data analysis step. Finally, **reliability** addresses the issue that the steps a researcher undertook should be repeatable by a third party with the same results. During this study, all interviews have therefore been recorded and then analyzed by two researchers. Drafts of the interview protocols were then sent back to the key informants for review and to ensure that the correct measures were taken.[456]

455 See Eisenhardt (1989a), p. 540.

456 See for this procedure Yin (2009), pp. 40ff. and Meyer (2001), pp. 345ff.

4.4 Analysis of Data and Findings

Due to the large amount of data the analysis follows the recommendation of Eisenhardt and Graebner.[457] The findings are presented in sections in such a way that each finding is supported by the data. To further proof depth and detail of empirical grounding, extensive summary and construct tables are used that complement the selective storytelling and show how the constructs are measured.

4.4.1 Clusters as Sources of Competitive Advantages and Disadvantages

The general assumption in the cluster literature is that they are beneficial to their member firms. As table 19 shows, the case study data confirms that clusters offer a variety of **competitive advantages** and **business opportunities**.

This is particularly evident in the case of Material, which is located in Shanghai. It pioneered the Chinese market as early as 1994 through a JV and in 2004 turned into a wholly foreign owned enterprise after it took control over the entire business.

The MNC purchases large amounts of raw material, i.e. stainless steel, non ferrous metals, and plastics, processes it, and then distributes the goods in smaller quantities. To achieve the economies of scale necessary for this business model, the desired customers are companies that demand large quantities of goods such as clients from the electronics, automotive, and equipment industry. As shown by figure 28, all of these industries are strongly concentrated in Shanghai. Therefore, the company's head of sales remarks states, "*How can I do business outside the cluster? There would be no events, no suppliers, and no customers, no associations and no chambers. Business development is easier in clusters, because the relevant people are easily accessible.*"

In consequence, Material recently appointed four relationship managers to approach senior employees of other MNCs. In this sense, the regular social events and the large number of MNCs in and around Shanghai increase the outcome of its efforts, "*Sure we profit from the cluster. Location choices are based on business potential, measured in number of potential customers.*"

Business opportunities are also pointed out by the CEO Asia Pacific of Sensor, a company that located its sales office for north China in Shenyang, "*China's buying power is concentrated along the coast. No company can afford to be underrepresented in these regions.*" This is in line with the information found on its homepage stating that it operates eight sales offices at the coastal regions besides only three in central China.

457 See Eisenhardt/Graebner (2007), pp. 28f.

Company	Location	Cluster impact	Examples	Case evidence
Frontgate	Beijing	Strong	"Our products are most needed in cold climate."	95 % of produced goods are sold in north China.
Image	Shanghai	Strong	"I tried to avoid Beijing and moved to Shanghai, because I rely on highly qualified employees with a medical background to explain my products to our customers."	80% of product portfolio younger than two years.
Importer	Beijing	Weak	"Recruiting automotive engineers in Beijing is very difficult. They are all in Shanghai and Guangzhou. Some of our employees commute between Shanghai and Beijing, which is very expensive."	Employee fluctuation of nearly 20 %.
Interior	Shanghai	Weak	"We have a hard time to find and keep capable suppliers and workers."	Cost level above industry average.
Pigment	Shanghai	Strong	"For lobbying…yes, you have to be in Beijing. But for business you have to be in Shanghai."	Successful change of regulation through lobbying.
Semiconductor	Xi'an	Strong	"We tried to recruit people from Chengdu and other regions but found that locals have more skills."	Employee fluctuation rate 5 %.
Sensor	Shanghai	Strong	"In Shanghai we have everything…suppliers, infrastructure and customers...our customers' headquarters are mainly located along the coast."	Eight strategic alliances with major local developers serving all provinces along the coast
Sharp-Ring	Shanghai	Strong	"In Shanghai many universities are located…so, we can find skilled employees that work in similar structures and have experience with western companies."	Average growth rate 50 %

Table 19 - Evidence from data illustrating the effect of clusters on performance

Among others, a strong cluster also supports efforts to recruit skilled employees. Semiconductor for example, due to the abundant availability of well educated university graduates and academics in the field of electrical engineering and physics, deliberately chose Xi'an as location for its R&D unit, *"We tried to recruit people from Chengdu and other regions, but found that locals have more skills."* As a result, the company introduced a variety of scholarship programs and conducts scientific research at the University of Xi'an to attract its best graduates. In this way, Semiconductor is able to tap into Xi'an's sophisticated knowledge infrastructure and R&D skills.

On the contrary, **weak industry or resource clusters** put a heavy burden on firms. One example of a company that is located outside of its industry's dominant cluster is Importer. The company sells special trucks for fire fighting, TV stations, the oil industry, and the chemical industry and relies heavily on its government relations. To build up and maintain good relationships, the company located its activities in Beijing, which hosts a small concentration of the automotive industry.

Being in Beijing allows Importer to conduct regular lobbying activities with European and German industry associations on restrictions, laws, and regulations. However, the scarcity of well educated automotive engineers in Beijing poses a serious constrain to its growth objectives. Due to the fact that many employees commute between their home and workplace, the company suffers from a high fluctuation rate counting for almost 20 % in 2008. This is particularly critical as it is already difficult to find skilled knowledge workers. Thus, retaining those that are already in employment became imperative for Importer.

Another negative example is Shanghai based Interior. It manufactures customized furniture for retail shops of western luxury brands. The China subsidiary was founded in 2005 and is located in Shanghai outside of major timber processing and furniture manufacturing clusters such as Guangzhou (see figure 28) or Tianjin and Shenyang.[458] Despite doubling its turnover from 2007 to 2008, the company suffers from a high cost level above the industry average. While it is easy to find management personnel, the company has difficulties to recruit workers that are skilled in wood processing. This has a particular negative business impact as 80 % of the company's staff consists of shop-floor workers, *"Shanghai might have been the right decision regarding management personnel. But they only account for 20 %. In Guangzhou the total costs of sourcing, land, and labor would have been much lower…although we doubled our turnover we could have done better. Many projects simply didn't pay off."*

Besides their advantages and opportunities, several Schools of Thought have also emphasized the significant **costs and disadvantages** that come along with locating in clusters. Marshall for example, points out that firms in clusters are ready to pay premiums for prime locations and highly skilled employees, thereby driving up costs for wages and ground rents.[459] As shown by Krugman, large clusters impose high congestion costs on their member firms acting as centrifugal factors that oppose further geographical concentration.[460] As a result, firms may find themselves in fierce competition with nearby firms. This rivalry is further increased by the fact that employees within clusters can move more easily from one job to another and spread the knowledge they gained during their employment throughout the community. According to Porter, competitive rivalry forces firms to upgrade and innovate or exit business by bankruptcy.[461] As can be seen in table 20, the case data confirms these find-

458 See appendix.
459 See Marshall (1920), p. 227.
460 See Krugman (1998), p. 8.
461 See Porter (1990), p. 127

ings. Disadvantages reach from high fluctuation of employees, rising salary levels and land costs, to scarcity of suppliers, congested logistics infrastructure, and threat of knowledge loss due to intense competition.

Company	Location	Cluster impact	Disadvantages
Cart	Shanghai	Strong	Congestion of capable suppliers. High labor costs due to competition for qualified employees. Threat of knowledge loss through spillover effects.
Frontgate	Beijing	Strong	High land and renting costs.
Image	Shanghai	Strong	High labor costs due to competition for qualified employees. Intense market competition.
Importer	Beijing	Weak	Congested logistics infrastructure. Difficult recruitment of skilled employees. High labor costs due to competition for qualified employees.
Interior	Shanghai	Weak	Scarcity of capable suppliers. Difficult recruitment of skilled employees. Availability of relevant industry information.
Material	Shanghai	Strong	High labor costs due to competition for qualified employees.
Pioneer	Shanghai	Strong	Due to Expo 2010 forced to relocate to an outer district of Shanghai and lost majority of its customers.
Sharp-Ring	Shanghai	Strong	High labor costs due to competition for qualified employees. Difficulty to build government relationships.
Topgear	Shanghai	Strong	High labor costs due to competition for qualified employees. High land and renting costs.

Table 20 - Evidence from data illustrating disadvantages when locating in clusters

Thus, being located in a dominant industry or resource-cluster provides various competitive advantages and business opportunities. Yet, they can also impose heavy costs on their member firms. In order to deal with these two sides of clusters, firms need a strong cluster-capability. Therefore, the next section will discuss the capability firms need to create and defend competitive advantages through clusters.

4.4.2 Skills that make up a Firm's Cluster-Capability

As the previous section shows, the case data confirms that clusters are characterized by a rich availability of human resources, suppliers, customers, and related industries and institutions, as well as intense rivalry among competitors. In order to succeed, firms have to make use of the various links that are present in clusters (see figure 15).

Due to their complexity, the analysis of the case data reveals that a firm's cluster-capability is not determined by a complex set of five skills, which mutually support each other: internal communication, external communication, relation, coordination, and human resources skills (see table 21). The next paragraphs, using selected examples, illustrate how firms with these skills are able to create and defend competitive advantages through clusters.

Dimensions	Activities	Company	Illustrative quota
Internal communication skills	Communication across departments	Sharp-Ring	"When our customers express a need, it is gathered by our sales staff and forwarded to the right department."
	Spontaneously exchange information	Tire	"We have a centralized marketing department that can swiftly provide us with up-to-date information."
External communication skills	Understand customer needs through face-to-face meetings	Flavor	"We regularly talk with our customers about their needs and new developments. We consider this as more effective than attending exhibitions and fairs."
	Exchange information with other cluster players	Pigment	"We update our information through meetings with chemical and industry park managers and marketing research consultants"
Relational skills	Invest in relationships	Interior	"Today, after putting a lot of effort into it, we have a supplier base."
	Build good relations to cluster members	Sensor	"We maintain good relations to professors, government institutes, and architects. Some of them are in standardization associations. So, it's easy for us to influence standards."
	Conduct joint product development	Flavor	"We develop some of our products in cooperation with nearby customers…they are involved in this process from the beginning."
Coordination skills	Evaluate local partners' resources and capabilities	Tire	"We have built strong relationships with a small base of trustworthy suppliers...to defend our competitive advantage we regularly analyze their resources and capabilities."
	Analyze local partners' goals and potentials	Interior	"We often meet with other companies from our industry to see what we can do together."
	Determine what to achieve with each relationship	Sensor	"We have very selective relationships with customers, universities, and other industry players. There is a commitment for cooperation, but only on a project-to-project base."
Human resources skills	Keep and develop human resources	Sharp-Ring	"Every company needs legends. Good and loyal people have to be supported and made known throughout the company."

Table 21 - Evidence from data illustrating cluster-capability

Internal and External Communication Skills

The majority of the companies possess strong **internal and external communication skills**, making them highly responsive to the information and knowledge that is available in clusters.

Importer for example, invests heavily in building up and maintaining good relationships to governmental bodies and firms along the horizontal dimension. By doing so, it conducts regular lobbying activities with industry associations and competitors on restrictions, laws, and regulations. Consequently, Importer is endued with valuable early information on the dynamic regulative landscape in China, which represents a major competitive advantage. As the Vice President (China) of Importer explains, "*All big automotive employers, customers, suppliers, logistics service providers, industry associations, and important government officials are in Beijing. This makes it easy for us to exchange information, build up relationships, influence public biddings, and ultimately make the sale.*"

Once it is gathered, it is only through internal communication that the company is able to translate real-time information into a competitive edge. "*We have two employees who conduct market intelligence on potential customers, the location of relevant industry clusters, and our major competitors. We also have four regional managers who regularly network with traders and customers. They forward this information to the market intelligence team who then gets the big picture...I think this is what puts us ahead.*"

Or as emphasized by the General Manager of Flavor, "*Spillovers don't come from related industries, but from our employees who share information with one another.*"

The data also shows that without relevant internal and external communication skills firms within clusters find it hard to introduce their products to their targeted customers such as in the case of Material. Although its business model is valued by its multinational client base, the company has difficulties to successfully sell it to potential Chinese clients, "*It's difficult to explain our business model to Chinese companies.*" Due to its missing communication skills, the company failed to explain its value-add to a potential client base although, "*for the future [it] is the safe and expanding market.*"

Relational Skills

Communication skills are further supported by **relational skills**, which the data shows are necessary to manage the diverse relationships to customers, government officials, and other cluster members.

Frontgate for example, a Beijing-based manufacturer of doors and gates, depends heavily on good relationships to governmental developers, architects, and design institutes. To develop and maintain a good network with its stakeholders, the company employs several relationship managers. As one outcome of these efforts the company was recently awarded its biggest real-estate construction project ever in Shanghai. Yet, this happened only after five years of relationship building in the local market.

Sharp-Ring, on the other hand, recently relocated its operations from Taicang at the outsets of the greater Shanghai area to Anting, a suburb of Shanghai, due to fierce competition for scarce employees. Although Taicang is known to be home to a large number of German companies, the key informant states that agreements, not to hire each others' employees away, didn't work out, "*In Taicang, as you might know, there is a 'German club'. But the competition for employees was so strong. We had, you would call them gentleman agreements between German companies in place, but frankly, they never worked!*" A lack of relational skills among the members of the Taicang cluster caused mistrust and finally forced the company to relocate its business.

Coordination Skills

One of the major advantages of clusters is the potential for cooperation. Firms in clusters can access each other's resources and optimize capacity utilization, achieve economies of scale, and influence market trends. Yet, the large pool of potential partners adds complexity to the selection process. To ensure that partners fit each other's resource profile and have congruent goals and objectives, firms need strong **coordination skills**.

One example of a company with strong coordination skills is Interior. As stated in the previous section, the company is located in Shanghai, outside its industry's dominant wood-processing cluster and therefore experiences significant sourcing difficulties. To overcome this hurdle, Interior seeks to pool its supply demand with other western companies and develop suppliers, which otherwise would not be possible. To this end, the company carefully analyzes with which partner to engage in such cooperation, "*We only purchase small amounts, and so most suppliers don't really care for us. To accumulate buying power, we sometimes look for western companies from our industry to pool demands. Since most of them are our competitors, we are doing this very carefully.*"

To effectively manage the flow of information between partners, Flavor appoints coordinators to important relationships. These individuals serve as single point of contact for customers and local business partners. Their main tasks are to facilitate the exchange of valuable information between the company and its partners, enhance transparency, and gather customer needs.

Thus, both Interior and Flavor are able to separate those firms that can add value to their existing operations from those that may turn out to be potentially harmful. Their strong coordination skills manage the flow of information and match the use of resources to the importance of the relationship.[462]

[462] See Yoshino/Rangan (1995), pp. 128f. and Douma et al. (2000), pp. 584f.

Human Resources Skills

In order to remain competitive in the long-run, companies have to be able to recruit and develop skilled employees. Within clusters this is particularly important as human resources [463] are seen as the real source of information and knowledge. Rivalry and competition in clusters is fierce and employees move easily between companies and by doing so spread the knowledge they gained.[464]

The case data provides evidence that effective **human resources skills** are decisive to accumulate knowledge and build competitive advantage within clusters. Evidence can once more be found in the case of Sharp-Ring, which was forced to relocate its business. As reported by its General Manager, the machine tool producer heavily invested in its employees, "*In our industry the competitive advantage lies in our workforce. To understand how a machine tool works, you need several years of practice. To identify improvement potential of an existing tool it takes you ten years of experience. But only after 15 years or so, you are able to actually develop a brand new tool.*" In order to protect its valuable knowledge, the company transferred advanced human resources practices[465] from Germany to its Chinese subsidiary, "*You have to build and support a knowledge culture. Employees want to feel valuable and this has to be done by examples and legends...Every company needs legends. Good and loyal people have to be supported and made known throughout the company.*"

Another example for the importance of good human resources practices within clusters is Xi'an based Semiconductor. The company conducts manufacturing and R&D in China and depends on highly skilled academics. Due to its advanced human resources capability the company was recently able to reduce its fluctuation rate in two consecutive years to a record-low of 5 %, "*We achieved this because our employees have attractive jobs and real projects, not these fake jobs. They do the same work as in the USA, or Europe...We value people with business impact.*"

Summing up, by providing rich insights into the specific skills that firms need to succeed in clusters, the discussion so far has fulfilled the first exploratory key objective of the fieldwork. Together, the five identified skills make up a firm's cluster-capability. It is conceptualized as a **higher-order capability** that builds upon a set of lower-order skills. Thus being of a higher-order nature, a firm's cluster-capability has a broader scope and synergy potential than its lower-order skills. It can therefore be expected that it adds great value to the firm.[466]

---

[463] In the context of the firm, *human resources* are defined as all of the knowledge, experience, skills, and commitments of a firm's employees (see Barney/Wright (1998), p. 32).

[464] See Hakanson (2005), p. 457.

[465] *Human Resources practices* are defined as all of the programs and policies that firms use to manage their human resources (see Barney/Wright (1998), p. 32).

[466] See section 3.2.2.

4.4.3 Theoretical Grounding of the Identified Skills

The second objective of the fieldwork aims at explaining *how* the identified skills assist firms in creating and defending competitive advantages. To this end it is helpful to recall the set of tasks that a firm's cluster-capability has to fulfill.[467] (1) The firm has to be able to utilize information sources that are prevalent in clusters. (2) The firm has to able to maintain and nurture access relationships. (3) Once resources become accessible to the firm, they have to be strategically exploited, upgraded, and augmented.

To assist in the explanatory stage of the analysis, the following discussion will also enfold a set of relevant literature to ground the identified skills in existing theory.

Task 1: Utilize Information

Several Schools of Thought and this study's underlying cluster definition highlight that clusters are an important source of information. Using the various links in clusters, i.e. formal, informal, vertical, and horizontal (see figure 15), firms can use their **internal and external communication skills** to stay responsive and open to their cluster environment.

In contrast with firms that seal themselves off, a firm's external communication skills emphasize interaction with its cluster environment. Staying in close contact to other cluster members such as governmental bodies, suppliers, competitors, and customers provides firms with the ability to identify current and future customer needs, upcoming market trends, changes in the regulatory framework, and developments that take place along the horizontal cluster dimension.[468]

Yet to effectively utilize and act on it, gathered information has to be internally communicated, disseminated, and made available among all relevant functions in an organization. Forwarding real-time information on partners, resources, and important cluster events, etc. at the right time to the right departments greatly enhances its value to the firm, avoids redundant processes, and reveals competitive synergies.[469]

The fulfillment of the first task, therefore, critically depends on the extent to which information is disseminated to relevant organizational units. The effectiveness of that process is greatly enhanced through individuals that stand either on the interface between the external cluster environment and the firm or between the different internal subunits. Typically, this is done by **gatekeeping or boundary-spanning individuals**, who acquire pieces of information from various sources and subsequently disseminate it to those individuals in the firm that can make the best use out of it (see figure 31).[470]

---

[467] See section 3.2.3.

[468] See also Kumar/Subramanian/Yauger (1998), pp. 203f.

[469] See Walter/Auer/Ritter (2006), pp. 547f.

[470] See Cohen/Levinthal (1990), p. 132. *Boundary spanners* are defined as those individuals who engage in significant transactions with out-group individuals. Their role is to facilitate interactions between different groups

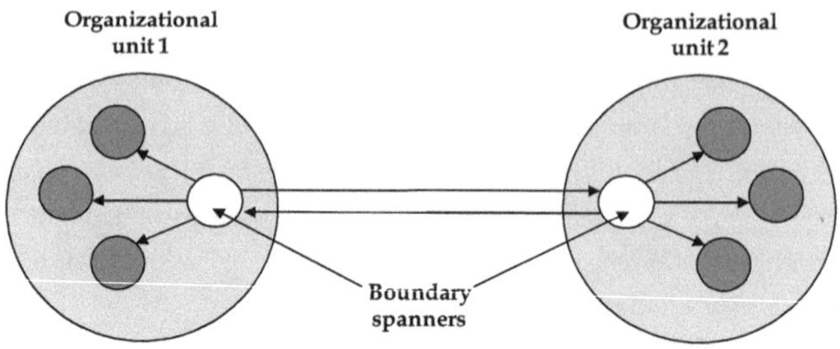

Figure 31 - Boundary spanners between organizational units

In the present case studies, firms with strong internal and external communication skills such as Importer, Tire, and Sharp-Ring consistently report of having specialized employees or central departments to gather and disseminate information. In most of the cases, specially trained sales staff and market intelligence teams gather real-time information and then share that information among all organizational units and top management teams.

Having strong communication skills both internally and externally, therefore, allows firms to effectively acquire information from external cluster sources and, by disseminating it to the right organizational unit, act swiftly in response.

Task 2: Maintain and Nurture Access Relationships

In clusters firms can form multiple relationships with other cluster members to access valuable resources, capabilities, and information. Existing literature and the present fieldwork show that managing these relationships is a complex task that depends on multiple skills.

First, **internal and external communication** is necessary to transmit information and knowledge from the firm to its partners in a credible, timely, and accurate way. It involves the use of various means of communication in case single conduits fail to effectively transmit what is intended to be said. It can include more formal pre-scheduled meetings, but also spontaneous exchange of information during social events. In addition, marketing and in-house events with reference cases and live demonstrations are an effective way of communication to a wider audience of partners. To the end that it is done in an open and honest way, communication enhances transparency and reduces some of the uncertainties partners may have about each other's motives, objectives, and competencies.[471] Such communication can also

and manage arising conflicts. Groups are sets of individuals who perceive themselves as constituting an identifiable social aggregate within or outside of organizations (see Richter et al. (2006), p. 1253). In the context of this study, boundary spanners can therefore be defined as individuals who facilitate and manage interactions either between different internal organizational units or between internal units and the firm's external cluster environment.

471 See Schreiner/Kale/Corsten (2009), p. 1401. In addition, internal communication also fosters an adequate climate to align business processes across partner firms and thereby increase partnership-specific investments (Walter/Auer/Ritter (2006), p. 550).

facilitate the exchange of more sensitive and competitively relevant information and thus generate greater advantages for the partner firms.[472]

Second, **coordination skills** ensure that firms meet their goals and objectives that have provided the motivation to commit to a given relationship. It involves the ability to identify and build consensus regarding task requirements, the strategic roles and responsibilities of the partners, and the allocation of resources.[473] To effectively coordinate a given partnership, firms can make use of two common mechanisms: formal and/or relational coordination mechanisms (see table 22).

Formal mechanisms include "*depersonalized exchanges, a reliance on financial parameters, and the drafting and implementation of formal contracts.*"[474] Relational mechanisms on the other hand, comprise social-based instruments that enhance trust, dependence, and the will to cooperate.[475] Their key tasks are to align actions and reduce the risk of opportunistic behavior by increasing mutual knowledge about the partners' interdependence. A lack of shared and accurate knowledge about how partners will act can cause coordination problems and mistrust and eventually lead to the failure of the partnership. Again, boundary spanners or coordinators such as those appointed by the case company Flavor can manage the information flow between partners and enhance the predictability of each other's actions.[476]

Formal coordination mechanisms	Relational coordination mechanisms
Task requirements	Appointed coordinators and boundary spanners
• Business plans	• Teams
• Service level agreements	• Task forces
• Procedures	• Committees
• Rules and regulations	• Direct managerial contact
• Performance indicators	Trust building
Goal fulfillment	• Shared decision making
• Incentive and reward systems	• Systems for conflict resolution
• Profit and loss accounts	• Joint problem solving
• Economic efficiency calculations	• Informal social networks
• Reporting accounts	

Table 22 - Overview of coordination mechanisms in inter-firm relationships
(Source: Own illustration based on Hoetker/Mellewigt (2009), pp. 1027ff)

472 See Paulraj/Lado/Chen (2008), p. 47.

473 See Schreiner/Kale/Corsten (2009), p. 1401. For an overview of specific instruments necessary to coordinate a complex portfolio of alliances see Hoffmann (2005), pp. 129ff.

474 Ferguson/Paulin/Bergeron (2005), p. 217.

475 See Hoetker/Mellewigt (2009), p. 1028.

476 See Gulati/Lawrence/Puranam (2005), p. 419.

Thus, the stronger a firm's coordination skills are, the better is it able to maintain existing relationships as they evolve and as firms develop a better understanding of the nature of their interdependence.

Finally, coordination and communication are greatly enhanced between firms with strong **relational skills** that can form personal contacts and constructively resolve conflicts.[477] Forming personal and resilient connections reduces the risk of opportunistic behavior.[478] It enables firms to access each other's information and resources and become more familiar with the way things are done. It includes providing timely responses to a partner's needs, being proactive and responsive, as well as the ability to put oneself in a partner's position in case conflicts arise. It also involves investing in a partnership beyond the simple call of duty, if it has proven to be valuable or is likely to do so in the future, as such behavior is likely to evolve reciprocity.[479]

This type behavior is also strongly resembled in the case of Interior, "*We constantly keep close contact to our important suppliers... sometimes we even help them out through, you know, little friendship things...there is this one supplier. They recently went into financial troubles. We helped them out through a small loan...and yes, they paid it back.*" When fueled with such relation-specific investments, the ties between firms that build upon strong relational skills can over time become an inimitable resource laying the foundation for future competitive advantage.[480]

Thus, the combined evidence suggests that the combination of communication, coordination, and relational skills allows firms to effectively manage the various relationships that can arise in clusters. Although each of the skills addresses specific issues, they are related to the same objective of ensuring stability and goal fulfillment.

Task 3: Upgrade and Augment Existing Resources

Similar to the management of access relationships, upgrading and augmenting a firm's resource base is a complex task that depends on multiple skills. According to the process model of Strategic Entrepreneurship (see figure 23), firms can upgrade their resource stock in two ways.[481]

First, firms can continuously gather **superior information** from external markets and disseminate it internally to put their stock of resources to the next best use and thereby enhance their value to the firm. Additionally, superior information enables firms to augment their existing resource stock by acquiring new resources where prices are too low, recombining

477 See Mohr/Spekman (1996), p. 36.

478 See Hoetker/Mellewigt (2009), p. 1028.

479 See Schreiner/Kale/Corsten (2009), p. 1402.

480 See Capaldo (2007), p. 601.

481 See section 3.3.1.2

them, and selling them where prices are too high. To do so, firms need superior external and internal communication skills.

Alternatively, firms can establish **inter-firm relationships** to access their partners' resources. Complementary resources in particular augment their resource profile and increase their strategic alternatives. Adding to communication skills, coordination and relational skills assist firms in this process.

Yet, clusters add an additional way in which firms can upgrade their existing resource base. The Geography of Innovation, the Innovative Milieu School, and the Nordic School of Innovation and Learning in particular highlight the importance of clusters for innovation and organizational learning.

As pointed out by Teece and colleagues, organizational learning is a key process in upgrading and augmenting a firm' resource base: *"It is in this [...] dimension, encompassing skill acquisition, learning and accumulation of organizational and intangible or invisible assets that we believe lies the greatest potential for contribution to strategy."*[482] The authors highlight the importance of skills, intangibles, and tacit knowledge for resource upgrading. As demonstrated throughout the discussion on clusters in chapter 2, these assets are person-embodied, context-dependent, and socially accessible only through interactions between individuals.[483] Similarly, Simon observes that, *"All learning takes place inside individual human heads; an organization learns in only two ways: (a) by the learning of its members, or (b) by ingesting new members who have knowledge the organization didn't previously have."*[484]

The availability of skilled human resources and the potential to establish intensive social interactions is a key advantage of clusters. Accessing it allows firms to upgrade and augment their resources and capabilities. The development of organizational capabilities, for example, depends on skilled individuals. No firm-capability can exist without the people who comprise and maintain it.[485] The extent to which an organizational capability provides value to the firm depends on how the firm accesses and integrates the specialized knowledge, skills, and abilities of its human resources, i.e. its **human resources skills**.[486] Thus, Wright and colleagues conclude that to understand a firm's organizational capability, one must understand the people, their individual skills, and the behavior in that they must engage in to implement that capability.[487]

482 Teece/Pisano/Shuen (1997), pp. 514f.

483 See Grant (1996), p. 111.

484 Simon (1991), p. 125.

485 See Wright (2001), p. 711.

486 See Grant (1996), p. 117. In this study, *human resources skills* are defined as a superior and coherent system that generates competitive advantage by aligning the firm's human resources practices to its employees' skills and behaviors (for a systems view on human resources practices see also Barney/Wright (1998), p. 36).

487 See Wright (2001), p. 712. Similarly, Chadwick and Dabu argue that all activities within organizational systems ultimately originate in human resources (see Chadwick/Dabu (2009), p. 255).

Yet, despite the fact that all learning takes place in individuals, figure 20 shows that it is also conditioned by the organizational context, its routines, and resources.[488] Therefore, a firm's human resources skills might not have direct effects on the development and upgrading of organizational capabilities. For example, good product development depends on more than just creative individuals. Such capabilities transcend individuals and are embedded in functional and cross-functional systems and processes.[489] People execute these processes, but they are not independent from them.[490]

However, a firm's human resources skills reach beyond its direct effects on individual employees in that it helps integrating their skills and knowledge into complex processes, systems, and ultimately organizational capabilities. Or as in the case of Sharp-Ring, it may lead to the development of certain organizational mindsets, complex relationships, and qualitative human resources that enable firms to develop and upgrade unique organizational capabilities.[491]

Summing up, "*the key strategic resources of a firm are the special knowledge and skills of its employees.*"[492] Firms therefore have to establish informal and external networks and allow the sharing and upgrading of information and knowledge.[493] This enables them to access the pool of skilled human resources that is available in clusters and upgrade their existing resource base to generate a continuous stream of competitive advantage.

Taken together, the results of the empirical fieldwork and the theoretical discussion have explained *how* the identified skills assist firms in creating and defending competitive advantages through clusters. This fulfills the second explanatory objective of the fieldwork.

4.5 Summary of Findings: The Conceptual Model

In conclusion, the identification of characteristics that help firms succeed in clusters provides the answer to the first research question: to succeed in clusters, firms need an EO and a strong cluster-capability that is composed of five lower-order skills, i.e. internal and external communication skills, relational skills, coordination skills, and human resources skills. In addition, firms need to align these variables according to their external cluster environment in order to achieve high levels of performance. The identified constructs and their hypothesized relationships are summarized in the conceptual model depicted in figure 32.

---

488 See Wright (2001), p. 714 and section 3.2.2.
489 See Eisenhardt (2000), p. 1108.
490 See Chadwick/Dabu (2009), p. 257.
491 See Wright (2001), pp. 709f.
492 Jacobson (1992), p. 804.
493 See Stevenson/Jarillo (2007), p. 166.

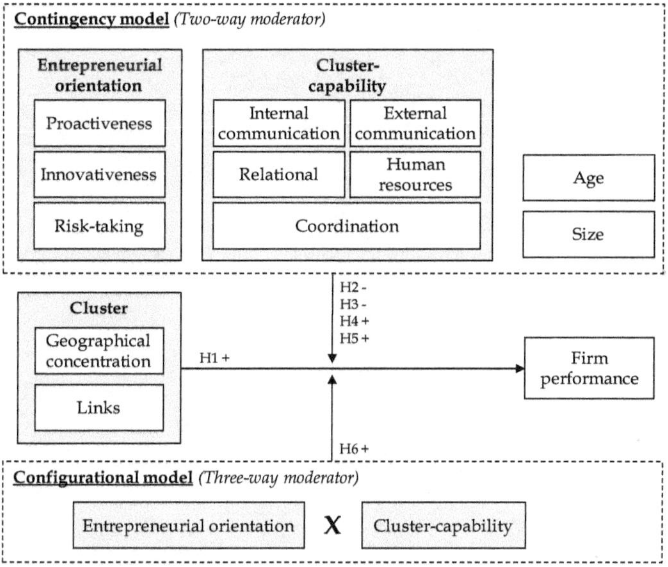

Figure 32 - The conceptual model

This conceptual model extends the theoretical model by illustrating the skills that together make up a firm's cluster-capability. It builds the foundation for answering the second research question through its empirical validation in chapter 5. This will also resolve the two competing assumptions by providing an answer about whether the contingency or the configurational perspective to strategy is better suited to explain how firms create and defend competitive advantages through clusters.

5 Empirical Analysis of the Internal Characteristics and their Influence on Firm Performance

The aim of the previous chapters was to arrive at a conceptual model about internal characteristics that enable firms to create competitive advantages through clusters. It is based on a theoretical discussion and a case study conducted in China. Taking this as a starting point, this chapter presents a survey that was carried out in China to empirically validate the hypothesized conceptual model. The outline of the next steps is illustrated in figure 33.

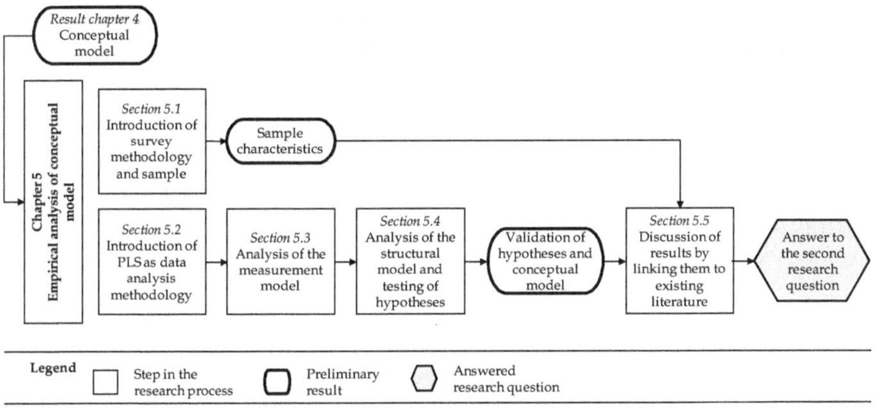

Figure 33 - Outline of chapter 5

At first, section 5.1 introduces the methodology that was followed during the data collection and provides relevant descriptive statistics of the final data sample. Section 5.2 discusses the partial least squares (PLS) approach to structural equation modeling (SEM) that was employed for the data analysis. Section 5.3 and 5.4 present the analysis of the measurement model and the structural model with a focus on hypotheses testing. In section 5.5, the results are then discussed in light of the sample characteristics and existing literatures. The chapter concludes by answering the second research question.

5.1 Research Methodology: Survey

5.1.1 Survey Design

The empirical analysis follows a survey-based research design using primary quantitative data. Research using **primary analysis** based on original data is particularly useful to test new theory in the form of newly developed constructs and hypothesized relationships.[494] **Secondary analysis** on the other hand, uses an existing, previously collected, and analyzed

[494] See Punch (2005), p. 75.

body of data. It has several advantages including time and cost savings as well as usually higher levels of quality. Yet, given the difficulty "*in finding ways of forcing the data, collected by someone else, quite often with entirely different theoretical and analytical orientations, to answer your questions*"[495] and the novelty of the underlying constructs that are to be tested, this study makes use of primary data collected through a survey.

Surveys capture naturally occurring variation in observable independent variables and their influence on equally observable dependent variables.[496] They can be conducted in a *standardized* and *non-standardized* way via *face-to-face* or *telephone interviews* and in written form using (e)-*mail* or *internet-based surveys*. Although a standardized written survey significantly restricts the respondent's flexibility, it is an efficient method of data collection that allows the comparison of findings across a large body of data.[497] Given these advantages, this study makes use of a standardized written e-mail survey.

The data itself is drawn from a larger *population*, i.e. the total target group that represents the research subject. Yet, as it is not possible to "*study everyone everywhere doing everything*"[498], research usually requires collecting data from a group of research subjects that are part of the wider population. This actual group from whom the data are collected represents the *sample* (see figure 34).

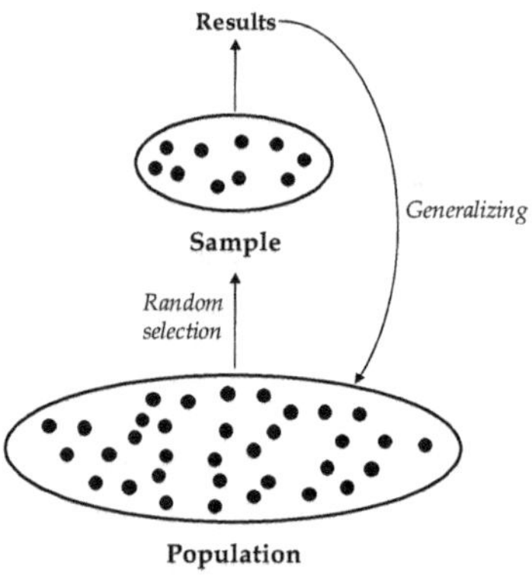

Figure 34 - Process of statistical sampling

The logic behind sampling is to analyze a small enough group and then generalize the findings from the sample back to the wider target population. This requires the sample to be representative of the population. *Representativeness* is achieved through random selection, in

495 Procter (1996), p. 262.

496 See Punch (2005), p. 71.

497 For a comprehensive introduction into different survey designs the interested reader may turn to Schnell/Hill/Esser (2008), pp. 358ff. and pp. 377ff.

498 Miles/Huberman (1994), p. 27.

which each element of the population has an equal probability to be included in the sample.[499]

To test the identified constructs and their hypothesized effects on firm performance, this study is based on an empirical survey that was conducted in China. As shown in chapter 4, China is particularly useful to study firms in clusters as the country's industries are mainly organized around clusters. After conducting the case study using German entrants in China as quasi-experiments, the aim is now to test the **external validity** of the derived conceptual model on home country firms in their respective domestic environment. In contrast to the case study, the empirical survey therefore targets only the population of wholly Chinese owned and Chinese-foreign owned JVs inside and outside of China's industrial clusters.

The actual data collection is conducted through a **questionnaire**. It includes a variety of measures that seek information about actual facts, behaviors, attitudes, values, and beliefs with the aim to capture independent, control, and dependent variables. It uses already existing measures and newly developed ones. Using appropriate scale transformation, measures turn information into **quantitative data** that is collected in the form of numbers. A widely popular scale that is also used in this study is the *Likert Scale*. It is based on the assumption that variables differ in degree and can be placed along a continuum with intervals showing less and more of its particular characteristic.[500]

The questionnaire in this study is structured according to the conceptual model presented in chapter 4 and consists of four parts. The first part seeks information regarding the respondent's firm EO. The second part consists of questions regarding a firm's cluster-capability. Part four addresses cluster related questions in which the respondents can assess the quality of their firm's cluster environment. Consequently, the survey questionnaire captures firms that are located in clusters of varying strength or even in none at all. The fourth and final part consists of general information and facts about the company and the respondent and includes the relevant control and dependent variables.

A critical factor in the questionnaire design stage is the use of different languages. Given that the targeted respondents are top-level managers of Chinese companies, the questionnaire was designed in English, but made available in Chinese. To ensure consistency between both versions, the questionnaire was translated using the *translation-backtranslation approach*.[501] Hence, a native Chinese speaker proficient in English first translated the questionnaire from English into Chinese. It was then translated back into English by a second independent native speaker and then checked for consistency. This was repeated until both versions turned out to be consistent. Using a Chinese version significantly increased the likelihood that the respondents filled out the questionnaire.

---

[499] See Punch (2005), pp. 101f.

[500] See Greving (2007), pp. 65ff and Simon (2007), p. 69.

[501] See van de Vijver/Leung (1997), p. 39 for an overview of the translation-backtranslation approach.

After the design of the questionnaire, a *pre-test* among 30 Chinese companies served to test the questionnaire for clarity, wording, and logic.[502] The companies that participated in the pre-test were not included in the final data sample. The incorporation of the feedback brought the design stage to a close.

5.1.2 Data Collection

The data was collected in cooperation with the DHL-Chair of Global Supply Chain Management at the Chinese-German School of Postgraduate Studies at Tongji University in Shanghai.

Similarly to the case study, the survey also followed the *key-informant* approach. Since the underlying research questions represent strategic issues, it requires respondents that are highly knowledgeable about their firm's overall goals, past, present, and future directions, critical decisions, as well as attitudes towards success and failure. The questionnaire was therefore attached to an Email written in Chinese and between October 2009 and February 2010 sent to C-level executives of 3,000 Chinese companies.

The contact information and email addresses of the targeted respondents were extracted from the database *Wan Fang*. To arrive at a meaningful sample, the drawing procedure followed a *sampling plan*.[503] The first step involved the selection of relevant industries to be studied. These include mainly the electronics, high-tech, machinery and industrial equipment, and consumer goods industry. In the second step, companies were grouped according to their geographical location so that the final sample consists of firms situated in diverse industry clusters. To ensure representativeness, the companies were then randomly drawn from an overall population of 250,000 database entries.

Three days after the questionnaire has been sent out, a follow-up was conducted via personal phone calls. The targeted executives or respective gatekeepers were contacted directly and asked, if they received the questionnaire. If not, the follow-up team updated the target person's contact information and resent the Email. At this occasion, the team pointed out the benefits of participating in this study and reassured the anonymity of the respondent's personal information. This significantly increased the participation and final response rate.[504] A second follow-up phase was conducted two weeks after the first Emails have been sent out to remind those contact persons that haven't responded yet to participate in the study. This final follow-up again increased the response rate significantly.

In total, 266 responses were obtained, which sums up to a response rate of 9 %. Given the effort that was necessary due to the repeated follow-up calls, the response rate is very satisfactory. In a final step, responses of low quality and responses with too many missing data points were removed from the final sample. After processing, the final sample consists of 227

502 See Kromrey (2009), pp. 384ff.

503 For more details on how to design a sampling plan see Punch (2005), p. 102.

504 As an incentive, the study participants received a summary of the results in Chinese and English.

responses. The minimum sample number for the PLS algorithm to work properly and yield robust estimates, is ten times the number of items of the most complex construct or ten times the number of exogenous constructs of the most complex endogenous construct. The threshold value is the highest of both numbers.[505] In the present conceptual model, the most complex endogenous construct is the dependent variable "Performance". Including the control variables it has 13 exogenous constructs. Therefore, the minimum sample number is 130, which is far below the number of 227 valid responses.

To further ensure data quality, the final sample was subjected to tests for Common Method Bias and Nonresponse Bias.

In this study, respondents answer questions regarding both independent and dependent variables at the same time. This can lead to *Common Method Bias* as responses by a single source can inflate or deflate correlation values between two or more variables.[506] Eliminating its key sources ex-ante can therefore significantly decrease its occurrence. First, ensuring anonymity reduces the respondent's urge to provide socially desirable, expected, or accommodating answers.[507] Second, separating dependent and independent variables from each other and arranging them into different parts of the questionnaire decreases the likelihood that the respondent artificially answers every question in the same way.[508] This study incorporates both elements in the design of the questionnaire. Ex-post, the *Harman-Single-Factor-Test* serves as a statistical test for Common Method Bias.[509] This widely used test subjects all items to exploratory factor analysis. A Common Method Bias is said to exist if a single factor emerges or a first factor explains the majority of the variance.[510] In this study, the Harman-Single-Factor-Test does not yield any evidence for the existence of Common Method Bias. Each principal construct from the principal component factor analysis explains a variance ranging from 13 % to 3 % and a total variance explained of 65 %.

Lastly, the final sample was tested for *Nonresponse-Bias*.[511] This test examines differences between the answers of early respondents and those that have not participated in the study. The test rests on the assumption that late respondents resemble the behavior and attitudes of non-respondents. The sample is therefore divided into early and late respondents. A Nonresponse bias is said to exist, if a t-test reveals significant differences between both groups in terms of demographic variables and key constructs. Yet, in the present study the questionnaires have been sent out over an extended period of time as opposed to a specific point in

505 See Henseler/Ringle/Sinkovics (2009), pp. 291f.

506 See Podsakoff et al. (2003), p. 879.

507 See Podsakoff et al. (2003), pp. 887f.

508 See Podsakoff/Organ (1986), p. 533.

509 Besides the Harman-Single-Factor-Test, there are also a variety of alternative methods to test for Common Method Bias. Despite some critiques, studies that compare the Harman-Single-Factor-Test with alternative test methods show that it consistently generates reliable test results (see for example Malhotra/Kum/Patil (2006), pp. 1867ff).

510 See Podsakoff/Organ (1986), p. 536.

511 See Armstrong/Overton (1977), p. 397; Lambert/Harrington (1990), pp. 6ff.

time. It was therefore not possible to divide the group into early and late respondents, which necessitates an alternative approach. Therefore, the first group consists of those responses that were obtained after the first Emails have been sent out and those that were obtained after the first follow-up call. The second group consists of those were repeated follow-up calls were necessary to obtain a response. This second group represents the late respondents. The comparison of both groups in terms of key variables revealed no significant differences indicating the absence of Nonresponse Bias.

5.1.3 Descriptive Sample Characteristics

Figure 35 shows the age of the surveyed companies. The average company is 15.5 years old, while the median company is 11 years old. The companies are therefore well established in their respective industries. Interestingly, almost half of the companies (46 %) are younger than 10 years, thus having been founded after China's entry into the WTO.

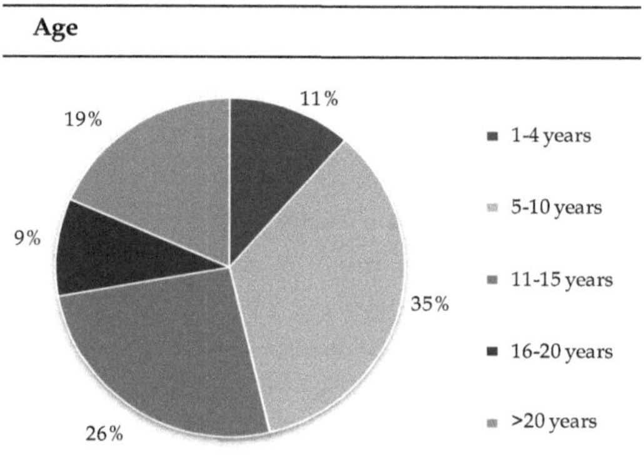

Figure 35 - Age distribution of surveyed companies

Designed as a cross-industry survey, the final sample of this study includes respondents from different manufacturing industries. As shown in figure 36, companies from the high-tech, computer, and electronics (25 %), as well as the industrial equipment (24 %) industries account for almost half of the respondents, while the metals (10 %) and the transportation equipment (9 %) industry come in third and fourth, respectively. The final sample therefore appropriately reflects the overall industry pattern of China's traditionally dominant key industries.

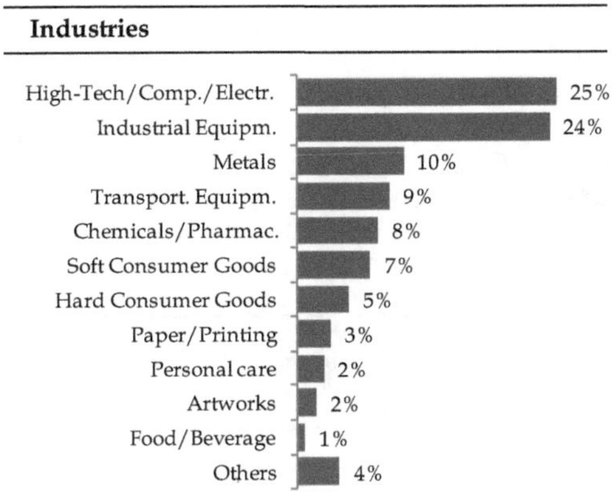

Figure 36 - Surveyed industries

In terms of their ownership structure, the majority of the companies are private owned and account for 65 %, while SOEs make up 22 % of the final sample (see figure 37).

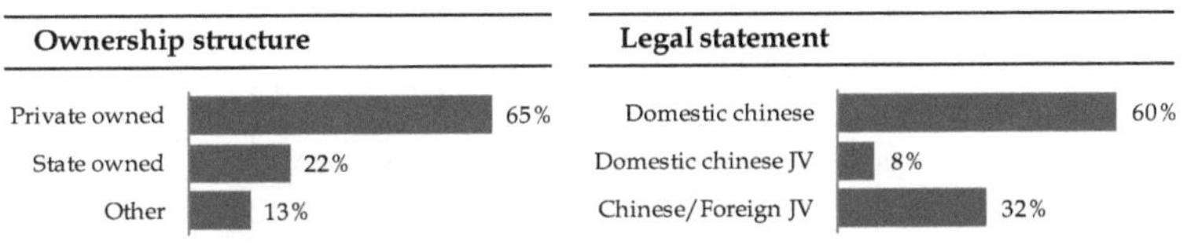

Figure 37 - Ownership structure and legal statement of surveyed companies

As stated earlier, the aim of the empirical survey is to test the general validity of the derived conceptual model on home country firms in their respective domestic environment. Wholly-foreign owned companies were therefore excluded from the investigation. As a result, the final sample consists largely of wholly domestic Chinese owned companies (60 %) and Chinese-foreign owned JVs (32 %), while JVs between domestic Chinese investors account for only 8 %.

When setting the threshold value for SMEs at a maximum of 500 employees and annual sales of 1bn RMB, the sample consists of an almost even number of SMEs and large companies (see figure 38).[512] Such a well-balanced sample is particularly important, as hypothesis 2 examines the effect of size on the relationship between clusters and firm performance.

[512] These criteria, which are commonly used in China, are set at higher threshold values than those used by e.g. the European Union (see European Commission (2005)), which defines companies as SMEs that employ less than 250 employees and earn less than 50 mill. EUR, ca. 467 mill. RMB (exchange rate EUR to RMB = 9.3528).

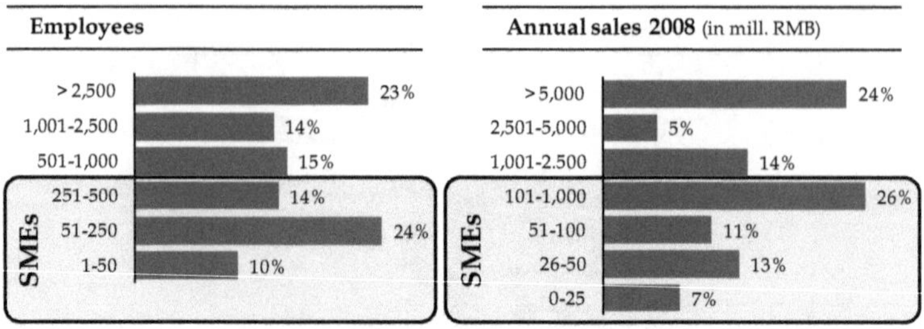

Figure 38 - Number of employees and annual sales of surveyed companies

Triggered by the emergence of globalization and rapid technological change, the cluster literature has repeatedly highlighted the importance of localized learning and the accumulation of knowledge in clusters to compete on innovation, productivity, and technological sophistication.[513] To reveal the degree to which the surveyed companies compete on knowledge, figure 39 illustrates the knowledge intensity of their products in terms of product customization and product complexity.

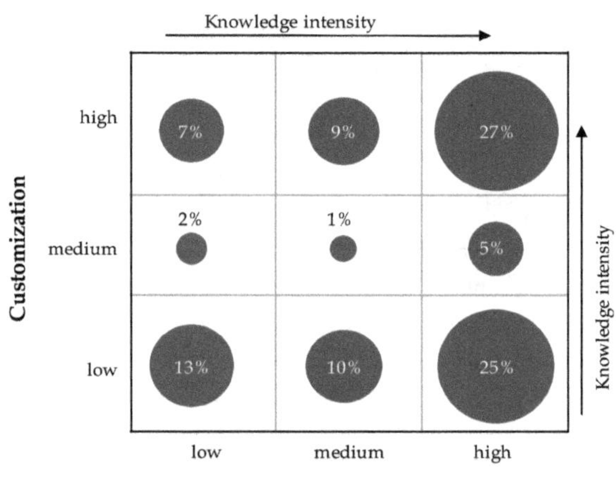

Figure 39 - Product knowledge intensity of surveyed companies

Starting from the upper left quadrant (low complexity; high customization) and the lower right quadrant (high complexity; low customization), the product knowledge intensity increases gradually and is at its highest for products in the upper right quadrant that are highly complex and customized. Accordingly, 27 % of the surveyed companies offer products that are highly complex and customized indicating a high degree of knowledge intensity. On the contrary, 13 % of the companies offer standardized products of low complexity. These

513 See chapter 2.

companies are commonly on the lower end of the value chain and belong to China's low-cost manufacturers. This reflects the notion that China's companies, and in particular its private owned ones, are increasingly moving up the value chain to compete on knowledge instead of low-cost leadership alone.

Summing up, the descriptive sample characteristics show that the final sample is well-balanced in terms of its most relevant characteristics and thus suitable to examine the effect of clusters on firm performance. The next section therefore first discusses the methodology that was employed for the data analysis and then presents the empirical validation of the conceptual model.

5.2 Data Analysis Methodology: Partial Least Squares

This study makes use of advanced **SEM** techniques to express and analyze causal networks of independent and dependent variables and their underlying relationships. These relationships represent the theorized hypotheses, making SEM most appropriate for theory development and testing. Also referred to as second generation of multivariate analysis[514], SEM techniques allow to (1) explicitly model measurement errors in observed variables, (2) incorporate unobservable latent constructs that are referred from multiple observable measures, (3) model multiple relationships between independent and dependent variables simultaneously, and (4) test developed theory with empirical data.[515] To analyze structural equation models, researchers can typically make use of either covariance-based SEM (CBSEM) or variance-based SEM techniques, i.e. PLS. This study makes use of PLS. The analysis of PLS path models is conducted in three steps as depicted in figure 40.

The analytical process starts with the operationalization of latent variables and is discussed in section 5.2.2. Latent variables or constructs can be defined as either being caused by their items (formative) or reflected by their items (reflective). Alternatively, constructs can be combined into and modeled as higher-order constructs of greater complexity. The second step, then, is discussed in section 5.2.3 and involves the evaluation of the measurement model, which differs for variables defined in a reflective and formative mode.

514 First generation techniques include linear regression, principal components analaysis, factor analysis, LOGIT, ANOVA, and MANOVA. In contrast to SEM, these techniques can only analyze individual linkages between independent and dependent variables at a time (see Gefen/Straub/Boudreau (2000), p. 4).

515 See Barroso/Cepeda Carrion/Roldan (2010), p. 429.

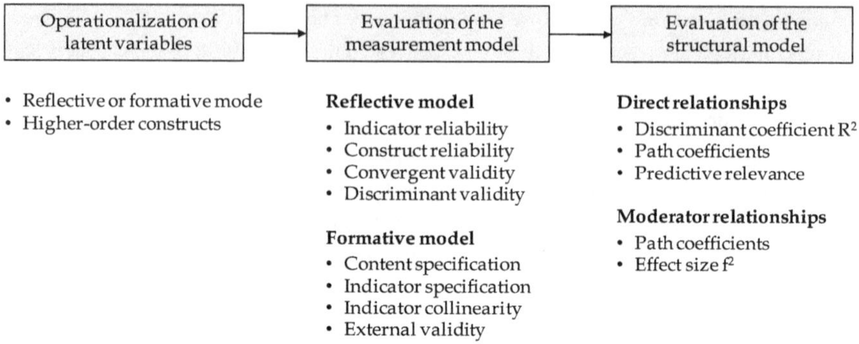

Figure 40 - Analysis of structural equation models using PLS

After the establishment of confidence in the measurement model, the analysis concludes with the actual analysis of the hypothesized relationships. This step is discussed in the sections 5.2.4 and 5.2.5. Before that, however, the next section addresses the reasons for choosing PLS and its analytical process.

5.2.1 Structural Equation Modeling Using Partial-Least-Squares

A structural equation model is formally defined by two submodels (see figure 41). The outer model represents the relationships between unobserved or latent variables and their multiple observable measures. The inner model specifies the relationships between latent variables.

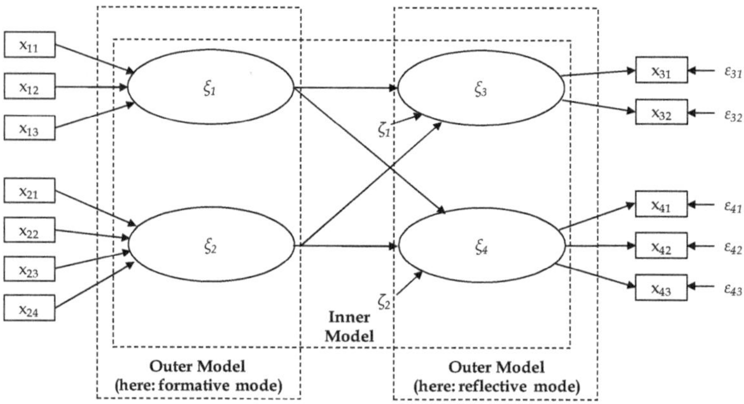

Figure 41 - Example of a simple structural equation model in its usual notation
(Source: Henseler/Ringle/Sinkovics (2009), p. 285)

The process of defining the relationships between latent variables and their assigned measures is also known as *operationalization*.[516] After the variables have been modeled, the actual analysis and interpretation of a structural equation model proceeds in two steps: (1) The assessment of the reliability and construct validity of the measurement model, and (2) the assessment of the structural model. This sequence ensures that the chosen measures are valid and reliable, before the quality of the structural model itself is evaluated.[517]

To assess a structural equation model, researchers can make use of either CBSEM or PLS techniques. Both differ in their objectives and analyses, the assumptions on which they are based, and the nature of the fit statistics they produce.

CBSEM estimates the loadings of observable measures and path values in order to minimize the difference between the sample covariances and those predicted by the underlying theoretical model. It therefore emphasizes the overall model fit and is oriented towards *testing a strong theory*. Thus as put forward by Jöreskog, in situations where prior theory is strong and the objective lies in further development and testing, CBSEM is the most appropriate statistical methodology.[518]

In contrast, **PLS** focuses on *prediction*. Its primary objective is to increase the variance explained of all dependent variables.[519] PLS is therefore preferred in exploratory study designs such as this one, because it is more concerned with the causal relationships between constructs. Further research characteristics that promote the applicability of PLS in this study are depicted in table 23.[520]

Research characteristics suitable for PLS	Presence in this study
• The research objective is exploratory in nature.	✓
• Prior theory requires development of new measures.	✓
• The sample size is relatively small.	✓
• Constructs are operationalized using formative measures.	✓
• The theoretical model involves moderator effects.	✓

Table 23 - Characteristics of this study that promote the use of PLS

This research is primarily concerned with new theory development and elaboration. The aim is to identify characteristics that allow firms to create and defend competitive advantages through clusters and examine how these characteristics influence performance under different cluster-contingencies. By identifying a set of skills that makes up a firm's cluster capability, this study is exploratory in nature. In contrast to the well established construct EO that

---

516 See Henseler/Ringle/Sinkovics (2009), pp. 284f.

517 See Hulland (1999), p. 198.

518 See Jöreskog (1982), p. 270.

519 See Henseler/Ringle/Sinkovics (2009), p. 297.

520 See Chin (2010), pp. 656ff.

relies on already existing measures, the remaining constructs require the development of entirely new ones. Furthermore, while adequate for this conceptual model the sample consist of 227 responses and would be considered as being rather small. In addition, some constructs are operationalized in a formative mode. Finally, the conceptual model also includes moderator effects. As discussed in section 5.2.5, moderator effects are calculated as the product of a predictor and a moderator variable. According to Chin, their error terms are therefore partially correlated with the error terms of the predictor and moderator variables. This is problematic for the application of CBSEM as it assumes uncorrelated error terms. In contrast, PLS does not assume uncorrelated error terms making it more appropriate to model and assess moderator effects.[521]

After this brief introduction into SEM and PLS in particular, the following sections present the operationalization of latent variables and the general procedure on how to evaluate a structural equation model using the PLS method.[522]

5.2.2 Operationalization of Latent Variables

As shown in the introductory to PLS, a structural equation model usually consists of latent variables with multiple observable measures. The nature of this relationship can be described either by a reflective or a formative mode. Figure 41 clarifies this issue. The arrows point either from the construct to the measures, i.e. reflective mode, or from the indicators to the construct, i.e. formative mode. A measurement model can either include formative or reflective indicators, or consist of both, depending on the nature of the latent variables. Whether or not a construct should be operationalized as being reflective or formative should be based on theoretical considerations regarding the hypothesized causal relationship to its indicators.[523]

Reflective indicators are believed to reflect the unobserved construct like a mirror, with the construct giving rise or causing the indicators, since "*the latent variable determines its indicators.*"[524] The causality is therefore from the construct to the indicators. The parameter value of reflective indicators depends on the value of the construct. As long as the indicators are reliable, their variance is completely determined by the variance of the construct. Hence, reflective indicators must be strongly correlated.[525]

---

521 See Chin/Marcolin/Newsted (2003), p. 197.

522 The assessment of the PLS path model was conducted using the software package SmartPLS (see Ringle/Wende/Will (2005)).

523 See Götz/Liehr-Gobbers/Krafft (2010), p. 693. Jarvis, MacKenzie, and Podsakoff (2003, pp. 202f.) have developed a set of conceptual criteria to assist researchers in determining whether a construct should be defined in a reflective or formative mode. Although useful, the decision ultimately comes down to a decision regarding the causal relationship between a construct and its measures (see Huber et al. (2007), pp. 19f).

524 Bollen/Lennox (1991), p. 306.

525 See Hulland (1999), p. 201; Huber et al. (2007), p. 20.

Formative indicators define or cause the construct. Thus, if one indicator changes its value the construct changes its value as well. On the other hand, if the construct changes its value then this translates into a change of value in at least one of its formative indicators. Consequently, formative indicators are not necessarily correlated. They are independent and share only their affiliation to the construct with each other. The variation of formative indicators can neither be traced back to the variation of the construct nor to the variation of other indicators of their construct.[526] Furthermore, a formative construct is completely defined by a linear combination of its indicators.[527] Omitting one indicator significantly changes the domain of the construct and could mean a significant change in its meaning.[528] Yet, since the formative construct cannot possibly be described completely by its indicators, the construct score does not represent its real value. Therefore, the error term is measured at the construct level.[529]

Consequences of the relationship between constructs and their indicators are that in formative relationships indicators cannot be exchanged by other indicators without the need to adapt the conceptual framework. Conversely, reflective indicators are only representatives of the constructs and thus can easily be exchanged by other indicators without the need to adapt the framework.

Additionally, constructs can also be conceptualized as **higher-order constructs** consisting of multiple dimensions of lower-order constructs. Whether a construct should be modeled as a first- or higher-order construct depends on the level of abstraction. Although it is possible to raise the level of abstraction indefinitely, its use in practice is commonly limited to second-order constructs due to increasing complexity. The key advantage of second-order constructs is the ability to distinguish between the different effects of their underlying first-order constructs. This makes second-order constructs particularly useful to test abstract theoretical concepts.[530]

Figure 42 illustrates four different possible operationalizations of second-order constructs.

526 See Huber et al. (2007), p. 20.

527 See Hulland (1999), p. 201.

528 See Henseler/Ringle/Sinkovics (2009), p. 290; Huber et al. (2007), p. 20.

529 See Huber et al. (2007), p. 5.

530 See Albers/Götz (2006), p. 672.

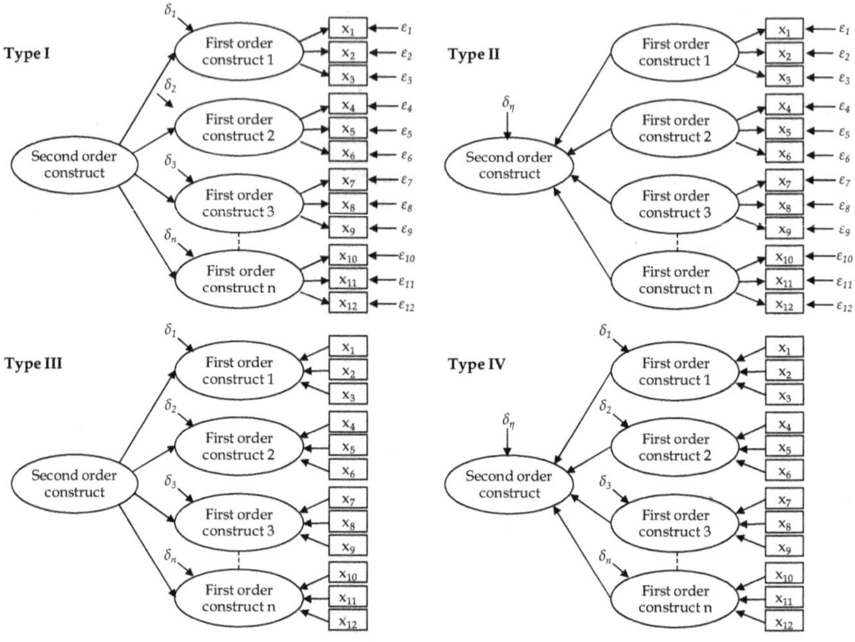

Figure 42 - Alternative second-order factor operationalizations
(Source: Jarvis/Mackenzie/Podsakoff (2003), p. 205)

The four types depend on whether the first- and second-order constructs are defined in a formative or reflective mode. Yet, not all of these models are regarded as being equally meaningful[531]:

- *Type I (reflective first-order, reflective second-order)*: This model consists of reflective first-order and a reflective second-order construct. Although it is the most common model in literature, it is also criticized by Albers and Götz as being unnecessary as the second-order construct can be measured directly by the indicators of the first-order constructs.[532]
- *Type II (reflective first-order, formative second-order)*: This model has reflective indicators for the first-order constructs and formative first-order constructs as indicators for the second-order construct. As the error term is measured on the first level, it is the most appropriate type to model independent dimensions of an abstract theoretical construct.
- *Type III (Formative first-order, reflective second-order)*: This model is particularly problematic, as the first-order constructs represent reflective, interchangeable indicators of

[531] See Jarvis/Mackenzie/Podsakoff (2003), p. 204.

[532] See Albers/Götz (2006), p. 673.

the second-order construct. They are therefore not independent dimensions of the second-order construct.

- *Type IV (Formative first-order, formative second-order)*: In this case, both the first-order and second-order constructs are defined in the formative mode. It is therefore particularly helpful to determine the influence of individual indicators and first-order constructs and is commonly used in studies on success factors.[533]

In the present study, the constructs "Cluster", "EO", and "Cluster-Capability" are defined as Type II second-order constructs. To model these constructs, literature suggests two widely used approaches. The first one was developed by Wold and is known as the hierarchical components model.[534] This approach uses the indicators of all first-order constructs as direct indicators for the second-order construct. It repeats the indicators and allows estimating the model by the standard PLS algorithm.[535] Yet, this approach requires that all first-order constructs are measured by the same number of indicators, a condition which is not met in this study.

An alternative approach that poses no limiting restrictions on the conceptual model is proposed by Yi and Davis. It uses a **Composite Second-Order Score** as single-item for the second-order construct.[536]

The composite second-order score is computed based on the factor scores of the formative latent first-order constructs. These scores are then used as formative indicators of the second-order constructs. They are multiplied with the loadings that relate each of the formative indicators to the second-order construct. Finally, the Composite Second-Order Score is derived by summing this product term across all first-order constructs according to the following equation:

$$Composite\ Second\text{–}Order\ Score = \sum_{i=1}^{n} F_i \lambda_i$$

where:

- F_i indicates the first-order factor scores,
- λ_i are the loadings relating each first-order construct to the second-order construct, and
- n indicates the number of first-order constructs.

Given its immediate applicability and the fact that it poses no restrictions on the conceptual model, this study makes use of Yi and Davis' approach to model second-order constructs.

---

533 See Albers/Götz (2006), p. 673.

534 See Lohmöller (1989), pp. 130ff.

535 See Reinartz/Krafft/Hoyer (2003), p. 19.

536 See Yi/Davis (2003), p. 160.

5.2.3 Evaluation of the Measurement Model

The analysis of a structural equation model starts with the evaluation of the measurement model. It attempts to assess whether the latent constructs are correctly measured by their assigned indicators and differs for reflective and formative constructs. For reflective constructs, it is necessary to examine the indicator loadings using traditional reliability and validity assessments. For formative constructs on the other hand, it is the weights that carry the critical information about the relative importance of each indicator. Their evaluation therefore relies on alternative assessments. Both evaluation approaches will be discussed in detail in the following sections.[537]

5.2.3.1 Evaluation of Reflective Measurement Models

In the case of reflective measurement models, each indicator is measured with an error. This error can be split into two parts, a random error and a systematic error. The random error includes all factors that affect the measurement results unsystematically. The systematic error in contrast occurs at each repetition and always at the same level. Against this background, a measurement model is said to be reliable if the random measurement error is zero and valid if the systematic error also equals zero.[538]

Starting with this basic definition, reflective constructs are traditionally evaluated using reliability and validity assessments:[539]

1. *Indicator reliability*: This reliability measure indicates, which part of an indicator's variance can be explained by its latent construct. In general, a latent variable should explain more than 50 % of the variance of its indicators. It is assessed by examining the loadings λ that relate the indicators to their respective constructs. As a rule of thumb, indicator loadings greater than 0.7 should be accepted. This implies that there is more shared variance between the construct and its measures than there is error variance. In general, items with loadings of less than 0.5 should be dropped.[540] In addition to the value of the loadings, their significance should also be examined.[541] For a two-tailed t-test and a 10 % significance level, items with t-statistics of less than 1.66 should be dropped.
2. *Construct reliability*: The Composite reliability is a measure of internal consistency and indicates the extent to which a construct's indicators jointly measure the construct, adequately. It requires indicators that are assigned to one construct to reveal a strong

537 See Barroso/Cepeda Carrion/Roldan (2010), pp. 432ff; Duarte/Raposo (2010), pp. 462f.

538 See Churchill (1987), pp. 381f.

539 See Götz/Liehr-Gobbers/Krafft (2010), pp. 694ff.

540 See Vinzi/Lauro/Tenenhaus (2003), p. 5 Bohrnstedt (1970), p. 92. Week loadings are frequently observed when newly developed measures are used (see Hulland (1999), p. 198).

541 See Huber et al. (2007), p. 87f.

intercorrelation. Values of 0.7 or higher are frequently suggested as acceptable. According to Fornell and Larcker, Composite reliability is defined as follows:[542]

$$Composite\ reliability = \frac{\left(\sum_i \lambda_{ij}\right)^2}{\left(\sum_i \lambda_{ij}\right)^2 + \sum_i var(\varepsilon_{ij})}$$

where λ_{ij} indicates the loading of indicator i of a latent variable, ε_i indicates the measurement error of indicator variable i, and j represents the flow index across all reflective measurement models.[543]

3. *Convergent validity*: This measure specifies that a set of indicators represents one and the same uni-dimensional construct. A common measure is the average variance extracted (AVE) and is defined by the following equation:[544]

$$AVE = \frac{\sum_i \lambda_i^2}{\sum_i \lambda_i^2 + \sum_i var(\varepsilon_i)}$$

An AVE value of at least 0.5 indicates satisfactory convergent validity and is a sign that a latent variable is able to explain more than half of the variance of its indicators.[545]

4. *Discriminant validity*: This measure indicates the extent to which indicators of a given latent variable differ from indicators of other latent variables in the same model. For adequate discriminant validity, a latent variable should share more variance with its indicators, than with indicators from other latent variables. This can be demonstrated by assessing the Fornell-Larcker criterion of a correlation matrix, which includes the correlations between all constructs in the lower left off-diagonal elements of the matrix and the square roots of the AVE calculated for each construct along the diagonal. For adequate levels of discriminant validity, the diagonal values should be greater than the values in the off-diagonal elements in the respective rows and columns.[546]

In summary, table 24 provides an overview of the criteria that are used in this study to evaluate reflective measurement models. Despite the importance of these well-established assessment criteria, it is also evident that in parts there is disagreement when it comes to the exact threshold values. Indicators should therefore not be eliminated exclusively on the basis of a quantitative assessment, but also based on theoretical considerations.

---

542 See Fornell/Larcker (1981), p. 45.

543 In addition to the composite reliability criterion, *Cronbach's alpha* is frequently suggested as additional measure of construct reliability. It is a generalized measure of a uni-dimensional, multi-item scale's internal consistency and indicates how well a set of indicators measures a uni-dimensional latent construct (see Götz/Liehr-Gobbers/Krafft (2010), p. 695). Yet, given that Cronbach's alpha provides severe underestimations of the internal consistency reliability (see Henseler/Ringle/Sinkovics (2009), p. 299), this study applies the composite reliability measure to assess construct reliability.

544 See Fornell/Larcker (1981), p. 45.

545 See Homburg/Giering (1996), p. 12.

546 See Fornell/Larcker (1981), p. 46; Hulland (1999), pp. 199f.

Criterion	Requirement
Reliability	
Indicator reliability	Indicator loadings > 0.7 (confirmatory) t-value > 1.66 (two-tailed t-test)
Construct reliability	Composite reliability > 0.7
Validity	
Convergent validity	AVE ≥ 0.5
Discriminant validity	Square root of AVE > Correlations

Table 24 - Assessment criteria for reflective measurement models

5.2.3.2 Evaluation of Formative Measurement Models

In contrast to reflective measurement models, latent variables defined in a formative mode can have indicators that have a positive, negative, or no correlation with one another.[547] Consequently, observed correlations among indicators allow for no meaningful interpretation, causing traditional reliability and validity measures to be irrelevant for the evaluation of formative measurement models.[548] Diamantapoulos and Winkelhofer therefore suggest evaluating formative models in terms of content specification, indicator specification, indicator collinearity, and external validity.[549]

1. *Content specification*: In formative models, failing to properly specify a construct's scope is equivalent to omitting parts of the content it is intended to capture. Content validity should therefore be ensured *before* the actual data collection by exhaustive literature research and expert interviews that result in definitions that capture a construct's entire breadth.[550]
2. *Indicator specification*: Under formative measurement, latent constructs are completely defined by their indicators. The chosen indicators must therefore cover the entire content of the latent variable. Similar to content specification, a census of all relevant indicators is required for a formative specification.[551] To further assess the degree to which each an indicator contributes to the latent variable by carrying the intended meaning, the value and significance of its weights can be examined.[552]
3. *Indicator collinearity*: To further separate the distinct influence of individual indicators, tests for multicollinearity assess to what degree indicators carry redundant information. This can be performed by calculating the variance inflation factor (VIF), which is defined as follows:

---

547 See Bollen/Lennox (1991), p. 307.
548 See Hulland (1999), p. 201.
549 See Diamantopoulos/Winkelhofer (2001), pp. 271ff.
550 See Diamantopoulos/Winkelhofer (2001), p. 271; Rossiter (2002), p. 306; Nunnally/Bernstein (1994), p. 484.
551 See Diamantopoulos/Winkelhofer (2001), p. 271.
552 See Henseler/Ringle/Sinkovics (2009), p. 302.

$$VIF = \frac{1}{1 - R^2}$$

where R^2 indicates the variance of an indicator that is explained by the remaining indicators. As a threshold, VIF values greater than 10 point to a critical level of multicollinearity.[553]

4. *External validity*: A further criterion to assess the suitability of the chosen indicators is to examine the degree to which they behave in a net of hypothesized relationships as expected. These relationships should be strong and significant. In general, there are three suggested procedures to examine external validity.[554] (1) Each indicator can be correlated to a global item that fully captures the content of the latent variable, and only those indicators that are significantly correlated with the item are retained. (2) The formative indicators can be augmented by reflective indicators to a multiple effect indicators for multiple causes (MIMIC) model. In this case, the reflective indicators serve as the external validation of the formative measurement model. (3) Based on a thorough theoretical base, the formative latent construct can be linked to other reflectively measured constructs with which it is expected to be linked. External validity is given in case a strong and significant relationship is detected.

Table 25 provides a summarized overview of the assessment criteria for formative measurement models.

Criterion	Requirement
Content specification	Literature research and expert interviews
Indicator specification	Indicator weights and t-values
Indicator collinearity	VIF < 10
External validity	(1) Correlation with a global item (2) MIMIC model (3) Strong and significant relationship with subsequent reflective constructs

Table 25 - Assessment criteria for formative measurement models

Despite these assessment criteria, the elimination of indicators should always be based on theoretical considerations and not on statistical assessments alone as such actions might significantly alter the content of the latent variable. Thus, as long as it is theoretically justified, both significant and insignificant indicators should be kept in the measurement model.[555]

553 See Gujarati (2003), p. 362.

554 See Diamantopoulos/Winkelhofer (2001), pp. 272f.

555 See Henseler/Ringle/Sinkovics (2009), p. 303.

5.2.4 Evaluation of the Structural Equation Model

After establishing the validity and reliability of the measurement model, the second step involves the evaluation of the structural model. This commonly involves three procedures, i.e. the assessment of the coefficient of determination R^2 of the endogenous latent variables, the directions and significance levels of the path coefficients, and the test for a model's predictive relevance Q^2.[556]

1. *Determination coefficient* R^2: Given the objectives of PLS, i.e. prediction and increasing the amount of variance explained, the essential criterion to evaluate a structural equation model is the coefficient of determination R^2 of the endogenous latent variables. It reflects the share of the latent's variable explained variance. Chin suggests R^2 values of 0.67, 0.33, and 0.19 as substantial, moderate, and weak, respectively.[557] Yet, other authors such as Götz, Liehr-Gobbers, and Kraft suggest that acceptable levels of R^2 are not generalizable and depend on the individual study.[558] In general, however, the larger the explained variance the better the model's goodness of fit.
2. *Path coefficients*: Also of critical importance are the directions and significance levels of the path coefficients. They represent the hypothesized relationships between latent variables. Paths that are insignificant or show signs that are contrary to the hypothesized direction do not support a hypothesis, while on the other hand significant paths showing the hypothesized direction empirically support the a priori proposed hypothesis. The significance can be tested by means of t-statistics. For a two-tailed t-test and a 10 % significance level, paths with t-statistics less than 1.66 are regarded as insignificant.[559]
3. *Predictive relevance*: Developed by Stone and Geisser, the Q^2 test assesses a model's predictive relevance, that is, how well a model and its estimated parameters reproduce actually observed values. It can only be applied to latent constructs that are defined in a reflective mode and is described by the following equation:

$$Q^2 = 1 - \frac{\sum_k E_{jk}}{\sum_k O_{jk}}$$

Where E_{jk} represents the squares of the prediction errors and O_{jk} represents the squares of the trivial prediction error provided by the mean of the remaining data. Index j indicates the observed endogenous measurement model, and k represents the index for all indicators of the measurement model. A Q^2 greater 0 indicates that the model has predictive relevance, while a Q^2 less than 0 suggests a lack thereof.[560] In

556 See Barroso/Cepeda Carrion/Roldan (2010), pp. 434f; Götz/Liehr-Gobbers/Krafft (2010), pp. 701f.; Henseler/Ringle/Sinkovics (2009), pp. 303ff.

557 See Chin (1998), p. 323.

558 See Götz/Liehr-Gobbers/Krafft (2010), p. 701 as well as Backhaus et al. (2003), p. 63.

559 See Huber et al. (2007), pp. 42f.

560 See Fornell/Cha (1994), p. 73.

addition, values of 0.02, 0.15, and 0.35 suggest small, moderate, and large predictive relevance of a certain latent variable, respectively.[561]

In summary, table 26 provides an overview of the assessment criteria and their threshold values for structural equation models as they are set in this study.

Criterion	Requirement
Determination coefficient R^2	R^2 in this study > 0.2 (No agreed threshold values.)
Path coefficients	t-value > 1.66 (two-tailed t-test) Coefficients in this study > 0.1 and with hypothesized direction (No agreed threshold values for coefficients)
Predictive relevance	$Q^2 > 0$

Table 26 - Assessment criteria for structural equation models

5.2.5 Modeling and Evaluation of Moderator Models

At the heart of this study lies the examination of variables that influence or moderate the hypothesized effect of clusters on firm performance. Moderators are commonly defined as "*a qualitative or quantitative variable that affects the direction and/or strength of the relation between an independent and dependent or criterion variable.*"[562] Thus, moderating effects are particularly useful to examine the contextual circumstances under which a hypothesized direct relationship between latent variables holds true.[563] The left-hand side of figure 43 shows a moderator model with three variables and X being the independent, M the moderating, and Y the dependent variable. The moderating effect d is indicated by an arrow that points onto the direct relationship between the exogenous and the endogenous variable b.

561 See Henseler/Ringle/Sinkovics (2009), p. 305.

562 Baron/Kenny (1986), p. 1174 in Wilson (2010), p. 621.

563 See Chin/Marcolin/Newsted (2003), p. 193; Homburg/Giering (2001), p. 47.

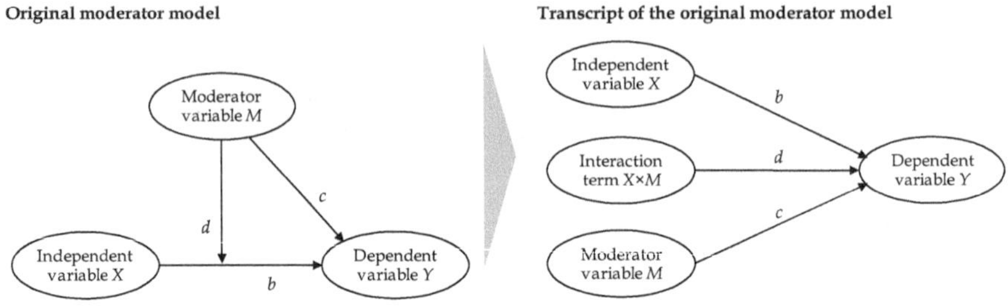

Figure 43 - Example of a simple PLS Moderator model
(Source: Henseler/Fassott (2010), p. 717 and p. 719)

In general, **two-way interaction effects** can be estimated using the product term approach for continuous variables and the group comparison approach for discrete variables. Because this study uses continuous variables, the following discussion will focus on modeling moderating effects as product terms.[564] In the *product term* approach, the moderator effect is added to the main effects model by including the product term between the independent and the moderating variable. The main effects model:

$$Y = a + b \times X + c \times M$$

thus becomes:

$$Y = a + b \times X + c \times M + d \times (X \times M)$$

where $X \times M$ represents the interaction term that is added to the PLS path model as additional latent variable. As a consequence, the slope of the independent variable X becomes dependent on the level of M; hence M is influencing the strength of the effect of X on Y. To properly evaluate the effect of the moderator effect, all components of the product term have to be included in the PLS model in a direct form. Otherwise, the size of the moderating effect would be overestimated. The right-hand side of figure 43 illustrates this approach.

The same approach can be applied to **three-way interactions**, in which there is an independent and two moderator variables that *together* influence the relationship between X and Y. Adding a second moderator N to the above equations thus leads to:

$$Y = aX + bM + cN + d(X \times M) + e(X \times N) + f(M \times N) + g(X \times M \times N)$$

To include three-way interactions in a PLS path model, all single effects, all two-way interactions, as well as the three-way interaction term have to be added as additional latent variables.

Once the interaction terms are included in the PLS path model, the interaction terms have to be properly modeled. This depends on the variables' mode of measurement. In case the independent and moderating variables are defined in a *reflective mode*, all indicators have first

564 The following discussion is based largely on the suggestions made by Henseler/Fassott (2010), pp. 716ff.

to be centered or standardized to avoid multicollinearity.[565] The product term is then built by multiplying each indicator of the independent variable with each indicator of the moderating variable(s). These product terms then serve collectively as indicators of the interaction term.

If at least one variable is defined in a *formative mode*, first the factor scores of the independent and the moderator variable(s) are calculated and then standardized. Finally, the interaction term is built by multiplying the standardized factor scores of the independent and the moderator variable(s).

In both cases, moderator effects are analyzed by estimating the path coefficients and their significance. The hypothesized relationship between *X*, *Y*, and *M* is supported, if the path coefficient *d* is significant; regardless of the coefficients *b* and *c*.[566] The moderator effect can be further assessed by its contribution to explain the variance of the dependent variable *Y*. It is performed by comparing the R^2 of the main effects model including all direct single effects with the R^2 of the full moderator model including the interaction term(s). This effect size f^2 is calculated according to the following formula:

$$f^2 = \frac{R^2_{model\ with\ moderator} - R^2_{model\ without\ moderator}}{1 - R^2_{model\ with\ moderator}}$$

Moderating effects with effect sizes of 0.02, 0.15, and abo ve 0.35 are regarded as weak, moderate, and strong, respectively. Yet, low effect sizes do not imply that the hypothesized model is irrelevant, as *"even a small interaction effect can be meaningful under extreme conditions, if the beta changes are meaningful, then it is important to take these conditions into account."*[567]

5.3 Analysis of the Measurement Model

According to the previously introduced PLS methodology, the data analysis starts with an assessment of the measurement model. In this respect, the current chapter is split into two parts. Section 5.3.1 deals with the operationalization and validation of the measurement models of the first-order constructs including the relevant control variables. Section 5.3.2 then presents the operationalization and validation of the second-order constructs, which are all defined in the Type II mode.

5.3.1 Operationalization and Validation of First-Order Constructs

On the first-order level, all independent latent variables are defined in a reflective mode as they give rise to observable measures such as behaviors and outcomes of uni-dimensional performance constructs. The causality is therefore from the construct to its indicators, which are only representatives of their constructs.[568] Thus, they can easily be exchanged by other

---

565 See Aiken/West (1991), p. 35.

566 See Baron/Kenny (1986), p. 730.

567 Chin/Marcolin/Newsted (2003), p. 311.

568 See Fornell/Bookstein (1982), p. 292.

indicators without the need to adapt the overall framework. In this study every latent construct is measured by at least two indicators to avoid the single-item problem.[569]

Control variables on the other hand, are measured using only a single item. They represent effects that influence a dependent variable and might confound those relationships that are actually being studied. Therefore, control variables are used to partial out or remove their effects by including them in the actual PLS path analysis.[570]

"Legal Statement" and "Ownership Structure" were included as control variables as both indicate slack resources that are available to the firm, its entrepreneurial dynamism, and the shareholder structure that might influence both. Particularly in China the ownership structure is important to control for as its state driven capitalism is mainly realized through its large SOEs and conglomerates.

To further account for industry effects and economic cycles that might impact performance levels, the respondents were asked to indicate their firm's performance over the three years 2006 to 2008 relative to their competitors.[571]

In addition to the control variables, the next sections discuss the operationalization and validation of all latent first-order constructs.

5.3.1.1 Cluster

The "Cluster" construct is defined as second-order construct. Based on the conceptual model, it is formed by two dimensions:

- "Geographical Concentration", and
- "Links in Clusters".

The validity and reliability of their operationalization is assessed according to the criteria for reflective measurement models as outlined in table 24.

Geographical Concentration

The operationalization of the "Geographical Concentration" construct is based on the *LQ* measure.[572] Accordingly, respondents were asked to compare the concentration of their own industry to the concentration of other industries in their region based on different indicators. These indicators involve (GC1) the number of companies operating in their industry, (GC2) the number of people employed by their industry, and (GC3) the GIOV generated by their own industry compared to the remaining industries in their region (see table 27).

---

569 See Churchill (1979), p. 66.

570 See Punch (2005), pp. 80ff.

571 See Spanos/Lioukas (2001), p. 916.

572 See section 4.2.2.

"Geographical Concentration": Indicator assessment			
		Criteria	
Indicators		Indicator loadings	t-value
Please compare your industry to other industries in your region.			
GC1	The number of companies operating in our industry compared to the number of companies operating in other industries.	0.75	8.99
GC2	The number of people employed in our industry compared to the number of people employed by other industries.	0.91	23.29
GC3	The percentage our industry contributes to the regional gross industrial output value compared to the total regional gross industrial output value.	0.94	40.9

"Geographical Concentration": Factor assessment	
Composite reliability	Average Variance Extracted
0.9	0.76

Table 27 - Assessment of the "Geographical Concentration" construct

The assessment results show that the loadings of all three indicators are above the 0.7 threshold and sufficiently significant. Similarly, the composite reliability (0.9) and the AVE (0.76) are also above their recommended values indicating acceptable levels of reliability and validity.

Links in Clusters

The operationalization of the "Links in Clusters" construct is based on figure 15, which consolidates the insights gained from the different Cluster Schools of Thought that have been discussed throughout chapter 2. As the construct is defined in a reflective mode, it is sufficient for its operationalization to include a selection of particularly useful examples. Based on the case study and the pre-tests, the indicators involve (LC1) the number of regional suppliers and customers, (LC2) the existing networks and relationships between those firms, (LC3) the extent to which employees attend local industry events, and (LC4) the degree of their inter-firm mobility (see table 28).

"Links in Clusters": Indicator assessment			
		Criteria	
Indicators		Indicator loadings	t-value
LC1	Our region is home to a large number of suppliers and potential customers.	0.83	29.88
LC2	We have build networks and alliances with our local business partners.	0.71	9.69
LC3	Our employees regularly participate in relevant local industry events.	0.88	32.78
LC4	In our local business environment it is common that employees who switch jobs move from one local company to another.	0.8	17.19

"Links in Clusters": Factor assessment	
Composite reliability	Average Variance Extracted
0.88	0.65

Table 28 - Assessment of the "Links in Clusters" construct

On the indicator level, all loadings and t-values show satisfactory values above their respective thresholds. On the construct level, the composite reliability measures 0.88 and the AVE 0.65 indicating acceptable levels of reliability and validity.

5.3.1.2 Entrepreneurial Orientation

The "Entrepreneurial Orientation" construct is defined as second-order construct that is formed by three distinct dimensions:

- "Proactiveness",
- "Innovativeness", and
- "Risk-Taking".

The validity and reliability of their operationalization is assessed according to the criteria for reflective measurement models as outlined in table 24.

Proactiveness

The "Proactiveness" construct was operationalized with four indicators of which three stem from well established scales. The first indicator was adapted from Venkatraman and reflects (PRO1) the firm's pursuit of opportunities through scanning and monitoring activities.[573] Two indicators were taken from Lumpkin and Dess, which reflect (PRO2) the firm's willingness to generate first mover advantages and (PRO3) move ahead of competitors with the introduction of new products or services.[574] The last indicator was newly developed based on

573 See Venkatraman (1989), p. 959.

574 See Lumpkin/Dess (2001), p. 451.

the case study results and reflects (PRO4) the firm's willingness to pursue industry leadership (see table 29).

"Proactiveness": Indicator assessment			
		Criteria	
Indicators		Indicator loadings	t-value
PRO1	Overall, my firm regularly scans the environment and gathers information from our local business partners to seek and identify new opportunities.	0.76	13.85
PRO2	In general, the top managers of my firm initiate preemptive actions in response to perceived opportunities which competitors then respond to.	0.77	16.48
PRO3	We are very often the first to introduce new products or services to our customers.	0.90	56.02
PRO4	In general, my firm is eager to be a leader rather than a follower.	0.83	24.46

"Proactiveness": Factor assessment	
Composite reliability	Average Variance Extracted
0.89	0.67

Table 29 - Assessment of the "Proactiveness" construct

The loadings of all four indicators are above the 0.7 threshold and sufficiently significant. The composite reliability (0.89) and the AVE (0.67) are also above their recommended values indicating acceptable levels of reliability and validity.

Innovativeness

Both indicators used to measure innovativeness were adapted from Lumpkin and Dess and reflect (IN1) the relative number of new products and services in the firm's portfolio and (IN2) the degree of changes in product and service lines (see table 30).[575]

[575] See Lumpkin/Dess (2001), p. 442.

"Innovativeness": Indicator assessment			
		Criteria	
Indicators		Indicator loadings	t-value
IN1	During the past three years my firm has marketed very many new lines of products and services.	0.91	35.08
IN2	Changes in product and service lines have been quite dramatic.	0.85	21.28

"Innovativeness": Factor assessment	
Composite reliability	Average Variance Extracted
0.87	0.77

Table 30 - Assessment of the "Innovativeness" construct

For the "Innovativeness" construct, both indicators show high indicator loadings as well as significant t-values. The measures for composite reliability and AVE are also above their thresholds indicating acceptable levels of reliability and validity.

Risk-Taking

Similar to the previous two dimensions, the "Risk-Taking" construct was also operationalized through well established measures. Both indicators were adapted from Lumpkin and Dess and reflect (RI1) the proclivity for high-risk projects within a firm and (RI2) the boldness of a firm's responsible employees (see table 31).

"Risk-Taking": Indicator assessment			
		Criteria	
Indicators		Indicator loadings	t-value
In my firm...			
RI1	...people have a strong proclivity for high-risk projects (with chances of very high returns).	0.79	4.33
RI2	...people believe that owing to the nature of the environment, bold wide-ranging acts are necessary to achieve the firm's objectives.	0.80	7.50

"Risk-Taking": Factor assessment	
Composite reliability	Average Variance Extracted
0.77	0.63

Table 31 - Assessment of the "Risk-Taking" construct

Again, all criteria are sufficiently fulfilled with all values being above their thresholds thus indicating reliability and validity.

5.3.1.3 Cluster-Capability

The "Cluster-Capability" construct is defined as second-order construct. Based on the case study results and the conceptual model it is defined by five dimensions:

- "Internal Communication Skills",
- "External Communication Skills",
- "Coordination Skills",
- "Relational Skills", and
- "Human Resources Skills".

The validity and reliability of the first-order constructs is assessed according to the criteria as outlined in table 24.

Internal Communication Skills

For the operationalization of the "Internal Communication" construct, this study adapted four indicators from a scale developed by Walter, Auer, and Ritter.[576] These indicators reflects (IC1) the regularity of meetings in which information is shared across departments, (IC2) the extent to which employees develop informal contacts among each other, (IC3) the communication quality within a firm, and (IC4) the spontaneity of the information exchange (see table 32).

"Internal Communication Skills": Indicator assessment			
		Criteria	
Indicators		Indicator loadings	t-value
In my firm…			
IC1	…we have regular meetings in which employees from different departments share information among each other.	0.74	2.27
IC2	…employees develop informal contacts among each other.	0.96	7.16
IC3	…communication often takes place across projects and departments.	0.97	20.16
IC4	…information is often spontaneously exchanged.	0.83	2.8
"Internal Communication Skills": Factor assessment			
Composite reliability		Average Variance Extracted	
0.93		0.77	

Table 32 - Assessment of the "Internal Communication Skills" construct

In summary, all assessment criteria are above their recommended thresholds. The indicator loadings range from 0.74 to 0.97 and are sufficiently significant. On the construct level, the

576 See Walter/Auer/Ritter (2006), p. 562.

composite reliability of 0.93 and the AVE of 0.77 indicate acceptable levels of reliability and validity.

External Communication Skills

The "External Communication" construct is operationalized based on well established scales and captures the extent to which a firm is able to effectively communicate with its local business partners. One indicator is adapted from Schreiner, Kale, and Corsten and indicates (EC1) a firm's ability to effectively explain its value-add to its local business partners.[577] Two indicators stem from a study conducted by Paulraj, Lado, and Chen and reflect (EC2) the extent to which a firm shares sensitive information and (EC3) maintains frequent face-to-face meetings with local business partners.[578] These indicators are complemented by a newly developed measure that is based on the case study results and which reflects (EC4) a firm's willingness to perform boundary spanning tasks by conducting in-house events for local business partners (see table 33).

"External Communication Skills": Indicator assessment			
		Criteria	
Indicators		Indicator loadings	t-value
EC1	On any given occasion, we can explain the value-adding proposition of our service and product offering to our local business partners.	0.82	25.17
EC2	We frequently share critical, sensitive information related to operational and strategic issues with our local business partners and government officials, with exception of direct competitors.	0.81	17.74
EC3	We maintain frequent face-to-face meetings with our local business partners to understand each other's strategic goals and objectives.	0.87	37.79
EC4	We provide regular trainings, seminars, and in-house events to promote our latest innovations among customers and important members of standardization associations.	0.85	34.8

"External Communication Skills": Factor assessment	
Composite reliability	Average Variance Extracted
0.9	0.7

Table 33 - Assessment of the "External Communication Skills" construct

On the indicator level, all criteria are well above their recommended thresholds. Similarly, on the construct level the composite reliability and the AVE are also well above their critical values indicating sufficient reliability and validity.

577 See Schreiner/Kale/Corsten (2009), p. 1419.

578 See Paulraj/Lado/Chen (2008), p. 51.

Coordination

The "Coordination Skills" construct reflects a firm's ability to successfully plan, manage, and control all activities, strategic roles, and responsibilities in inter-firm relations and allocate resources where they are needed the most.

Five of the original indicators are adapted from Walter, Auer, Ritter[579] and one is based on the study conducted by Sarkar, Echambadi, and Harrison[580]. These indicators measure (CS1) the extent to which a firm plans ahead before establishing a partnership, (CS2) assesses the strategic complementarity of its partners along critical dimensions, (CS3) the degree to which it defines the goals and objectives it likes to achieve with each partnership, (CS4) allocates the resources to where they have the biggest impact, (CS5) informs itself of its partner's resources and capabilities, and (CS6) appoints boundary spanners to coordinate its inter-firm relationships (see table 34).

"Coordination Skills": Indicator assessment			
		Criteria	
Indicators		Indicator loadings	t-value
CS1	We judge in advance with which potential local business partners to talk about building up relationships.	0.88	48.74
CS2	We inform ourselves of our local business partner's goals, potentials, and strategies.	0.89	52.32
CS3	We analyze what we would like and desire to achieve with which local business partner.	0.91	78.14
CS4	We match the use of resources (e.g. personnel, finance, and management support) to the importance of the individual relationship.	0.79	20.32
CS5	We regularly analyze our local business partner's resources and capabilities.	0.86	45.53
CS6	We appoint coordinators who are responsible for the relationships with our local business partners and government officials.	0.74	18.97

"Coordination Skills": Factor assessment	
Composite reliability	Average Variance Extracted
0.94	0.72

Table 34 - Assessment of the "Coordination Skills" Construct

On the indicator level, all criteria exceed their recommended thresholds. Similarly, on the construct level the composite reliability and the AVE are also well above their critical values indicating sufficient reliability and validity.

579 See Walter/Auer/Ritter (2006), p. 561.

580 See Sarkar/Echambadi/Harrison (2001), pp. 702f.

Relational Skills

The "Relational Skills" construct indicates a firm's ability to establish and maintain close relationships with its local business partners. It is measured by two items from Walter, Auer, and Ritter[581], two items that are adapted from Phan, Lawrence, and Puranam[582], and two items that were newly developed based on the insights gained from the case study. They reflect the firm's (RS1) ability to build relationships in which both parties can achieve their strategic goals and objectives, (RS2) the willingness to invest in relationships, (RS3) the commitment to given arrangements, (RS4) problem solving skills, (RS5) bonding aspects, and (RS6) the degree of empathy the firm is able to show (see table 35).

"Relational Skills": Indicator assessment			
		Criteria	
Indicators		Indicator loadings	t-value
RS1	We have the ability to use relationships with our local business partners in a way that both parties achieve their strategic goals and objectives.	0.87	40.95
RS2	If necessary, we invest in local partnerships which we think will prove valuable in the future.	*eliminated*	
RS3	Even in difficult times, we respect past commitments we have made to our local business partners.	*eliminated*	
RS4	We almost always solve problems constructively with our local business partners.	0.85	32.44
RS5	We have the ability to build good personal relationships with our local business partners and government officials.	0.87	39.18
RS6	We can put ourselves in our local business partner's position.	0.91	59.83

"Relational Skills": Factor assessment	
Composite reliability	Average Variance Extracted
0.93	0.77

Table 35 - Assessment of the "Relational Skills" Construct

After the initial assessment, two indicators showed low loadings and were therefore eliminated. After purification, all indicator loadings are well above their critical values ranging from 0.85 to 0.91 and sufficiently significant. Furthermore, on the construct level the composite reliability and AVE measures are also above their thresholds indicating reliability and validity.

581 See Walter/Auer/Ritter (2006), p. 562.

582 See Phan/Styles/Patterson (2005), p. 177.

Human Resources Skills

The "Human Resources Skills" construct is operationalized with nine items of which the first one was newly developed based on the insights gained in the case study. It reflects (HRS1) the extent to which a firm supports good and loyal employees. The remaining eight indictors stem from the field of strategic human resources management. Four items are adapted from Ngo, Lau, and Foley's study situated in China and reflect (HRS2) the emphasis on an individual's contribution in determining bonuses, (HRS3) the competitiveness of compensation packages, (HRS4) the emphasis on long-term employments, and (HRS5) the extent to which employees are subjected to job rotations.[583] The remaining four indicators stem from Michie and Sheehan and reflect (HRS6) the amount of training and development provided to employees, (HRS7) the communication of clear career paths, (HRS8) the degree of employee participation, and (HRS9) the company-wide transparency of strategic goals and objectives (see table 36).

"Human Resources Skills": Indicator assessment			
		Criteria	
Indicators		Indicator loadings	t-value
HRS1	We support good and loyal people and make them known throughout our company.	*eliminated*	
HRS2	In determining individual bonuses, we emphasize the individual's contributions more than job title.	0.76	16.27
HRS3	Our compensation package is designed to be more competitive than those of other nearby located firms.	0.79	25.02
HRS4	Our compensation package is designed to reward long-term employees.	*eliminated*	
HRS5	Employees transfer to new functional areas and/or new units are used as a development activity in our firm.	0.85	32.07
HRS6	We provide a considerable amount of training to our employees.	0.88	45.52
HRS7	Within our firm, individuals have clear career paths.	0.87	38.94
HRS8	We encourage our employees to suggest improvements in the way things are done.	0.87	40.88
HRS9	Our staff is informed about our strategic goals and the competitive pressures we face.	0.82	27.49

"Human Resources Skills": Factor assessment	
Composite reliability	Average Variance Extracted
0.94	0.7

Table 36 - Assessment of the "Human Resources Skills" Construct

[583] See Ngo/Lau/Foley (2008), p. 90.

After their initial assessment, HRS1 and HRS2 showed low and non-significant indicator loadings and were therefore eliminated. After purification, a repeated assessment showed satisfactory levels of all assessment criteria. The indicator loadings are all significant and range from 0.76 to 0.88. Furthermore, on the construct level all values are above their thresholds indicating reliability and validity.

5.3.1.4 Performance

For the operationalization of performance, this study relies on two subjective measures that are widely used in the field of strategic management and entrepreneurship, i.e. profitability and sales performance. Thus, performance is treated as a two dimensional phenomenon, where sales performance represents a firm's entrepreneurial aspiration to grow and develop new markets and profitability the internal economic rents stemming from the efficient use of its resources and its ability to generate returns for its shareholders.[584]

Besides the subjective measures of performance, it was not possible to obtain financial performance measures. During the pre-test, respondents were highly reluctant to provide their firms' financial figures and almost collectively refused to answer the respective questions. Despite these initial setbacks, the questions remained in the final version of the questionnaire. However, as indicated by the pre-test only a small minority of the final sample provided financial figures and where they did, these included almost solely revenue figures, while profitability figures remained undisclosed. This study therefore relies exclusively on subjective performance measures. Yet, there is a long tradition in the field of strategic management and entrepreneurship to use subjective performance measures as they have been found to significantly correlate with a firm's actual financial data.[585]

Profitability

The "Profitability" construct is operationalized with three indicators reflecting (PP1) return on investment, (PP2) profit margin, and (PP3) net profits (see table 37).

[584] See Venkatraman/Ramanujam (1986), p. 803f.

[585] See for example Sarkar/Echambadi/Harrison (2001), p. 706; Spanos/Lioukas (2001), pp. 916f. and the cited literature.

"Profitability": Indicator assessment		
	Criteria	
Indicators	Indicator loadings	t-value
Please assess your firm's performance relative to your competitors over the three years 2006/2007/2008 in terms of...		
PP1 ...return on investment	0.91	63.91
PP2 ...profit margin	0.95	116.19
PP3 ...net profits	0.94	78.29
"Profitability": Factor assessment		
Composite reliability	Average Variance Extracted	
0.95	0.87	

Table 37 - Assessment of the "Profitability" Construct

At the item level, all indicator loadings are well above their threshold and highly significant. On the construct level high values for composite reliability and AVE indicate acceptable levels of reliability and validity.

Sales Performance

The "Sales Performance" construct is measured with two indicators reflecting (SP1) sales volume and (SP2) growth in sales volume (see table 38).

"Sales Performance": Indicator assessment		
	Criteria	
Indicators	Indicator loadings	t-value
Please assess your firm's performance relative to your competitors over the three years 2006/2007/2008 in terms of...		
SP1 ...sales volume.	0.87	23.82
SP2 ...growth in sales volume.	0.9	39.95
"Sales Performance": Factor assessment		
Composite reliability	Average Variance Extracted	
0.88	0.78	

Table 38 - Assessment of the "Sales Performance" Construct

Besides these indicators, it is common for the sales performance construct to also include measures of market share and growth in market share. As the participants of the pre-test noted, most Chinese companies don't strategize for growth in market share as this would require resource consuming actions against competitors, which is not feasible given that most of China's industries are still growing in absolute terms with high single or even double-digit figures. Thus, most companies tend to grow with the market and focus rather on growth in sales volume. Market share indicators were therefore not adapted in this study.

As shown in table 38, the two indicators of the "Sales Performance" construct show both high loadings and significance levels. The composite reliability and AVE also all exceed their thresholds indicating reliability and validity.

5.3.1.5 Test for Discriminant Validity on the Construct Level

Lastly, after the operationalization and validation of all first-order constructs, discriminant validity on the construct level was assessed using the Fornell-Larcker criterion across all first-order constructs (see table 39).

A comparison of all correlations in the off-diagonal rows and columns with the square roots of the AVEs on the diagonal indicates adequate levels of discriminant validity on the construct level. Furthermore, as the correlation matrix in the off-diagonal does not show extremely high correlations of 0.9 and above, there is also no evidence of common method variance. This gives further evidence that common method bias is not an issue in this study.[586]

	1	2	3	4	5	6	7	8	9	10	11	12	13	14	15	16
1. GC	0.87															
2. LC	0.40	0.81														
3. PRO	0.11	0.30	0.82													
4. IN	0.21	0.27	0.28	0.88												
5. RI	-0.07	0.04	0.03	0.20	0.80											
6. ICS	-0.06	0.00	0.09	0.13	0.04	0.88										
7. ECS	0.24	0.52	0.38	0.30	0.03	0.08	0.84									
8. CS	0.09	0.47	0.39	0.13	0.02	0.05	0.66	0.85								
9. RS	0.21	0.55	0.38	0.23	0.05	0.06	0.72	0.78	0.88							
10. HRS	0.14	0.48	0.40	0.14	-0.02	0.03	0.63	0.77	0.70	0.83						
11. PP	0.30	0.46	0.34	0.37	0.04	0.14	0.50	0.49	0.47	0.47	0.93					
12. SP	0.29	0.33	0.34	0.34	0.15	0.12	0.40	0.38	0.40	0.35	0.65	0.88				
13. OWN	-0.13	-0.03	-0.06	-0.13	-0.02	-0.02	-0.06	-0.01	0.00	-0.03	-0.03	-0.03	1			
14. LEG	0.12	0.04	-0.04	0.03	0.07	0.03	0.07	-0.05	-0.09	-0.09	-0.05	0.06	0.04	1		
15. AGE	0.22	0.12	0.07	0.20	0.03	-0.15	0.12	0.02	0.06	-0.01	0.02	0.04	-0.21	-0.07	1	
16. EMP	0.14	0.10	0.05	0.09	0.02	-0.04	0.04	0.02	0.00	-0.02	0.02	0.00	-0.05	0.05	0.18	1

Table depicts square root of AVE in grey shading on diagonal, and correlations on off-diagonal

Table 39 - Discriminant validity on the construct level

586 See Ettlie/Pavlou (2006), p. 133 and Lai et al. (2008), p. 31

5.3.2 Operationalization and Validation of Second-Order Constructs

After the assessment of the measurement models, the next step consists of the operationalization and validation of the respective second-order constructs. The formative Type II second-order constructs are subject to the same assessment criteria as first-order formative constructs. The validation therefore proceeds along the guidelines outlined in table 25.

5.3.2.1 Cluster as Second-Order Construct

According to the approach suggested by Yin and Davis, the factor scores of the "Geographical Concentration" and "Links in Clusters" constructs were computed and represented as formative indicators of the second-order "Cluster" construct. The relationship between each dimension and the second-order construct are defined by the factor loadings and their respective t-values. As shown in figure 44[587], both dimensions load positive and significant on the "Cluster" construct.

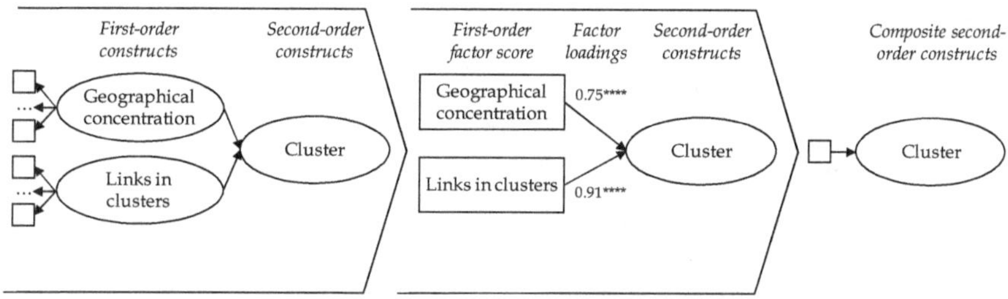

Figure 44 - "Cluster" as second-order construct

To avoid the problem of highly biased parameter estimations, the "Cluster" construct was assessed with regards to multicollinearity among its indicators by calculating the VIF. Its values measure 1.12 for both "Links in Clusters" and "Geographical concentration" thus being far below the threshold of 10 indicating the absence of multicollinearity.

Lastly, in order to assess the external validity of the second-order "Cluster" construct, an external global item was correlated with the factor scores of its two dimensions. An overall item that comprehensively summarizes the content of the formative construct is "*overall our region provides us with all the resources (e.g. capital, suppliers, human resources, etc.) and access to markets we need for operating our business*". The respective Spearman correlation coefficients are 0.25 and 0.67 and are both significant on the 1 % level indicating external validity.[588]

587 The illustration follows the guidelines first introduced by Köhler (2011), p. 209.

588 Spearman's rank correlation coefficient is a non-parametric measure of statistical correlation between two variables. It is particularly useful, if the data does not follow a bivariate normal distribution as is the case in this study (see Hartung/Elpelt/Klösener (2009), pp. 553ff)

5.3.2.2 Entrepreneurial Orientation as Second-Order Construct

The "Entrepreneurial Orientation" construct is defined by three dimensions, i.e. "Proactiveness", "Innovativeness", and "Risk-Taking". In the first step, the factor scores of all three constructs were computed and then represented as formative indicators of the second-order construct. The loadings relate each of the indicators to the second-order construct. As shown in figure 45, all formative indicators load positive and significant on the "Entrepreneurial Orientation" construct.

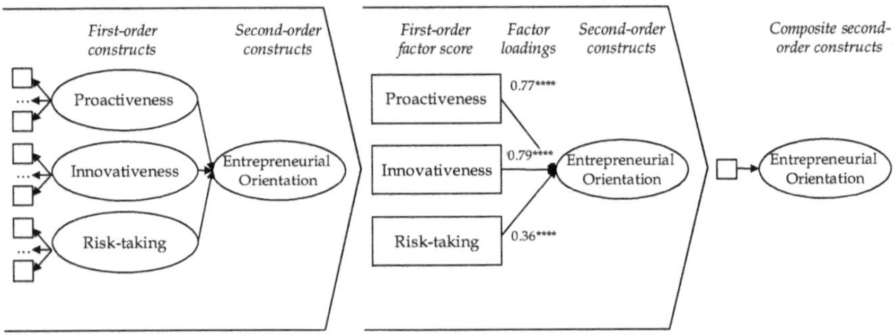

Figure 45 - "Entrepreneurial Orientation" as second-order construct

In the second step, the VIF for all indicators was calculated to assess multicollinearity. The values range from 1.06 for "Risk-Taking" to 1.16 for "Innovativeness" thus indicating the absence of multicollinearity.

In order to assess the external validity of the "Entrepreneurial Orientation" constructs, all first-order factor scores were correlated with the global item *"in this firm entrepreneurial behavior is a central principle."* The Spearman correlation coefficients range from 0.211 to 0.532 and are significant on the 1 % level. Thus, the "Entrepreneurial Orientation" construct is sufficiently defined by its underlying dimensions indicating external validity.

5.3.2.3 Cluster-Capability as Second-Order Construct

According to conceptualization, the "Cluster-Capability" construct is defined by five dimensions. To calculate its composite second-order score, the factor scores of its underlying first-order constructs were computed and then represented as formative indicators. In a subsequent PLS run, the loadings were estimated and then multiplied with their respective factor scores. As shown in figure 46, all loadings are positive and significant.

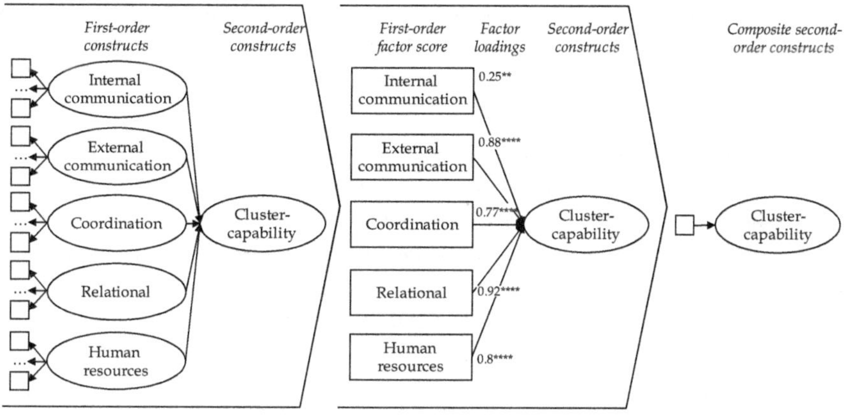

Figure 46 - "Cluster-Capability" as second-order construct

To avoid the problem of multicollinearity, the "Cluster-Capability" construct was assessed using the VIF. For all five dimensions, its values range from 1.28 for "Internal Communication" to 3.24 for "Relational Skills" thus being far below its threshold indicating the absence of multicollinearity.

Finally, the dimensions of the "Cluster-Capability" construct were correlated with the global item "*overall we have the resources and capabilities we need to get the most out of our local business environment*" to assess its external validity. The Spearman correlation coefficients range from 0.576 to 0.714 and are significant on the 1 % level. Thus, the "Cluster-Capability" construct is sufficiently defined by its underlying dimensions indicating external validity.

5.4 Analysis of the Structural Model and Hypothesis Testing

After the assessment of the measurement models established confidence in their reliability and validity, the next step involves the analysis of the structural model with a focus on hypothesis testing. The analysis consists of three parts.

The first part is related to the assessment of the **baseline model** as depicted in figure 16 and articulated in hypothesis H1. It represents the general view in the literature that clusters of a diverse set of linked industries are always beneficial to their member firms.

The second part includes the assessment of the **contingency model** as shown in figure 32 and articulated in hypotheses H2 to H5. It postulates that the relationship between clusters and firm performance is moderated by a whole set of contingency factors. H2 and H3 include the assumption that a firm's age and size negatively impact the relationship between clusters and firm performance. This reflects the notion that large vertically integrated firms and firms with already well established supply chains and stable product-markets rely less on clusters for their competitiveness than small and new firms. Instead, they are said to be negatively impacted by the presence of diverse and linked industries as they contribute to the competitiveness of the cluster without gaining much in return. H4 and H5 then include the postulated effect of a firm's EO and cluster-capability that are hypothesized to have a positive moderating effect on firm performance.

Finally, hypothesis H6 somewhat challenges the validity of the contingency model with respect to EO and cluster-capability. It postulates that it is a **configurational model** also depicted in figure 32 by the three-way moderator effect that is best suited to explain the way in which clusters influence firm performance. Here it is said that those firms achieve the highest levels of performance that operate in a balanced trade-off[589], i.e. that simultaneously act entrepreneurial and have the necessary capabilities to exploit the opportunities being perceived.

To examine the validity of these hypotheses, the results for the estimates of the parameters and quality criteria with respect to sales performance are shown in table 40, and those for profitability in table 41. Following Chin, the tables report the path coefficients with their respective t-values, the coefficient determination R^2, the Stone-Geisser criterion Q^2 for predictive relevance, and the effect size f^2 to explore whether the changes in the coefficient determinations have substantive impact.[590]

Model 1, which represents the **baseline model**, yields a positive and significant effect of clusters on sales performance (β = 0.35) and profitability (β = 0.45). The R^2 values of 0.12 and 0.2 indicate that both models have moderate explanatory power, while the Q^2 values suggest acceptable predictive relevance. Thus, while both measures provide support for hypothesis H1, they also suggest that there are more variables that govern the relationship between clusters and firm performance.

Next, model 2 represents the main effects model including the effects of EO and cluster-capability on firm performance. With regards to the control variables, only the legal statement (β = -0.07) and firm age (β = -0.06) have a weakly significant and low negative effect on profitability while both are non significant for sales performance. The effect of the legal statement suggests that in China JVs with domestic/domestic and foreign/domestic shareholders generally exhibit lower profitability than wholly Chinese owned companies lending further support for the common wisdom that JVs in China tend to notoriously underperform.

589 See figure 22.

590 See Chin (2010), pp. 674ff.

Sales Performance					
Variables		Model 1	Model 2	Model 3	Model 4
Baseline model					
	OWN	-0.01			
	LEG	0.02			
	AGE	-0.02			
	EMP	-0.05			
	CL	0.35 ****			
Main effects model					
	OWN		0.01	0.01	0.01
	LEG		0.05	0.04	0.03
	AGE		-0.03	-0.03	-0.01
	EMP		-0.04	-0.06	-0.05
	CL		0.18 ****	0.19 ****	0.14 ***
	EO		0.29 ****	0.27 ****	0.22 ****
	CAP		0.24 ****	0.24 ****	0.25 ****
Contingency model					
(Two way)	CL*AGE			-0.06	-0.09 *
	CL*EMP			0.18 ***	0.18 ***
	CL*EO			-0.21 ****	-0.23 ****
	CL*CAP			0.13 ***	0.15 ***
	EO*CAP				0.03
Configurational model					
(Three way)	CL*EO*CAP				0.16 ****
R^2		0.12	0.28	0.34	0.36
f^2			0.23	0.08	0.03
Q^2		0.10	0.20	0.26	0.27

Path coefficients (t-values) *p < 0.10; **p < 0.05; ***p < 0.025; ****p < 0.01

Table 40 - PLS path analysis results for "Sales Performance"

Model 3 represents the **contingency model** as indicated by the two-way interaction effects. This addition increased the explained variance in both sales performance ($R^2 = 0.34$; $\Delta R^2 = 0.06$) and profitability ($R^2 = 0.44$; $\Delta R^2 = 0.03$). The effect size for sales performance ($f^2 = 0.08$) and for profitability ($f^2 = 0.05$) indicate that the change in R^2 is significant and thus has substantive impact. This is also indicated by the predictive relevance Q^2 of the contingency model that measures 0.26 for sales performance and 0.39 for profitability.

		Profitability			
Variables		Model 1	Model 2	Model 3	Model 4
Baseline model					
	OWN	0.0			
	LEG	-0.1 **			
	AGE	-0.07 *			
	EMP	-0.03			
	CL	0.45 ****			
Main effects model					
	OWN		0.02	0.01	0.02
	LEG		-0.07 *	-0.08 **	-0.09 **
	AGE		-0.06 *	-0.04	0.0
	EMP		-0.02	-0.02	-0.02
	CL		0.24 ****	0.24 ****	0.18 ****
	EO		0.24 ****	0.23 ****	0.14 ****
	CAP		0.36 ****	0.38 ****	0.37 ****
Contingency model					
(Two way)	CL*AGE			-0.04	-0.11 ***
	CL*EMP			0.05	0.05
	CL*EO			-0.17 ****	-0.17 ****
	CL*CAP			0.13 **	0.15 ****
	EO*CAP				-0.04
Configurational model					
(Three way)	CL*EO*CAP				0.24 ****
R^2		0.2	0.41	0.44	0.48
f^2			0.37	0.05	0.08
Q^2		0.17	0.34	0.39	0.41

Path coefficients (t-values) *p < 0.10; **p < 0.05; ***p < 0.025; ****p < 0.01

Table 41 - PLS path analysis results for "Profitability"

With regards to the magnitude and significance of the two-way interaction effects, the effect of size on the relationship between clusters and performance is only significant for sales performance, but in the opposing direction (β = 0.18) thus giving no support for hypothesis H2. Furthermore, the negative interaction effect of clusters and age is non-significant for both sales performance and profitability thus also giving no support for hypothesis H3. Further on, hypothesis H4 postulated a positive interaction effect between clusters and EO. The data shows that the effect is indeed strongly significant for both performance measures, yet surprisingly in the opposing direction with β = -0.21 for sales performance and β = -0.17 for profitability providing no support for hypothesis H4. Lastly, hypothesis H5 stipulates a positive interaction effect between clusters and cluster-capability. This is strongly supported by both sales performance (β = 0.13) and profitability (β = 0.13). In sum, while the contingency model provides strong explanatory power, the hypothesized relationships assumed to influence the effect of clusters on firm performance are only partially supported.

Lastly, the **configurational model** is represented by model 4 and the three-way interaction effect between clusters, EO, and cluster-capability. This inclusion again increased the explained variance in sales performance (R^2 = 0.36; ΔR^2 = 0.02) and profitability (R^2 = 0.48; ΔR^2 = 0.04). The effect size for sales performance (f^2 = 0.03) and profitability (f^2 = 0.08) both indicate a significant change in R^2. Furthermore, the predictive relevance Q^2 in both cases is also above its threshold and measures 0.27 for sales performance and 0.41 for profitability.

The three-way interaction itself is highly significant and strongly positive for both sales performance (β = 0.16) and profitability (β = 0.24). This gives strong support for hypothesis H6, which postulates that a configurational model is better suited to explain the complex relationship between clusters, EO, and cluster-capability than a contingency model.

To advance further interpretations, the interaction effects were plotted based on the estimated regression coefficients and according to the approach suggested by Aiken and West.[591] The impact of EO and cluster-capability on firm performance is examined at high and low scores of both variables (set at one standard deviation above and below the mean) each in a strong and weak cluster environment (also set at one standard deviation above and below the mean). The plot considers the three main effects, the three two-way interaction effects (including the effect between EO and cluster-capability), and the three-way interaction term. This results in a total of four plots each for sales performance and profitability as shown in figure 47.

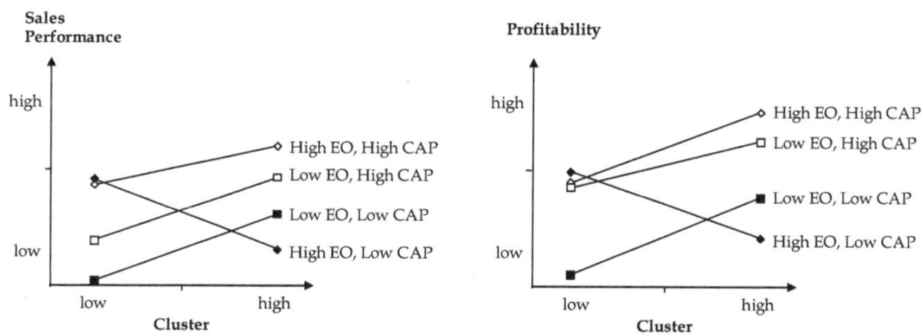

Figure 47 - Interaction effect of EO and cluster-capability on the relationship between clusters and firm performance

For **sales performance**, the left-hand side of figure 47 shows that in *weak cluster environments* (i.e. at low cluster levels), which offer few resources and opportunities, entrepreneurial firms

591 See Aiken/West (1991), pp. 12ff.

are the highest performers. This is even independent of whether the firms exhibit high or low levels of cluster-capability. At the other end of the extreme, the lowest performers are, as would be expected, those firms that are neither entrepreneurial nor score high on their cluster-capability. Lastly, non-entrepreneurial yet cluster capable firms perform mediocre when put into relation with the highest and lowest performers.

In *strong cluster environments* (i.e. at high cluster levels), on the other hand, the picture turns significantly. Strong clusters are characterized by a geographical concentration of related firms and institutions that are deeply embedded in the fabric of their local communities as they form extensive links among each other. Here, it is the entrepreneurial firms with a strong cluster-capability that achieve the highest levels of sales performance (hypothesis H6 supported). They are followed by those firms that show no signs of entrepreneurial activities, but appear to be particularly capable of exploiting the advantages clusters have to offer (hypothesis H5 supported). Surprisingly, entrepreneurial firms that score low on their cluster-capability show the lowest levels of sales performance and perform even worse than non-entrepreneurial and non-capable firms; this running counter to the previously held assumption that in rich clusters EO has a positive effect on performance (hypothesis H4 not supported).

For **profitability**, the right hand side of figure 47 shows that the slopes run very similar to those of sales performance. The only noteworthy exception is that in *weak cluster environments* non-entrepreneurial firms with a strong cluster-capability score higher on profitability than sales performance. In fact, there is not much difference among the high performing firms whether they score high on their EO, cluster-capability, or on both. When it comes to profitability, therefore, firms seem to be able to choose whether they want to invest in their EO or cluster-capability as both yield similar results. Given these circumstances, developing both simultaneously does not seem desirable. This, however, is different in *strong cluster environments*, where the leverage to achieve high levels of performance lies again in a firm's cluster-capability, and very much like in the case of sales performance.

To summarize these findings, table 42 provides a comprehensive overview of the research hypotheses and the results regarding the two performance measures.

No.	Hypotheses	SP	PP
Baseline model			
1	Clusters that comprise a diverse set of geographically concentrated and linked industries have a positive influence on firm performance.	✓	✓
Contingency model			
2	The relationship between clusters and firm performance will be negatively moderated by firm size.	✗	✗
3	The relationship between clusters and firm performance will be negatively moderated by firm age.	✗	✗
4	The relationship between clusters and firm performance will be positively moderated by a firm's entrepreneurial orientation.	✗	✗
5	The relationship between clusters and firm performance will be positively moderated by a firm's cluster-capability.	✓	✓
Configurational model			
6	The relationship between clusters and firm performance will be positively moderated by a firm's entrepreneurial orientation together with its cluster-capability.	✓	✓

Table 42 - Results of the analysis of the structural model and hypothesis testing

With this in mind, the next section turns to a critical discussion of the results by linking them with a set of relevant literatures. A particular focus lies in explaining the contradictions between the findings of this study and existing theory.

5.5 Discussion of the Results

Clusters

The findings of this study suggest that strong clusters have a positive impact on firm performance as indicated by the results of the baseline model and the interaction analysis performed in figure 47. This is particularly evident in the case of those firms that are neither entrepreneurial nor cluster capable. These firms despite the fact that they put no particular effort in going after opportunities or in investing in capabilities to fully exploit them still score higher on performance in strong clusters than in weak ones. This lends strong support for Porter's claim that clusters *"help any company in any industry to compete in the most sophisticated ways."*[592]

Thus, to a certain degree all firms in clusters seem to get their share of opportunities regardless of the effort they put into exploring them. It is then, however, up to the firms themselves to decide whether they want to invest in their cluster-capability to exploit these opportunities to the fullest extent, or additionally to venture out and explore as many opportunities as they can, knowing that they have the ability to appropriate the created returns through their superior cluster-capability.

---

[592] Porter (1998a), p. 86. See also the discussion of Porter's Competitiveness School on clusters in section 2.2.5.

Size and Age

The results of the interaction effects of size and age are mixed. While large firms located in strong clusters are able to generate higher sales than firms outside of clusters, age has no significant impact on firm performance.

The **non-significant interaction effect between clusters and age** contradicts the results of Wennberg and Lindqvist who found that new firms have higher levels of performance when they are located in stronger clusters. As noted by the authors, the ready availability of resources, labor, and specialized skills partially provided by incumbents (i.e. older firms) may allow young firms to significantly reduce their overhead costs, which in turn may raise their profitability levels.[593]

To explain this contradiction, it is helpful to turn to figure 35, which indicates that the average age of the surveyed companies is 15.5 years, while the median is 11 years. Furthermore, 89 % of the companies are older than 6 years, while 44 % are older than 11 years. The sample therefore consists largely of firms that already have well established supply chains and that operate in familiar product-markets, while new firms and start-ups are rather underrepresented. Therefore, all else being equal the results suggest that there is an age-threshold for the effect of clusters beyond which they have no impact on firm performance. Once firms have evolved beyond the initial start-up phase, age seems to lose its status as a competitive differentiator as both mid-aged and older firms are equally impacted by the effects of clusters.[594]

The effect of the **positive interaction between clusters and size** on sales performance, on the other hand, may be due to the characteristics of the Chinese business context. Such as in many emerging markets, China's economy is in a stage of long-term transition to a market-driven capitalism. Yet, despite the country's progress and significant reforms, it still suffers from an "*institutional void resulting from a lack of market-supporting institutions.*"[595] Examples include the difficulty to enforce legal rights, settle payments, protect intellectual property, or obtain information on markets and regulations. This forces firms and their employees to rely on their personal contacts with people they know and trust personally to get things done, rather than on an abstract notion of institutional-based trust.[596] Besides responding to threats, Zhang and Li in their earlier cited study have documented how firms in China use personal contacts to increase their sales performance.[597] It may therefore well be that in China large firms can capitalize on their *slack human resources* and build extensive links into their local

593 See Wennberg/Lindqvist (2010), p. 225 and 238. See also the discussion of their findings in section 2.4.2.

594 To advance further interpretations, it would have been helpful to split the sample into e.g. firms that are younger than 4 years and firms that are older than 4 years. Yet, the sample consists only of 26 firms that are younger than 4 years, while the complexity of the path model demands a sample of at least 130 companies to provide reliable estimates.

595 Luo (2003), p. 1317.

596 See Zucker (1986), p. 88f.

597 See Zhang/Li (2008), p. 629 and the discussion of their study presented in section 2.4.2.

cluster environment to generate higher levels of sales performance. In this case, networking allows gaining access to opportunities that are controlled by local government officials in power or executive employees from nearby firms.[598] Due to their size, large firms may also be more *visible* for potential investors ready to provide capital to seize opportunities that abound in strong cluster environments.[599]

When put in context, the relevance of size for sales performance may therefore very much stem from the importance of *social capital* within the Chinese business context.[600] In contrast, due to the strong institutional context large firms in developed markets such as Europe and the USA rely more on formal business relationships. These are build on institutional-based trust grounded in the rule of law and the enforcement of legal rights making complex market-based transactions across large distances possible without the need to personally know each other.[601] Thus, while large firms in Europe and the USA can rely solely on their internal returns to scale[602], large firms in China remain much more dependent on their local business environment.

Entrepreneurial Orientation and Cluster-capability

With regards to the interaction effects between clusters, EO, and cluster-capability the results suggest that a configurational model offers more useful explanations than a contingency model.

In **weak cluster environments** firms that want to achieve high levels of *sales performance* rely heavily on their EO. As noted by Zahra and Covin, in such severely constrained environments opportunities are scarce and competition is fierce, while mere survival may be perceived as accomplishment.[603] In this case, a firm's EO may provide an important differentiation mechanism against competitors. It helps firms to seek and find the few growth opportunities present in their environment and thereby create a competitive advantage. The results of this study lend strong support for this argument and are further backed up by Wiklund and Shepherd who found that EO had its biggest positive impact on firm performance in resource constraint environments.[604]

For *profitability* as noted earlier, the only noteworthy exception is that in weak cluster environments non-entrepreneurial firms with a strong cluster-capability score higher on profita-

598 See Park/Luo (2001), pp. 473ff.

599 As shown by Li (2005, pp. 437f.) in his study on the importance of managerial ties in China, this also holds true for foreign invested firms.

600 See Luo (2003), p. 1326.

601 As shown by Zucker (1986), the growing complexity of the newly industrialized economy of the USA at the end of the 19th century required the production of trust that went beyond personal ties. This led to the creation of a general institutional framework that built a common base for transactions between distant economic actors.

602 See the results of Kukalis (2010) as discussed in section 2.4.2.

603 See Zahra/Covin (1995), p. 48.

604 See Wiklund/Shepherd (2005), p. 85 and the discussion of their findings in section 3.1.3.

bility than on sales performance. While at first this finding might be surprising as high levels of profitability due to a firm's cluster-capability would rather be associated with a strong cluster environment, it can be explained from a resource-based perspective. The part of Strategic Entrepreneurship that emphasizes the importance of exploitation as introduced by the RBV focuses traditionally on such things as refinement, execution, competency, skillfulness, effectiveness, and efficiency. In environments that are scarce in resources and opportunities firms with high levels of internal and external communication, the ability to establish and coordinate relationships, and upgrade their human resources seem to be particularly able to efficiently exploit the few opportunities they are being offered. Evidence for this is also provided by the case study company Importer, which is located outside of its industry's main wood processing clusters. Although it experiences significant difficulties in its sourcing activities, the company uses its strong cluster-capability to establish cooperative relationships with other western companies to pool supply demand and develop capable suppliers.[605] Thus, while entrepreneurial firms may identify more opportunities than non-entrepreneurial but capable firms, the latter may be better able to fully capitalize on their exploitation. This suggests that for firms, which pursue profitability goals, having a strong cluster-capability may be desirable regardless of whether they are located in a strong or weak cluster environment.

In contrast, in **strong cluster environments**, as it is to be expected, the leverage to achieve high levels of sales and profitability performance lies in the firm's cluster-capability. This also explains the lowest performers in strong clusters, i.e. entrepreneurial yet incapable cluster-firms. These results, although initially surprising, are consistent with prior findings by Covin and Slevin. The authors suggest that because of the abundance of opportunities in rich environments, the sole pursuit of an EO represents an unnecessary risk.[606] These firms seem to be trapped into an excessive resource consuming frenzy of experimentation, search, and innovation without having the ability to appropriate the rents they create.[607] As a consequence, they suffer heavy costs due to their venturing out, but miss out on developing and exploiting the opportunities they discover. Similar findings are also reported by Wiklund and Shepherd who suggest that in opportunity rich environments performance might be improved by an inwardly focused strategy that puts emphasis on efficient exploitation.[608] Thus, although entrepreneurship is a desirable quality it must be developed and applied with great care. It is equally necessary to commit fully to a valuable opportunity and devote enough resources to turn it into a rent-creating competitive advantage.

These results and the findings derived from the analysis of the configurational model to Strategic Entrepreneurship are summarized in table 43.

605 See section 4.4.2.

606 See Covin/Slevin (1989), pp. 83ff.

607 See figure 22.

608 See Wiklund/Shepherd (2005), p. 86.

	Sales Performance		Profitability	
	Entrepreneurial Orientation	Cluster-Capability	Entrepreneurial Orientation	Cluster-Capability
Weak Clusters	✓		✓	(✓)
Strong Clusters		✓		✓

Table 43 - Configuration-based leverages for increasing performance in clusters

With the analysis of the structural model and the final discussion of the generated insights, this study has provided an answer to the second research question. After identifying an EO and a set of skills as relevant for creating and defending competitive advantages through clusters, table 43 illustrates how these firm-level characteristics influence performance under different cluster-contingencies. In *weak cluster environments*, the leverage to achieve high levels of performance whether it is sales or profitability lies in the firm's EO. Additionally, firms that pursue profitability oriented goals may also profit from the development of a dedicated cluster-capability. In *strong cluster environments*, on the other hand, firms profit the most from a cluster-capability as it enables the pursuit of a low-risk strategy, which capitalizes on the opportunities that abound in clusters. Furthermore as shown in figure 47, firms that venture out to explore new opportunities knowing that they have a strong cluster-capability at their disposal to capitalize on their returns achieve the highest levels of performance.

With this in mind, the next chapter addresses the third and final research question and provides managerial recommendations on how to implement the findings of this study into organizational reality.

6 Recommendations for Implementing the Identified Internal Characteristics into Organizational Reality

The results of the empirical analysis lend strong support for the validity of the configurational model. The Configurational School to strategy argues that firms achieve lasting competitive advantages, if they manage to achieve a "good fit" between their environment, strategy, internal capabilities, and organizational structure. These four variables give rise to distinct *configurations* also known as *gestalts* or *archetypes*, which represent organizational forms that have proven to lead to firm success.[609]

Although not initially investigated, the Configurational School to Strategy suggests a distinct organizational structure that aligns the variables clusters, EO, and cluster-capability in an ideal fashion. It provides an answer to the third research question and is depicted in figure 48.

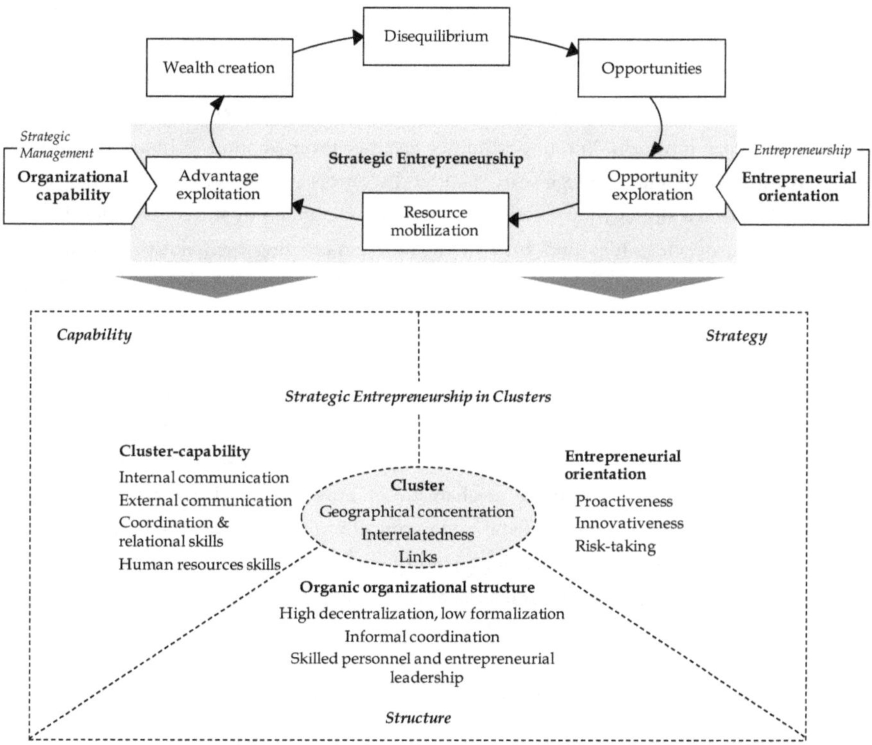

Figure 48 - A configuration for cluster-firms

---

609 See Miller (1990), p. 772.

In line with the exploratory nature of this study the proposed configuration is strongly grounded in its empirical results and the well established literature of the Configurational School to strategy. It should be noted, however, that the same four variables can give rise to different configurations. This is the notion of *functional equivalence* in Luhmann's modern systems theory, which argues that different means can be used to arrive at the same end.[610] This is in line with the pragmatist view to social science, which is followed in this study, and that acknowledges that there may exist answers to the research questions other than those provided here. Thus, firms may have a vast repertoire of instruments to succeed in clusters. Given that literature has yet to come up with a set of firm-level characteristics other than those explored here, the suggested organizational form should not be viewed as the one and only feasible in clusters. Rather, it should be seen as the concentrated essence of the results gained in this study that provides practical recommendations on how to implement the findings into organizational reality.

According to the Configurational School, distinct organizational forms arise through a complex causal relationship that has its origin in the firm's environment. For firms in strong clusters, the environment is characterized by a dense population of related firms and institutions that form extensive links among each other. The level of competition is high as competitors frequently introduce new products and services and customers demand a continuous stream of sophisticated innovation. Yet, opportunities and resources abound.[611] In such a complex and dynamic environment change is frequent and requires firms to be highly responsive to their cluster. From a strategy perspective adaptation is facilitated by the entrepreneurial ability to perceive opportunities and turn them into rent-creating competitive advantage.[612] From a *structural perspective*, the Configurational School suggests the adoption of organic organizational structures.[613]

The **organic firm** strives to adapt to its environment by embracing flexible structures.[614] To solve complex problems, it delegates authority to personnel with the greatest expertise, emphasizes open and lateral communication, and facilitates dense, diffuse, and reciprocal network relationships across organizational units.[615] By doing so, it stands at the opposite side of a continuum that subtends more mechanistic or bureaucratic structures. **Bureaucratic firms** are the idealized archetype of the large vertically integrated firm that appears to be optimal for stable and routine technology environments. Their structure comprises centralized authority, hierarchical chains of command, and downward lines of communication.[616]

610 See Luhmann (1987), pp. 84ff.

611 This is the notion of co-opetition as introduced by Porter in his diamond concept (see section 2.2.5)

612 See the results in section 5.5.

613 See Mintzberg (1973), p. 49; Miller/Friesen (1978), p. 926; Mintzberg (1980), p. 337; Deutschmann (1995), p. 40.

614 The organic firm is also known as adhocracy or adaptive firm (see for example Mintzberg (1973), pp. 46f).

615 See Miller/Friesen (1978), p. 932; Mintzberg (1980), p. 338.

616 See Schrader/Lincoln/Hoffman (1989), p. 45.

In contrast, in the organic mode little emphasis is put on **hierarchy** or **formalization**. Authority is broadly delegated and a function of expertise not position.[617] The highest leadership retains power for key decisions, yet discretion is given to lower level units as they have the knowledge to rapidly adapt to new situational demands.[618] Hence, tasks are distributed flexibly, not based on rigid job descriptions and to a certain degree everybody is involved in strategy-making.[619]

To move a system so decentralized towards common organizational goals, management employs a wide array of **informal instruments of coordination and control**. They can be summarized into three sets of mechanisms: mutual adjustment, internal networks, and corporate culture.

Mutual adjustment refers to direct real-world interaction and contact among key staff that takes place within and across departmental units. It includes informal contact among employees, temporary or permanent task-forces, teams, cross-functional committees, coordinators, boundary spanners, and liaison officers. These open channels of communication enable wide information and knowledge sharing among the members of the organization. The aim is to facilitate direct links between experts who share common problems and might develop joint solutions together.[620] On the other hand, the causality may also work in reverse. Intense lateral communication coordinates and binds teams with the rest of the organization by sharing goals, information, knowledge, values, and norms.[621]

In both cases, these patterns of interaction give rise to cohesive yet open *informal networks* among managers from different organizational units. Personal relationships, intensive direct communication, and frequent face-to-face meetings enable self-regulative processes of continuous adjustment and redefinition of individual tasks and responsibilities. Thus, work groups are often formed temporarily to take on particular projects and then dissolve again.[622]

Both mechanisms are complemented by a *corporate culture* of shared strategic objectives, symbols, norms, and values. They are conveyed through processes of socialization such as openly communicating the way things are done, workplace cooperation, company training, continuing education, and targeted recruitment policy. Although costly to develop, a corporate culture that promotes mutual adjustment and informal networks is a subtle yet powerful tool to coordinate the actions of the entire organization in the absence of formal organizational structures.[623]

---

617 See Miller/Friesen (1978), p. 927; Santoro/Chakrabarti (2002), p. 1168.

618 See Miller/Friesen (1978), p. 927.

619 See Mintzberg (1980), p. 337; Travica (1998), p. 1227.

620 See Martinez/Jarillo (1989), p. 492.

621 See Green/Covin/Slevin (2008), p. 361 and Travica (1998), p. 1239.

622 See Schrader/Lincoln/Hoffman (1989), p. 63.

623 See Deutschmann (1995), pp. 41ff.

It is evident then, that organic firms are driven by professional and highly skilled **personnel** that favor cooperation, involvement, informality, and participative, knowledge-driven decision-making. Professionalism means that jobs are horizontally specialized requiring intensive training, but little formalization. To reflect the demands of the environment, employees are deployed in small multidisciplinary project teams to boost the production of innovative goods and services.[624] The emphasis on expertise and entrepreneurship also extends upwards to the firm's top management. As shown by Miller and Toulouse, organic firms are likely to pick executives that fit their strategy and structure. That is, executives who feel that they are well in charge of things and who purse innovative future-oriented strategies.[625] This congruence may work in both ways as executives also influence the structure of their firms to become congruent with their own personality: Entrepreneurial executives create organic firms, and in turn organic firms are more likely to have entrepreneurial executives.[626]

Thus, high decentralization with power and discretion given to lower level units, a low degree of task and role formalization, the use of informal coordination mechanisms, and the presence of highly skilled personnel and entrepreneurial leaders are the decisive characteristics of organic firm structures. They combine with an entrepreneurial strategy and a strong cluster-capability to form a distinct organizational configuration for cluster-firms (see figure 48).

At its core lies the notion that in clusters opportunities abound, but also that firms need distinct characteristics to perceive these opportunities, mobilize the required resources in response, and manage them strategically to defend their competitive advantage in the long-run.[627]

Firms meet these requirements by adopting an entrepreneurial strategy based on proactiveness, innovativeness, and risk-taking. This allows them to adapt their actions to the cluster environment and compete on innovation and technological sophistication. To support their venturing out and avoid getting lost in excessive experimentation, firms have to be able to appropriate the rents they create. This is met by a strong cluster-capability made up of the abilities to communicate effectively internally and externally, develop and coordinate inter-firm relationships, and recruit, train, and retain skilled human resources. To implement both elements into organizational reality, firms should adopt organic structures. High decentralization and low formalization help firms to confront a dynamic cluster environment and stay responsive to suppliers, customers, competitors, and upcoming market trends. Informal instruments of coordination become the main mechanisms to align the actions of dispersed organizational members towards common goals. Finally, skilled personnel and an entrepre-

624 See Mintzberg (1980), p. 337 and Laursen (2002), p. 144.
625 See Miller/Toulouse (1986), p. 1405.
626 See Miller/Kets de Vries (1982), pp. 247ff.
627 See chapter 3.

neurial leadership reflect the fine balance between entrepreneurial opportunity and strategic advantage seeking behavior.

To further prove the external validity of the proposed organizational form, empirical descriptions of successful cluster-firms can be seen as tentative evidence for its practical suitability. In the absence of more systemic firm-level data, the discussion relies upon a very limited set of case study data.

Throughout the Italian District School, researchers have given instructive descriptions of typical district firms. Brusco for example, differentiates between three types of firms.[628] The first manufacture finished products and deliver them directly to end customers. They sometimes orchestrate a collective of firms of the second type, which are vertically specialized and carry out one or several production steps. The third type of firms operates outside the respective industrial sector. Despite their size, all firms are described in an organic fashion as being highly decentralized through networks of semi-autonomous work units, subcontractors, and internal cooperative relationships.[629] They are typically being led by entrepreneurial patriarchs or professional managers who recruit highly skilled workers and artisans to act swiftly on changing market demands. In fact, *"technical know-how forms an integral part of the overall social heritage."*[630] Coordination within and among firms is achieved primarily through informal means such as trust-based cooperation, shared values, and a sense of community.[631] A philosophy that is commonly associated with organic firms.

Additional insights can be derived from Saxenian's case-based comparison between a thriving Silicon Valley and Boston's stagnating and declining Route 128. In Boston, large vertically integrated firms lock-up technical skills and capacities and are highly reluctant to engage in inter-firm cooperation. Employees socialize mostly within firm-boundaries and are expected to slowly climb up the corporate hierarchy. The key to Silicon Valley's success on the other hand, lies in the organic nature of its firms. Here, firms of all sizes including multinationals such as Hewlett-Packard and Intel favor open networks of communication and exchange within and across firm boundaries. Technical expertise is valued above all and firms are commonly led by highly entrepreneurial individuals. This corresponds to decentralized organizational structures such as internal venture capital models, significant amounts of autonomy given to product-based business units, and coordination based on common corporate goals.[632]

Taken together, the empirical results and the theoretical discussion of the proposed archetype provide the answer to the third and final research question: successful cluster-firms purse entrepreneurial strategies that are supported by a strong cluster-capability. Both ele-

---

628 See Brusco (1992), pp. 178ff.

629 See Zeitlin (1992), p. 284.

630 Brusco (1992), p. 182.

631 See Asheim (2000), pp. 417f.

632 See Saxenian (1994), pp. 54ff.

ments are implemented into organizational reality by adopting organic organizational structures of high decentralization and low formalization. They make extensive use of informal coordination mechanisms, which are costly to develop but particularly effective in the dynamism of strong cluster environments. Furthermore, entrepreneurial leaders and skilled personnel ensure a balanced trade-off between the exploration of new opportunities and the exploitation of the rents that are being created.

With this in mind, the concluding chapter will provide a comprehensive summary of the results gained in this study, address some of their limitations, and suggest areas of theoretical extension.

7 Conclusion

7.1 Summary of Results

At the outset of this study laid the notion that up until recently the cluster discourse paid little attention to the individual cluster-firm. Instead, researchers, practitioners, and policy makers alike focused almost exclusively on the cluster as a whole, which came at the expense of the individual firm. Thus, while there is a well established body of knowledge on the capacity of clusters to promote regional development and national prosperity, there is little account of internal characteristics that enable the firm to create and defend competitive advantages through clusters. Given that the forces of globalization and rapid technological change will lead to more geographical concentration of economic activity rather than less, top managers need to know what they can do to profit from this trend.

Early on in the research process, however, this study exposed that there is no common agreement in the literature on a unified and meaningful definition of clusters. Instead, different concepts such as agglomerations, regional networks, learning regions, etc. are all treated as they were only one, i.e. clusters. This made it necessary to first review the Schools of Thought that have contributed the most to the current understanding of the cluster phenomenon and identify the elements that could be integrated into a meaningful definition. These elements include the notion that economic activity of firms and institutions tends to specialize and cluster geographically, that in some instances these actors are interrelated, and that were they are this represents the precondition to build formal and informal links to achieve common goals. The definition resulting from this endeavor views clusters as a *"geographical concentration of linked firms and institutions that are related to each other in terms of a common resource-base and/or product-market."*

This definition made it possible to bring order into chaos and separate studies that investigate the relationship between clusters and firm performance from those that claim to do so, but whose methods do not. A comprehensive review of these studies led to a baseline model that guided the remainder of the research process. It exposed the need to investigate:

(1) *What internal characteristics allow firms to create and defend competitive advantages through clusters?*

To answer this research question, this study applied the fields of entrepreneurship and strategic management as the theoretical frameworks of analysis. Using a contingency and a configurational perspective to strategy, the theoretical discussion revealed that firms need an *entrepreneurial orientation* to perceive the opportunities that abound in clusters and mobilize the required resources in response. A distinct *cluster-capability* is then necessary to appropriate the rents that are created and defend the competitive advantages in the long-run.

Using theoretical deduction and a well established body of existing literature, entrepreneurial orientation was shown to consist of a firm's willingness to act proactively towards opportunities, depart from existing lines of operations by committing a considerable amount of resources to innovations, and take well calculated and managed risks. These characteristics provide firms in clusters with the ability to find opportunities that others have overlooked, thereby differentiating them from their competitors. With regards to a distinct cluster-capability, the literature has yet to come up with a set of skills that may be of relevance in clusters. This required an inductive case study based exploration to identify the skills that build up to a distinct cluster-capability. Using data from 14 German manufacturing companies in China's industrial clusters, the research process gave a comprehensive account of skills that firms need in clusters. It also explained how these skills assist firms in turning opportunities into competitive advantages and defending them in the long-run. The findings show that a cluster-capability is a higher-order capability that consists of the skills to effectively communicate with external cluster actors to gather information on upcoming market trends, changing customer needs, and new combinations that could potentially disrupt industry structure and lead to new market niches, disseminate this information to internal organizational units that can make the most use out of it, coordinate and maintain access relationships, and continuously recruit, develop, and retain skilled personnel and entrepreneurial leaders.

The literature on clusters, the theoretical model, and the case study data suggested that the extent to which firms actually apply these characteristics depends on the qualities of their local environment. This triggered further investigation into the question:

> (2) *How do these internal characteristics influence firm performance under different cluster contingencies?*

This second research question was approached through an empirical survey that was conducted in China among 227 domestic firms. Using a PLS path model, the findings first confirmed the general assumption of the literature that clusters have a positive effect on firm performance. That is, unless they pursue an entrepreneurial strategy that is not backed up by a well-developed cluster-capability. These firms, it was found, show particularly low performance outcomes. Although initially surprising, linking these findings with previous studies showed that pursuing an entrepreneurial strategy in clusters is a risky venture that can lead to a resource-consuming frenzy of experimentation, search, and innovation. Unless firms are equally able to appropriate the returns they create, the sole pursuit of an entrepreneurial strategy leads to failure. Thus, entrepreneurship is useless in clusters when capability is lacking.

On the other hand, firms that support their venturing out with a strong cluster-capability and devote enough resources to turn potentially valuable opportunities into lasting competitive advantages are able to achieve the highest levels of performance. This suggests that while the leverage in weak cluster environments lies in a firm's entrepreneurial orientation, firms in strong clusters should first develop a distinct cluster-capability. It is a low-risk strategy with relatively high returns as it capitalizes on the opportunities and resources that abound in strong cluster environments. Only upon developing a strong cluster-capability made up of skills to communicate externally and internally, coordinate and maintain access relationships, and recruit and retain skilled personnel should firms attempt to venture out in search for new combinations and unmet demands.

In sum, the results of the testing stage and the answers it provided lend strong support for the proposition that firms need to align their internal characteristics to external cluster-contingencies. Within the literature on strategy and entrepreneurship, one strand that emphasizes this need is the Configurational School to strategy. It postulates that firms are described by a distinct point in a four dimensional space made up of environment, strategy, capability, and structure. Although not initially investigated, the explored firm-characteristics and cluster-contingencies provided valuable hints towards a feasible organizational structure that could provide an answer to the final research question:

(3) How can these internal characteristics be implemented into organizational reality?

Based on the results gained from both empirical studies and an enfolded set of relevant literatures, it was possible to sketch out a configuration for cluster-firms and provide practical recommendations on how to implement it into organizational reality. Successful cluster-firms pursue entrepreneurial strategies that are backed up by a strong cluster-capability. To implement both elements into organizational reality, firms should adopt organic organizational structures. Decisive design elements include a high degree of decentralization and low formalization. They are necessary to cope with the dynamism of strong cluster environments and stay responsive to unmet needs, upcoming market trends, and competitive developments. Informal instruments of coordination such as mutual adjustment, internal social networks, and a corporate culture that promotes cooperation and knowledge sharing are the main mechanisms to coordinate dispersed project teams towards common organizational goals. The effects of these efforts are amplified in firms that recruit, develop, and retain highly skilled personnel and entrepreneurial leaders. Evidence that provides tentative support for this proposition can be found in firms located in Italy's industrial districts and California's high technology districts that are commonly described in an organic fashion.

In sum, the results and findings of this study provide a consolidated answer to the overriding research question:

How do firms create and defend competitive advantages through clusters?

They do so, by proactively scanning their cluster environment to seek out new opportunities and innovate in response to unmet demand and newly evolving market niches. A willingness to take well-managed and calculated risk leads entrepreneurial firms to depart from existing lines of operations and find opportunities that others have overlooked. Their early mover advantages are further backed up by a distinct cluster-capability that enables them to appropriate the returns they create and turn them into lasting competitive advantages. By doing so, successful cluster-firms pursue a balanced trade-off between exploration and exploitation that is reflected in their organic organizational structure.

7.2 Limitations

Like any scientific research attempting to capture the full extent of complex social phenomena, the model and propositions developed here need further exploration and testing. The case study and the survey were both designed as cross-industry studies. While this enhances the external validity and generalizability of the results, more fine-grained industry specific studies could reveal additional insights. The question remains as to what extent the results of the studies hold true, if they are performed exclusively in knowledge-based industries or even service industries such as finance, consulting, media, or logistics.

Another limitation concerns the data that was collected during the empirical survey. As noted earlier, information on both the dependent and independent variables were gathered from the same key informants. While all necessary precautions were taken to avoid common method bias, it would be interesting to repeat the investigation with actual financial performance measures. Yet, the results from the data collection revealed that Chinese managers are highly reluctant to provide financial performance data. Future studies attempting to use actual financial data should therefore probably be conducted in more open cultural settings.

The lack of quantitative data also posed a challenge in identifying clusters and delineating their boundaries. As an emerging market country, China lacks a consistent statistical data set. To identify clusters that would eventually serve as research locations for the case study, the investigation therefore had to be limited to selected municipalities and provincial capitals that provided the most coherent set of data. While this posed no major challenge for the case study investigation as measures were taken to complement the quantitative top-down approach with a qualitative bottom-up approach, it did pose an obstacle to the empirical survey. Similar to the studies conducted by Kukalis, Wennberg and Lindqvist, as well as Gilbert and colleagues[633], it would have been desirable to *a priori* identify and delineate all clusters that are present in China and subsequently select firms that would participate in the survey based on whether they are located inside or outside of their respective industry clusters. This could then be complemented by a self-assessment of the key informants. This approach could reveal whether there are differences in firm behavior or performance when firms are located in second- or third-tier clusters as opposed to leading edge clusters such as Shanghai. While increasing the robustness of the findings, it could also reveal to what extent managers' perceptions conform to the actual reality of their local cluster environment.

It would therefore be desirable to replicate this study in different cultural settings.

---

633 See Kukalis (2010); Wennberg/Lindqvist (2010); Gilbert/McDougall/Audretsch (2008).

7.3 Outlook on Further Research

This research study represents a first step towards bringing the cluster discourse back to the firm. To this end, it has identified several characteristics that allow firms to create and defend competitive advantages through clusters. The fact, that the configurational model explains 36 % and 48 % of variance of sales performance and profitability, respectively, suggests that there are more firm-level characteristics that govern the relationship between clusters and firm performance.

For example, the identification of relevant cluster-skills was based on a case study of German companies in China's industrial clusters. While this had the advantage of treating the sample as quasi-experiments, it could very well be that there are more skills that are relevant in clusters. China is a country that traditionally bases high importance on personal relationships and informal networks. Therefore, all case study companies confirmed that these skills are particularly important to establish links in clusters. Although the results were grounded in existing literature, these insights could have come to the expense of other skills such as absorptive capability. Furthermore, this very fact also means that all companies in China whether or not they succeed in developing them put particular emphasis on relational skills. These skills are therefore likely to be less a differentiator than they might be in cultural settings that put greater emphasis on market-based transactions and arms-length relationships. This means that their impact on performance is likely to be understated. Thus, further research needs to be done to assess the true impact of relational skills on the relationship between clusters and performance as well as identify additional skills that may also be of relevance in clusters.

Second, the results of the empirical analysis showed that firms pursuing entrepreneurial strategies while lacking a strong cluster-capability exhibit the lowest performance outcomes. Thus, while proactiveness, innovativeness, and risk-taking remain important levers in weak cluster environments, it is evident that firms in strong clusters need to pursue other strategies that are valuable in and of themselves. In strong cluster environments resources and opportunities abound and potential investors are more likely to provide capital to help seize these opportunities. Therefore, future research should examine low-risk strategies that are designed in response to such rich environments. For example, the industrial district literature shows that firms in districts purse asset-light strategies by conducting extensive outsourcing to lower their fixed costs and remain flexible in case markets shift unexpectedly, while larger firms and intermediary agents orchestrate networks of vertically specialized suppliers.[634] Similarly, the work on California's technology districts shows how large firms outsource a significant amount of R&D activities to nearby universities and start-up firms thus holding the costs of innovation and the associated risks off their balance sheets.[635] Fu-

[634] See Brusco (1992), pp. 178ff.

[635] See Saxenian (1990), pp. 54ff. and Storper (1997), pp. 9ff.

ture research could put these strategies under further scrutiny and explore the content of a distinct "*Cluster Orientation*", that is, a strategy designed to seek and identify the opportunities that abound in clusters and undertake low-risk ventures in their response.

Third, the proposed configuration for cluster-firms opens up another promising avenue for further research. Future studies could take the proposed organizational structures and coordination mechanisms as starting point and test their empirical validity in various cluster-contingencies. Beyond what has been proposed here, an additional structural element that could be of relevance for firms in clusters relates to Kale and colleagues' concept of a dedicated alliance function.[636] Similarly, it could be of benefit for cluster-firms to create a dedicated "*Cluster Function*". Such a function could act as a central boundary spanning coordination unit that facilitates interactions between the cluster-firm and its local environment. For local partners willing to enter into access relationships it could provide a single point of contact, while internally it could be used as a powerful signal of commitment towards the local environment and as a consolidation point to facilitate learning about the dynamics that take place in the cluster, improve the allocation of resources towards important local projects, and evaluate cluster related outcomes. Future studies may therefore wish to explore the content of a potential cluster function and put its empirical validity to a test.

Lastly, throughout this study the presented literatures on clusters as well as the findings derived from both studies show the importance of skilled human resources and entrepreneurial leaders in implementing entrepreneurial strategies and developing a strong cluster-capability. Thus, future studies could examine if a particular type of people and personalities are more suited to interact with their firm's local cluster environment than others. For example, it could very well be that managers who feel that they are well in charge of things are more likely to open up their departments and firms to outside influences than managers who depend on their position to exercise power and authority.

In conclusion, by putting the individual firm back into the center of attention this study has opened up new and promising avenues for studying the cluster phenomenon. Thus, future studies may go beyond these initial findings and explore all areas related to the individual firm to extend our current understanding on how firms compete in clusters.

[636] See Kale/Dyer/Singh (2002), p. 752.

List of References

Acs, Z.J./Audretsch, D.B./Feldman, M.P. (1994): R&D spillovers and recipient firm size. In: Review of Economics and Statistics 76(1994)2, pp. 336-340.

Aiken, L.S./West, S.G. (1991): Multiple regression: Testing and interpreting interactions. Thousand Oaks 1991.

Albers, S./Götz, O. (2006): Messmodelle mit Konstrukten zweiter Ordnung in der betriebswirtschaftlichen Forschung. In: Die Betriebswirtschaft 66(2006)6, pp. 669-677.

Aldrich, H.E./Zimmer, C. (1986): Entrepreneurship through social networks. In: Sexton, D. L./Smilor, R. W. (eds.): The Art and science of entrepreneurship. Cambridge 1986, pp. 2-23.

Almeida, P./Kogut Bruce, (1997): The exploration of technological diversity and the geographic localisation of innovation. In: Small Business Economics 9(1997)1, pp. 21-31.

Alvarez, S.A./Barney, J.B. (2006): Resource-based theory and the firm. In: Hitt, M. A./Ireland, D. R./Camp, M. S./Sexton, D. L. (eds.): Strategic entrepreneurship: Creating a new mindset. Oxford 2006, pp. 89-105.

Amin, A. (1989): A model of the small firm in Italy. In: Goodman, E./Bamford, J./Saynor, P. (eds.): Small firms and industrial districts in Italy. London 1989, pp. 111-122.

Amit, R./Schoemaker, P.J.H. (1993): Strategic assets and organizational rent. In: Strategic Management Journal 14(1993)1, pp. 33-46.

Anderson, C.R./Zeithaml, C.P. (1984): Stage of the product life cycle, business strategy, and business performance. In: Academy of Management Journal 27(1984)1, pp. 5-24.

Armstrong, H./Taylor, J. (2000): Regional economics and policy. 3. ed., Oxford 2000.

Armstrong, S.J./Overton, T.S. (1977): Estimating nonresponse bias in mail surveys. In: Journal of Marketing Research 14(1977)3, pp. 396-400.

Asheim, B.T. (2000): Industrial districts: The contributions of Marshall and beyond. In: Clark, G. L./Gertler, M. S./Feldman, M. P. (eds.): The Oxford handbook of economic geography. Oxford 2000, pp. 413-431.

Audia, P.G./Rider, C.I. (2010): Close, but not the same: Locally headquartered organizations and agglomeration economies in a declining industry. In: Research Policy 39(2010)3, pp. 360-374.

Audretsch, D.B./Feldman, M.P. (1996): R&D spillovers and the Geography of Innovation and Production. In: The American Economic Review 86(1996)3, pp. 630-640.

Audretsch, D.B./Stephan, P.E. (1996): Company-scientist locational links: The case of biotechnology. In: American Economic Review 86(1996)3, pp. 641-652.

Aydalot, P. (1986): Milieux innovateurs en Europe. Paris 1986.

Aydalot, P./Keeble, D. (1988): High technology industry and innovative environments: The European experience. London 1988.

Aziz, K.A./Norhashim, M. (2008): Cluster-based policy making: Assessing performance and sustaining competitiveness. In: Review of Research Policy 25(2008)4, pp. 349-375.

Backhaus, K./Erichson, B./Plinke, W./Weiber, R. (2003): Multivariate Analysemethoden: Eine anwendungsorientierte Einführung. 10. ed., Berlin 2003.

Bahlmann, M.D./Huysmann, M.H. (2008): The emergence of a knowledge-based view of clusters and its implications for cluster governance. In: The Information Society 24(2008)5, pp. 304-318.

Baird, I.S./Thomas, H. (1985): Toward a contingency model of strategic risk taking. In: Academy of Management Review 10(1985)2, pp. 230-243.

Baptista, R./Swann, P. (1998): Do firms in clusters innovate more? In: Research Policy 27(1998)5, pp. 525-540.

Barney, J.B. (1991): Firm resources and sustained competitive advantage. In: Journal of Management 17(1991)1, pp. 99-120.

Barney, J.B. (1986): Strategic factor markets: Expectations, luck and business strategy. In: Management Science 32(1986)10, pp. 1231-1241.

Barney, J.B./Clark, D.N. (2007): Resource-based theory: Creating and sustaining competitive advantage. Oxford 2007.

Barney, J.B./Wright, M./Ketchen, D.J. (2001): The resource-based view of the firm: Ten years after 1991. In: Journal of Management 27(2001)6, pp. 625-641.

Barney, J.B./Wright, P.M. (1998): On becoming a strategic partner: The role of human resources in gaining competitive advantage. In: Human Resource Management 37(1998)1, pp. 31-46.

Baron, R.M./Kenny, D.A. (1986): The moderator-mediator variable distinction in social psychological research: Conceptual, strategic, and statistical considerations. In: Journal of Personality and Social Psychology 51(1986)1, pp. 1173-1182.

Barroso, C./Cepeda Carrion, G./Roldan, J.L. (2010): Applying maximum likelihood and PLS on different sample sizes: Studies on SERVQUAL model and employee behavior model. In: Esposito Vinzi, V./Chin, W. W./Henseler, J./Wang, H. (eds.): Handbook of partial least squares - concepts, methods and applications. Berlin 2010, pp. 427-447.

Bathelt, H./Malmberg, A./Maskell, P. (2004): Clusters and knowledge: Local buzz, global pipelines and the process of knowledge creation. In: Progress in Human Geography 28(2004)1, pp. 31-56.

Beaudry, C. (2001): Entry, growth and patenting in industrial clusters: A study of the aerospace industry in the UK. In: International Journal of the Economics of Business 8(2001)3, pp. 405-436.

Beaudry, C./Breschi, S./Swann, P. (2002): Clusters, innovation and growth. A comparative study of European countries. In: Dunning, J./Mucchielli, J. (eds.): Multinational Firms: The Global-Local Dilemma. London 2002, pp. 190-213.

Becattini, G. (1989): Sectors and/or districts: Some remarks in the conceptual foundations of industrial economics. In: Goodman, E./Bamford, J./Saynor, P. (eds.): Small firms and industrial districts in Italy. London 1989, pp. 123-135.

Becattini, G. (1990): The Marshallian industrial district as a socioeconomic notion. In: Pyke, F./Becattini, G./Sengenberger, W. (eds.): Industrial districts and inter-firm co-operation in Italy. Geneva 1990, pp. 37-51.

Becker, M.C. (2004): Organizational routines: A review of the literature. In: Industrial and Corporate Change 13(2004)4, pp. 643-677.

Bell, J. (1995): The internationalisation of small computer software firms: A further challenge to "stage" theories. In: European Journal of Marketing 29(1995)8, pp. 60-75.

Bettis, R.A./Hitt, M.A. (1995): The new competitive landscape. In: Strategic Management Journal 16(1995)5, pp. 7-19.

(BMI) Business Monitor International (2008): The China business forecast report. London 2008.

(BMWi) Bundesministerium für Wirtschaft und Technologie (2010): Direktinvestitionen lt. Zahlungsbilanzstatistik. Available at: http://www.bmwi.de (accessed: 19.03.2011).

Bohrnstedt, G.W. (1970): Reliability and validity assessment in attitude measurement. In: Summers, G. F. (eds.): Attitude measurement. London 1970, pp. 80-99.

Bollen, K./Lennox, R. (1991): Conventional wisdom on measurement: A structural equation perspective. In: Psychological Bullettin 110(1991)2, pp. 305-314.

Bramanti, A./Ratti, R. (1997): The multi-faced dimensions of local development. In: Ratti, R./Bramanti, A./Gordon, R. L. (eds.): The dynamics of innovative regions: The GREMI approach. Brookfield 1997, pp. 3-46.

Brenner, T. (2007): A methodology to identify local industrial clusters and its application to Germany. In: Hanusch, H./Pyka, A. (eds.): Elgar companion to neo-Schumpeterian economics. Cheltenham 2007, pp. 556-573.

Breschi, S./Lissoni, F. (2001): Knowledge spillovers and local innovation systems: A critical survey. In: Industrial and Corporate Change 10(2001)4, pp. 975-1005.

Brülhart, M. (2008): An account of global intra-industry trade, 1962-2006. Discussion paper of the faculty of Economics, Lausanne 2008.

Brusco, S. (1990): The idea of the industrial district: Its genesis. In: Pyke, F./Sengenberger, W. (eds.): Industrial districts and inter-firm co-operation in Italy. Geneva 1990, pp. 10-19.

Brusco, S. (1992): Small firms and the provision of real services. In: Pyke, F./Sengenberger, W. (eds.): Industrial districts and local economic regeneration. Geneva 1992, pp. 177-196.

Burrell, G./Morgan, G. (1979): Sociological paradigms and organisational analysis. Ashgate 1979.

Cainarca, G.C./Colombo, M.G./Mariotti, S. (1992): Agreements between firms and the technological life cycle model: Evidence from information technologies. In: Research Policy 21(1992)1, pp. 45-62.

Cairncross, F. (1997): The death of distance: How the communications revolution will change our lives. Boston 1997.

Camagni, R. (1991a): "Local milieu", uncertainty and innovation networks: Towards a dynamic theory of economic space. In: Camagni, R. (eds.): Innovation networks: Spatial perspectives. London 1991, pp. 121-143.

Camagni, R. (1991b): Introduction: From the local 'milieu' to innovation through cooperation networks. In: Camagni, R. (eds.): Innovation networks: Spatial perspectives. London 1991, pp. 1-9.

Canina, L./Enz, C.A./Harrison, J. (2005): Agglomeration effects and strategic orientations: Evidence from the U.S. lodging industry. In: Academy of Management Journal 48(2005)4, pp. 565-581.

Capaldo, A. (2007): Network structure and innovation: The leveraging of a dual network as a distinctive relational capability. In: Strategic Management Journal 28(2007)6, pp. 585-608.

Castells, M./Hall, P. (1994): Technopoles of the world: The making of twenty-first-century industrial complexes. London 1994.

Caves, R.E./Porter, M.E. (1977): From entry barriers to mobility barriers: Conjectural decisions and contrived deterrence to new competition. In: Quarterly Journal of Economics 91(1977)2, pp. 241-262.

Cavusgil, S.T./Knight, G./Riesenberger, J.R. (2008): International business: Strategy, management, and the new realities. 1. ed., Upper Saddle River 2008.

Chadwick, C./Dabu, A. (2009): Human resources, human resource management, and the competitive advantage of firms: Toward a more comprehensive model of causal linkages. In: Organization Science 20(2009)1, pp. 253-272.

Chapman, K./Walker, D. (1987): Industrial location: Principles and policies. Oxford 1987.

Cherryholmes, C.H. (1992): Notes on pragmatism and scientific realism. In: Educational Researcher 21(1992)6, pp. 13-17.

Chetty, S./Agndal, H. (2007): Social capital and its influence on changes in internationalization mode among small and medium-sized enterprises. In: Journal of International Marketing 15(2007)1, pp. 1-29.

Chin, W.W. (1998): The partial least squares approach to structural equation modeling. In: Marcoulides, G. A. (eds.): Modern methods for business research. Mahwah 1998, pp. 295-358.

Chin, W.W. (2010): How to write up and report PLS analyses. In: Esposito Vinzi, V./Chin, W. W./Henseler, J./Wang, H. (eds.): Handbook of partial least squares - concepts, methods and applications. Berlin 2010, pp. 655-690.

Chin, W.W./Marcolin, B.L./Newsted, P.R. (2003): A partial least squares latent variable modeling approach for measuring interaction effects: Results from a Monte Carlo simulation study and electronic-mail emotion/adoption study. In: Information Systems Research 14(2003)2, pp. 189-217.

China National Bureau of Statistics (2011): China statistical yearbooks 2003 - 2009. Available at: http://www.stats.gov.cn/tjsj/ndsj/2009/html/R1701e.htm (accessed: 30.01.2011).

China Statistics Press (2002): Beijing statistical yearbook 2002. Beijing 2002.

China Statistics Press (2007a): China labour statistical yearbook 2007. Beijing 2007.

China Statistics Press (2007b): Shanghai statistical yearbook 2007. Shanghai 2007.

China Statistics Press (2007c): Shanghai statistical yearbook on industry, traffic and transport 2007. Shanghai 2007.

China Statistics Press (2007d): Beijing statistical yearbook 2007. Beijing 2007.

China Statistics Press (2007e): Xi'an statistical yearbook 2007. Xi'an 2007.

China Statistics Press (2007f): Guangzhou statistical yearbook 2007. Guangzhou 2007.

China Statistics Press (2008): China statistical yearbook 2008. Beijing 2008.

China Statistics Press (2010): China statistical yearbook 2010. Available at: http://som.xjtu.edu.cn/somlab/zhonguotongjinianjian/2010/indexeh.htm (accessed: 30.01.2011).

Choosin, T./Kwan, P./Cheung, F. (1996): The distribution system in China: Past, present and future. In: Bettignies, H. D. (eds.): Business transformation in China. London 1996, pp. 115-129.

Churchill, G.A. (1979): A paradigm for developing better measures of marketing constructs. In: Journal of Marketing Research 16(1979)1, pp. 64-73.

Churchill, G.A. (1987): Marketing research: Methodological foundations. 4. ed., Fort Worth 1987.

Cohen, W.M./Levinthal, D.A. (1990): Absorptive capacity: A new perspective on learning and innovation. In: Administrative Science Quarterly 35(1990)1, pp. 128-152.

Collis, D.J. (1994): How valuable are organizational capabilities? In: Strategic Management Journal 15(1994)8, pp. 143-152.

Cortright, J. (2006): Making sense of clusters: Regional competitiveness and economic development. Discussion paper of the faculty of Metropolitan Policy Program, The Brookings Institution 2006.

Cova, B./Mazet, F./Salle, R. (1996): Milieu as a pertinent unit of analysis in project marketing. In: International Business Review 5(1996)6, pp. 647-664.

Covin J.G./Slevin, D.P. (1989): Strategic management of small firms in hostile and benign environments. In: Strategic Management Journals 10(1989)1, pp. 75-87.

Crevoisier, O. (2004): The innovative milieus approach: Toward a territorialized understanding of the economy? In: Economic Geography 80(2004)4, pp. 367-379.

Crouch, C./Farrell, H. (2001): Great Britain: Falling through the holes in the network concept. In: Crouch, C./Le Gales, P./Trigilia, C./Voelzkow, H. (eds.): Local production system in Europe: Rise or demise? Oxford 2001, pp. 161-211.

Cyert, R.M./March, J.G. (1963): A behavioral theory of the firm. Englewood Cliffs 1963.

Czamanski, S./Czamanski, D.Z. (1976): Study of spatial industrial complexes. Halifax 1976.

D'Aveni, R.A. (1994): Hypercompetition: Managing the dynamics of strategic maneuvering. New York 1994.

Dahl, M.S./Pedersen, C.O. (2004): Knowledge flows through informal contacts in industrial clusters: Myth or reality? In: Research Policy 33(2004)10, pp. 1673-1686.

de Blasio, G./Di Addario, S. (2005): Do workers benefit from industrial agglomeration. In: Journal of Regional Science 45(2005)4, pp. 797-827.

Denzin, N.K./Lincoln, Y.S. (1994): Handbook of qualitative research. Thousand Oaks 1994.

Deutschmann, C. (1995): The "adhocracy" as viewed by modernization theory. In: International Journal of Political Economy 25(1995)3, pp. 37-49.

Diamantopoulos, A./Winkelhofer, H.M. (2001): Index construction with formative indicators: An alternative to scale development. In: Journal of Marketing Research 38(2001)2, pp. 269-277.

Dierickx, I./Cool, K. (1989): Asset stock accumulation and sustainability of competitive advantage. In: Management Science 35(1989)12, pp. 1504-1513.

DiMaggio, P./Powell, W.W. (1991): The iron cage revisited: Institutional isomorphism and collective rationality. In: Powell, W. W./DiMaggio, P. (eds.): The new institutionalism in organizational analysis. Chicago 1991, pp. 63-82.

Dimitratos, P./Lioukas, S./Carter, S. (2004): The relationship between entrepreneurship and international performance: The importance of domestic environment. In: International Business Review 13(2004)1, pp. 19-41.

Doloreux, D. (2002): What we should know about regional systems of innovation. In: Technology in Society 24(2002)3, pp. 243-263.

Dong, Z./Tann, J. (2005): A regional innovation system in a small-sized region: A clustering model in Zhongguancun Science Park. In: Technology Analysis & Strategic Management 17(2005)3, pp. 375-390.

Douma, M.U./Bilderbeek, J./Idenburg, P.J./Looise, J.K. (2000): Strategic Alliances: Managing the dynamics of fit. In: Long Range Planning 33(2000)4, pp. 579-598.

Duarte, P.A./Raposo, M.L. (2010): A PLS model to study brand preference: An application to the mobile phone market. In: Esposito Vinzi, V./Chin, W. W./Henseler, J./Wang, H. (eds.): Handbook of partial least squares - concepts, methods and applications. Berlin 2010, pp. 449-485.

Dunning, J.H. (2000): Regions, globalization, and the knowledge economy: The issues stated. In: Dunning, J. H. (eds.): Regions, globalization, and the knowledge-based economy. Oxford 2000, pp. 7-41.

Eisenhardt, K.M. (1989a): Building theories from case study research. In: Academy of Management Review 14(1989)4, pp. 532-550.

Eisenhardt, K.M. (1989b): Making fast strategic decisions in high-velocity environments. In: Academy of Management Journal 32(1989)3, pp. 543-576.

Eisenhardt, K.M. (2000): Dynamic capabilities: What are they? In: Strategic Management Journal 21(2000)10-11, pp. 1105-1121.

Eisenhardt, K.M./Graebner, M.E. (2007): Theory building from cases: Opportunities and challenges. In: Academy of Management Journal 50(2007)1, pp. 25-32.

(EIU) Economist Intelligence Unit (2008): Country commerce - China. New York 2008.

Enright, M.J. (1996): Regional clusters and economic development: A research agenda. In: Staber, U. H./Schaefer, N. V./Sharma, B. D. (eds.): Business networks: Prospects for regional development. Berlin 1996, pp. 190-213.

Enright, M.J. (2003): Regional clusters: What we know and what we should know. In: Bröcker, J./Dohse, D./Soltwedel, R. (eds.): Innovation clusters and interregional competition. Berlin 2003, pp. 99-129.

Erikson, R.A. (1974): The regional impact of growth firms: The case of Boeing 1963-1968. In: Land Economics 50(1974)2, pp. 127-136.

Ettlie, J.E./Pavlou, P.A. (2006): Technology-based new product development partnerships. In: Decision Sciences 37(2006)2, pp. 117-147.

European Commission (2002): Final Report of the Expert Group on Enterprise Clusters and Networks. Brussels 2002.

European Commission (2005): Small and medium-sized enterprises (SMEs): SME definition. Available at: http://ec.europa.eu/enterprise/policies/sme/facts-figures-analysis/sme-definition/index_en.htm (accessed: 30.12.2010).

Feldman, M.P. (2000): Location and innovation: The New Economic Geography of Innovation, Spillovers, and Agglomeration. In: Clark, G. L./Feldman, M. P./Gertler, M. S. (eds.): The Oxford Handbook of Economic Geography. Oxford 2000, pp. 373-394.

Feldman, M.P./Florida, R. (1994): The geographic sources of innovation: Technological infrastructure and product innovation in the United States. In: Anals of the Association of Economic Geographers 84(1994)2, pp. 210-229.

Ferguson, R.J./Paulin, M./Bergeron, J. (2005): Contractual governance, relational governance, and the performance of interfirm service exchanges: The influence of boundary-spanners closeness. In: Journal of the Academy of Marketing Science 33(2005)2, pp. 217-234.

Feser, E.J. (1998): Old and new theories of industrial clusters. In: Steiner, M. (eds.): Clusters and regional specialisation: On geography, technology and networks. London 1998, pp. 18-40.

Feser, E.J./Bergman, E.M. (2000): National industry cluster templates: A framework for applied regional cluster analysis. In: Regional Studies 34(2000)1, pp. 1-19.

Feser, E.J./Luger, M.I. (2003): Cluster analysis as a mode of inquiry: It's use in science and technology policymaking in North Carolina. In: European Planning Studies 11(2003)1, pp. 11-24.

Fingleton, B./Igliori, D./Moore, B. (2005): Cluster dynamics: New evidence and projections for computing services in Great Britain. In: Journal of Regional Science 45(2005)2, pp. 283-311.

Florida, R. (1995): Toward the learning region. In: Futures 27(1995)5, pp. 527-536.

Folta, T.B./Cooper, A.C./Baik, Y. (2006): Geographic cluster size and firm performance. In: Journal of Business Venturing 21(2006)2, pp. 217-242.

Fontana, A./Frey, J.H. (1994): Interviewing: The art of science. In: Denzin, N. K./Lincoln, Y. S. (eds.): Handbook of qualitative research. Thousand Oaks 1994, pp. 361-376.

Fornell, C./Bookstein, F.L. (1982): A comparative analysis of two structural equation models: LISREL and PLS applied to market data. In: Fornell, C. (eds.): A second generation of multivariate analysis. 1982, pp. 289-324.

Fornell, C./Cha, J. (1994): Partial least squares. In: Bagozzi, R. P. (eds.): Advanced methods of marketing research. Cambridge 1994, pp. 52-78.

Fornell, C./Larcker, D.F. (1981): Evaluating structural equation models with unobservable variables and measurement errors. In: Journal of Marketing Research 18(1981)1, pp. 39-50.

Foss, N.J./Ishikawa, I. (2007): Towards a dynamic resource-based view: Insights from Austrian capital and entrepreneurship theory. In: Organization Studies 28(2007)5, pp. 749-772.

Fülbier, R. (2004): Wissenschaftstheorie und Betriebswirtschaftslehre. In: Wissenschaftliches Studium 33(2004)5, pp. 266-271.

Gefen, D./Straub, D.W./Boudreau, M. (2000): Structural equation modeling and regression: Guidelines for research practice. In: Communications of the Association for Information Systems 4(2000), pp. 1-79.

Gilbert, B.A./McDougall, P.P./Audretsch, D.B. (2008): Clusters, knowledge spillovers and new venture performance: An empirical examination. In: Journal of Business Venturing 23(2008)4, pp. 405-422.

Gilbert, C.G. (2005): Unbundling the structure of inertia: Resource versus routine rigidity. In: Academy of Management Journal 48(2005)5, pp. 741-763.

Glaser, B.G. (1992): Basics of grounded theory analysis. Mill Valley 1992.

Glaser, B.G./Strauss, A.L. (1967): The discovery of grounded theory. Chicago 1967.

Götz, O./Liehr-Gobbers, K./Krafft, M. (2010): Evaluation of structural equation models using the partial least squares (PLS) approach. In: Esposito Vinzi, V./Chin, W. W./Henseler, J./Wang, H. (eds.): Handbook of partial least squares - concepts, methods and applications. Berlin 2010, pp. 691-711.

Gordon, I.R./McCann, P. (2000): Industrial clusters: Complexes, agglomeration and/or social networks? In: Urban Studies 37(2000)3, pp. 513-532.

Gordon, S. (1991): The history and philosophy of social science. London 1991.

Grabher, G. (2002): Cool projects, boring institutions: Temporary collaboration in social context. In: Regional Studies 36(2002)3, pp. 205-214.

Granovetter, M.S. (1973): The strength of weak ties. In: American Journal of Sociology 78(1973)6, pp. 1360-1380.

Granovetter, M.S. (1974): Getting a job: A study of contacts and careers. Cambridge 1974.

Granovetter, M.S. (1983): The strength of weak ties: A network theory revisited. In: Sociological Theory 1(1983), pp. 201-233.

Grant, R.M. (1991): The resource-based theory of competitive advantage: Implications for strategy formulation. In: California Management Review 33(1991)3, pp. 114-135.

Grant, R.M. (1996): Toward a knowledge-based theory of the firm. In: Strategic Management Journal 17(1996)Winter Special Issue, pp. 109-122.

Grant, R.M. (2005): Contemporary strategy analysis. 5. ed., Malden 2005.

Green, K.M./Covin, J.G./Slevin, D.P. (2008): Exploring the relationship between strategic reactiveness and entrepreneurial orientation: The role of structure-style fit. In: Journal of Business Venturing 23(2008)3, pp. 356-383.

Greving, B. (2007): Messen und skalieren von Sachverhalten. In: Albers, S./Klapper, D./Konradt, U. (eds.): Methodik der empirischen Forschung. Wiesbaden 2007, pp. 65-78.

Guan, J.C./Yam, R.C./Tang, E.P./Lau, A.K. (2009): Innovation strategy and performance during economic transition: Evidences in Beijing, China. In: Pesearch Policy 38(2009)5, pp. 802-812.

Gujarati, D.N. (2003): Basic Econometrics. 4. ed., Irwin 2003.

Gulati, R./Lawrence, P.R./Puranam, P. (2005): Adaptation in vertical relationships: Beyond incentive conflict. In: Strategic Management Journal 26(2005)5, pp. 415-440.

Gulati, R./Nohria, N./Zaheer, A. (2000): Strategic networks. In: Strategic Management Journal 21(2000)3, pp. 203-215.

Hakanson, L. (2005): Epistemic communities and cluster dynamics: On the role of knowledge in industrial districts. In: Industry and Innovation 12(2005)4, pp. 433-463.

Hammersley, M./Atkinson, P. (1995): Ethnography: Principles in practice. 2. ed., London 1995.

Handfield, R.B./Withers, B. (1993): A comparison of logistics management in Hungary, China, Korea and Japan. In: Journal of Business Logistics 14(1993)1, pp. 81-109.

Hartung, J./Elpelt, B./Klösener, K. (2009): Statistik: Lehr- und Handbuch der angewandten Statistik. 15. ed., München 2009.

Hayek, F.A.v. (1948): Individualism and economic order. London 1948.

Hayek, F.A.v. (1978): Competition as a discovery procedure. In: Hayek, F. A. v. (eds.): New studies in philosophy, politics, economics and the history of ideas. Chicago 1978, pp. 179-190.

Head, K./Ries, J./Swenson, D. (1995): Agglomeration benefits and location choice: Evidence from Japanese manufacturing investments in the United States. In: Journal of International Economics 38(1995)3-4, pp. 223-247.

Heckscher, E.F. (1919): The effect of foreign trade on the distribution of income. In: Ekonomisk Tidskrift 21(1919), pp. 497-512.

Heininger, N./Gehnen, R. (2008): German Business Expansion in China 2008-2010. Shanghai 2008.

Held, D./McGrew, A./Goldblatt, D. (1999): Global transformations: Politics, economics and culture. Stanford 1999.

Helfat, C.E. (2003): Stylized facts regarding the evolution of organizational resources and capabilities. In: Helfat, C. E. (eds.): The SMS Blackwell handbook of organizational capabilities - emergence, development, and change. Malden 2003, pp. 1-14.

Helfat, C.E./Peteraf, M.E. (2003): The dynamic resource-based view: Capability lifecycles. In: Strategic Management Journal 24(2003)10, pp. 997-1010.

Henseler, J./Fassott, G. (2010): Testing moderator effects in PLS path models: An illustration of available procedures. In: Esposito Vinzi, V./Chin, W. W./Henseler, J./Wang, H.

(eds.): Handbook of partial least squares - concepts, methods and applications. Berlin 2010, pp. 713-735.

Henseler, J./Ringle, C.M./Sinkovics, R.R. (2009): The use of partial least squares path modeling in international marketing. In: Advances in International Marketing 20(2009)1, pp. 277-319.

Herd, R. (2010): OECD economic surveys: China 2010. Paris 2010.

Hewings, G.J.D./Jensen, R.C. (2000): Regional, interregional and multiregional input-output analysis. In: Nijkamp, P. (eds.): Handbook of regional and urban economics. Amsterdam 2000, pp. 295-355.

Hill, E.W./Brennan, J.F. (2000): Methodology for identifying the drivers of industrial clusters: The foundation of regional competitive advantage. In: Economic development quarterly 14(2000)1, pp. 67-96.

Hitt, M.A./Ireland, D.R./Camp, M.S./Sexton, D.L. (2001): Entrepreneurial strategies for wealth creation. In: Strategic Management Journal 22(2001)6-7, pp. 479-491.

Hitt, M.A./Ireland, D.R./Camp, M.S./Sexton, D.L. (2006): Strategic entrepreneurship: Integrating entrepreneurial and strategic management perspectives. In: Hitt, M. A./Ireland, D. R./Camp, M. S./Sexton, D. L. (eds.): Strategic entrepreneurship: Creating a new mindset. Oxford 2006, pp. 1-16.

Hitt, M.A./Ireland, R.D./Hoskisson, R.E. (2009): Strategic management: Competitiveness and globalization. 8. ed., Mason 2009.

Hoetker, G./Mellewigt, T. (2009): Choice and performance of governance mechanisms: Matching alliance governance to asset type. In: Strategic Management Journal 30(2009)10, pp. 1025-1044.

Hoffmann, W.H. (2005): How to manage a portfolio of alliances. In: Long Range Planning 38(2005)2, pp. 121-143.

Holden, M.T./Lynch, P. (2004): Choosing the appropriate methodology: Understanding research philosophy. In: Marketing Review 4(2004)4, pp. 397-409.

Homburg, C./Giering, A. (1996): Konzeptualisierung und Operationalisierung komplexer Konstrukte. In: Marketing Zeitschrift für Forschung und Praxis 18(1996)1, pp. 5-24.

Homburg, C./Giering, A. (2001): Personal characteristics as moderators of the relationship between customer satisfaction and loyalty: An empirical analysis. In: Psychology and Marketing 18(2001)1, pp. 43-66.

Hoopes, D.G./Madsen, T.L. (2008): A capability-based view of competitive heterogeneity. In: Industrial and Corporate Change 17(2008)3, pp. 393-426.

Hoover, E.M. (1971): An introduction to regional economics. New York 1971.

Howells, J.R. (2002): Tacit knowledge, innovation and Economic Geography. In: Urban Studies 39(2002)5-6, pp. 871-884.

Huber, F./Herrmann, A./Meyer, F./Vogel, J./Vollhardt, K. (2007): Kausalmodellierung mit Partial Least Squares. Wiesbaden 2007.

Hulland, J. (1999): Use of partial least squares (PLS) in strategic management research: A review of four recent studies. In: Strategic Management Journal 20(1999)2, pp. 195-204.

Ireland, D.R./Hitt, M.A./Sirmon, D.G. (2003): A model of strategic entrepreneurship: The construct and its dimensions. In: Journal of Management 29(2003)6, pp. 963-989.

Ireland, D.R./Hitt, M.A./Vaidyanath, D. (2002): Alliance Management as a source of competitive advantage. In: Journal of Management 28(2002)3, pp. 413-446.

Jacobson, R. (1992): The "Austrian" of strategy. In: Academy of Management Review 17(1992)4, pp. 782-807.

Jaffe, A.B. (1989): Real effects of Academic Research. In: The American Economic Review 79(1989)5, pp. 957-970.

Jaffe, A.B./Trajtenberg, M./Henderson, R. (1993): Geographic localization of knowledge spillovers as evidenced by patent citations. In: The Quarterly Journal of Economics 108(1993)3, pp. 577-598.

Jarvis, C.B./Mackenzie, S.B./Podsakoff, P.M. (2003): A critical review of construct indicators and measurement model misspecifications in marketing and consumer research. In: Journal of Consumer Research 30(2003)2, pp. 199-218.

Javidan, M. (1998): Core competence: What does it mean in practice? In: Long Range Planning 31(1998)1, pp. 60-71.

Jöreskog, K.G. (1982): The LISREL approach to causal model-building in the social sciences. In: Jöreskog, K.G./World, H. (eds.): Systems under indirect observation: Causality, structure, prediction. Amsterdam; New York 1982, pp. 81-100.

Kale, P./Dyer, J.H./Singh, H. (2002): Alliance capability, stock market response, and long-term alliance success: The role of the alliance function. In: Strategic Management Journal 23(2002)8, pp. 747-767.

Keats, B.W. (1990): Diversification and business economic performance revisited: Issues of measurement and causality. In: Journal of Management 16(1990)1, pp. 61-72.

Kirsch, W. (1990): Unternehmenspolitik und strategische Unternehmensführung. München 1990.

Kirzner, I.M. (1973): Competition and entrepreneurship. Chicago 1973.

Kirzner, I.M. (1978): Wettbewerb und Unternehmertum. Tübingen 1978.

Kirzner, I.M. (1997): Entrepreneurial discovery and the competitive market process: An Austrian approach. In: Journal of Economic Literature 35(1997)1, pp. 60-85.

Köhler, H. (2011): Supply Chain Risiken im Low Cost Country Sourcing. Reduktion von Lieferrisiken in China und der Türkei. Diss. Darmstadt 2011.

Kogut, B./Zander, U. (1992): Knowledge of the firm, combinative capabilities, and the replication of technology. In: Organization Science 3(1992)3, pp. 383-397.

Korhonen, S./Niemela, J.S. (2005): A conceptual analysis of capabilities: Identifying and classifying sources of competitive advantage in the wood industry. In: The Finnish Journal of Business Economics 54(2005)1, pp. 11-47.

Kraatz, M.S./Zajac, E.J. (2001): How organizational resources affect strategic change and performance in turbulent environments: Theory and evidence. In: Organization Science 12(2001)5, pp. 632-657.

Krätke, S. (2002): Network analysis of production clusters: The Potsdam/Babelsberg film industry as an example. In: European Planning Studies 10(2002)1, pp. 27-54.

Kromrey, H. (2009): Empirische Sozialforschung: Modelle und Methoden der Datenerhebung und Datenauswertung. 12. ed., Stuttgart 2009.

Krugman, P. (1991a): Increasing returns and Economic Geography. In: Journal of Political Economy 99(1991)3, pp. 483-499.

Krugman, P. (1991b): Trade and geography. Cambridge 1991.

Krugman, P. (1991c): History versus expectations. In: Quarterly Journal of Economics 106(1991)2, pp. 651-667.

Krugman, P. (1998): What's new in the economic geography? In: Oxford Review of Economic Policy 14(1998)2, pp. 7-17.

Krugman, P. (2000): Where in the world is the New Economic Geography? In: Clark, G. L./Gertler, M. S./Feldman, M. P. (eds.): The Oxford Handbook of Economic Geography. Oxford 2000, pp. 49-60.

Kuhn, T.S. (1996): The structure of scientific revolutions. 3. ed., Chicago 1996.

Kuijs, L. (2009): China through 2020: A macroeconomic outlook. Beijing 2009.

Kukalis, S. (2010): Agglomeration economies and firm performance. In: Journal of Management 36(2010)2, pp. 453-481.

Kumar, K./Subramanian, R./Yauger, C. (1998): Examining the market orientation-performance relationship: A context-specific study. In: Journal of Management 24(1998)2, pp. 201-233.

Lai, F./Li, D./Wang, Q./Zhao, X. (2008): The information technology capability of third-party logistics providers: A resource-based view and empirical evidence from China. In: Journal of Supply Chain Management 44(2008)3, pp. 22-38.

Lam, T. (2006a): Overview of the industrial clusters in China. Hong Kong 2006.

Lam, T. (2006b): Industrial clusters in the Pearl River Delta. Hong Kong 2006.

Lambert, D.M./Harrington, T.C. (1990): Measuring nonresponse bias in customer service mail surveys. In: Journal of Business Logistics 11(1990)2, pp. 5-25.

Laursen, K. (2002): The importance of sectoral differences in the application of complementary HRM practices for innovation performance. In: International Journal of the Economics of Business 9(2002)1, pp. 139-156.

Lazerson, M.H./Lorenzoni, G. (1999): The firms that feed industrial districts: A return to the Italian source. In: Industrial and Corporate Change 8(1999)2, pp. 235-266.

Lee, C./Lee, K./Pennings, J.M. (2001): Internal capabilities, external networks, and performance: A study on technology-based ventures. In: Strategic Management Journal 22(2001)6-7, pp. 615-640.

Levitt, B./March, J.G. (1988): Organizational learning. In: Annual Review of Sociology 14(1988)3, pp. 319-340.

Li, J.J. (2005): The formation of managerial networks of foreign firms in China: The effects of strategic orientations. In: Asia Pacific Journal of Management 22(2005)4, pp. 423-443.

Liao, T. (2010): Cluster and performance in foreign firms: The role of resources, knowledge, and trust. In: Industrial Marketing Management 39(2010)1, pp. 161-169.

Liu, W. (2006): Knowledge exploitation, knowledge exploration, and competency trap. In: Knowledge and Process Management 13(2006)3, pp. 144-161.

Lohmöller, J. (1989): Latent variable path modeling with partial least squares. Heidelberg 1989.

Longhi, C./Keeble, D. (2000): High-technology clusters and evolutionary trends in the 1990s. In: Keeble, D./Wilkinson, F. (eds.): High-technology clusters, networking and collective learning in Europe. Aldershot 2000, pp. 21-56.

Low, M.B./MacMillan, I.C. (2007): Entrepreneurship: Past research and future challenges. In: Cuervo, A./Ribeiro, D./Roig, S. (eds.): Entrepreneurship: Concepts, theory and perspective. Berlin 2007, pp. 131-154.

Luger, M./Shetty, S. (1985): Determinants of foreign plant start-ups in the United States: Lessons from policymakers in the Southeast. In: Vanderbilt Journal of Transnational Law 18(1985)2, pp. 223-245.

Luhmann, N. (1987): Soziale Systeme: Grundriß einer allgemeinen Theorie. 1. ed., Frankfurt 1987.

Lumpkin, G./Dess, G.G. (2001): Linking two dimensions of entrepreneurial orientation to firm performance: The moderating role of environment and industry life cycle. In: Journal of Business Venturing 16(2001)5, pp. 429-451.

Lumpkin, G.T./Dess, G.G. (1996): Clarifying the entrepreneurial orientation construct and linking it to firm performance. In: Academy of Management Review 21(1996)1, pp. 135-172.

Lundvall, B. (1996): The social dimension of the learning economy. Discussion paper of the faculty of Business Studies, Aalborg University 1996.

Lundvall, B./Johnson, B./Andersen, E.S./Dalum, B. (2002): National systems of production, innovation and competence building. In: Research Policy 31(2002)2, pp. 213-231.

Luo, Y. (2003): Industrial dynamics and managerial networking in an emerging market: The case of China. In: Strategic Management Journal 24(2003)13, pp. 1315-1327.

Mahoney, J.T./Pandian, R.J. (1992): The resource-based view within the conversation of strategic management. In: Strategic Management Journal 13(1992)5, pp. 363-380.

Maillat, D./Léchot, G./Lecoq, B./Pfister, M. (1997): Comparative analysis of the structural development of milieux: The watch industry in the Swiss and French Jura Arc. In: Ratti, R./Bramanti, A./Gordon, R. (eds.): The dynamics of innovative regions: The GREMI approach. Brookfield 1997, pp. 109-138.

Malhotra, N.K./Kum, S.S./Patil, A. (2006): Common method variance in IS research: A comparison of alternative approaches and a reanalysis of past research. In: Management Science 52(2006)12, pp. 1865-1883.

Marangoni, G./Solari, S. (2006): Flexible specialization 20 years on: How the 'good' industrial district in Italy have lost their momentum. In: Competition & Change 10(2006)1, pp. 73-87.

March, J.G. (1991): Exploration and exploitation in organizational learning. In: Organization Science 2(1991)1, pp. 71-87.

Marino, L./Strandholm, K./Steensma, K.H./Weaver, M.K. (2002): The moderating effect of national culture on the relationship between entrepreneurial orientation and strategic alliance portfolio extensiveness. In: Entrepreneurship Theory and Practice 26(2002)4, pp. 145-160.

Markusen, A. (1996): Sticky places in slippery space: A typology of industrial districts. In: Economic Geography 72(1996)3, pp. 293-313.

Marshall, A.A. (1920): Principles of Economics. 8. ed., London 1920.

Marshall, A.A. (1927): Industry and Trade. 3. ed., London 1927.

Martin, R./Sunley, P. (1996): Paul Krugman's geographical economics and its implications for regional development theory: A critical assessment. In: Economic Geography 72(1996)3, pp. 259-292.

Martin, R./Sunley, P. (2003): Deconstructing clusters: Chaotic concept or policy panacea. In: Journal of Economic Geography 3(2003)1, pp. 5-35.

Martinez, J.I./Jarillo, C.J. (1989): The evolution of research on coordination mechanisms in multinational corporations. In: Journal of International Business Studies 20(1989)3, pp. 486-514.

Maskell, P. (2001): Towards a knowledge-based theory of the geographical cluster. In: Industrial and Corporate Change 10(2001)4, pp. 921-943.

Maskell, P./Lorenzen, M. (2004): The cluster as market organisation. In: Urban Studies 41(2004)5-6, pp. 991-1009.

Mathews, J.A. (2002): A resource-based view of Schumpeterian economic dynamics. In: Journal of Evolutionary Economics 12(2002)1, pp. 29-54.

Mathews, J.A. (2010): Lachmannian insights into strategic entrepreneurship: Resources, activities and routines in a disequilibrium world. In: Organization Studies 31(2010)2, pp. 219-244.

Maurer, I./Ebers, M. (2006): Dynamic of social capital and their performance implications: Lessons from biotechnology startups. In: Administrative Science Quarterly 51(2006)2, pp. 262-292.

Maurseth, P.B./Verspagen, B. (2002): Knowledge spillovers in Europe: A patent citation analysis. In: Scandinavian Journal of Economics 104(2002)4, pp. 531-545.

McCann, B.T./Folta, T.B. (2011): Performance differentials within geographic clusters. In: Journal of Business Venturing 26(2011)1, pp. 104-123.

McCann, P./Sheppard, S. (2003): The rise, fall and rise again of industrial location theory. In: Regional Studies 37(2003)6&7, pp. 649-663.

McNamara, G./Vaaler, P.M./Devers, C. (2003): Same as it ever was: The search for evidence of increasing hypercompetition. In: Strategic Management Journal 24(2003)9, pp. 261-278.

Meyer, C.B. (2001): A case in case study methodology. In: Field Methods 13(2001)4, pp. 329-352.

Meyer, D.G./Neck, H.M./Meeks, M.D. (2006): The entrepreneurship-strategic management interface. In: Hitt, M. A./Ireland, D. R./Camp, M. S./Sexton, D. L. (eds.): Strategic entrepreneurship: Creating a new mindset. Oxford 2006, pp. 19-44.

Michael, S./Storey, D./Howard, T. (2006): Discovery and coordination in strategic management and entrepreneurship. In: Hitt, M. A./Ireland, D. R./Camp, M. S./Sexton, D. L. (eds.): Strategic entrepreneurship: Creating a new mindset. Oxford 2006, pp. 45-65.

Miles, M.B. (1979): Qualitative data as an attractive nuisance: The problem of analysis. In: Administrative Science Quarterly 24(1979)4, pp. 590-601.

Miles, M.B./Huberman, M.A. (1994): Qualitative data analysis: An expanded sourcebook. Thousand Oaks 1994.

Miller, D. (1990): Organizational configurations: Cohesion, Change, and prediction. In: Human Relations 43(1990)8, pp. 771-789.

Miller, D./Friesen, P.H. (1978): Archetypes of strategy formulation. In: Management Science 24(1978)9, pp. 921-933.

Miller, D./Kets de Vries, M.F. (1982): Top executive locus of control and its relationship to strategy-making, structure, and environment. In: Academy of Management Journal 25(1982)2, pp. 237-253.

Miller, D./Toulouse, J. (1986): Chief executive personality and corporate strategy and structure in small firms. In: Management Science 32(1986)11, pp. 1389-1409.

Miller, P./Botham, R./Gibson, H./Martin, R./Moore, B. (2001): Business clusters in the UK: A first assessment. London 2001.

Millonig, K. (2002): Wettbewerbsvorteile durch das Management des institutionalen Kontextes. Diss. Berlin 2002.

Mintzberg, H. (1973): Strategy-making in three modes. In: California Management Review 16(1973)2, pp. 44-53.

Mintzberg, H. (1980): Structure in 5'S: A synthesis of the research on organizational design. In: Management Science 26(1980)3, pp. 322-341.

Mohr, J.J./Spekman, R.E. (1996): Perfecting partnerships. In: Marketing Management 4(1996)4, pp. 34-43.

Molina-Morales, X.F./Martinez-Fernandez, T.M. (2004): How much difference is there between industrial cluster firms? A net value creation approach. In: Research Policy 33(2004)3, pp. 473-486.

Molina-Morales, X.F./Martinez-Fernandez, T.M. (2008): Shared resources in industrial districts: Information, know-how and institutions in the Spanish tile industry. In: International Regional Science Review 31(2008)1, pp. 35-61.

Molina-Morales, X.F./Martinez-Fernandez, T.M. (2009): Too much love in the neighborhood can hurt: How an excess of intensity and trust in relationships may produce negative effects on firms. In: Strategic Management Journal 30(2009)9, pp. 1013-1023.

Montgomery, C.A. (1982): The measurement of firm diversification: Some new empirical evidence. In: Academy of Management Journal 25(1982)2, pp. 299-307.

Morgan, G./Smircich, L. (1980): The case of qualitative research. In: Academy of Management Review 5(1980)4, pp. 491-500.

Morgan, K. (2004): The exaggerated death of geography: Learning, proximity and territorial innovation systems. In: Journal of Economic Geography 4(2004)1, pp. 3-21.

Morris, M.H./Trotter, D. (1990): Institutionalizing entrepreneurship in a large company: A case study at AT&T. In: Industrial Marketing Management 19(1990)2, pp. 131-139.

Morschett, D./Schramm-Klein, H./Zentes, J. (2009): Strategic International Management. Wiesbaden 2009.

National Bureau of Statistics (2005): China input-output table 2002. Beijing 2005.

Ngo, H./Lau, C./Foley, S. (2008): Strategic Human Resource Management, firm performance, and employee relations climate in China. In: Human Resource Management 47(2008)1, pp. 73-90.

Nunnally, J.C./Bernstein, I.H. (1994): Psychometric Theory. 3. ed., New York 1994.

Oakey, R.P./Rothwell, R./Cooper, S. (1988): The management of innovation in high-technology small firms: Innovation and regional development in Britain and the United States. New York 1988.

Ohlin, B. (1933): Interregional and international trade. Cambridge 1933.

Park, S.H./Luo, Y. (2001): Guanxi and organizational dynamics: Organizational networking in Chinese firms. In: Strategic Management Journal 22(2001)5, pp. 455-477.

Paulraj, A./Lado, A.A./Chen, I.J. (2008): Inter-organizational communication as a relational competency: Antecedents and performance outcomes in collaborative buyer-supplier relationships. In: Journal of Operations Management 26(2008)1, pp. 45-64.

Pehrsson, A. (2006): Business relatedness and performance: A study of managerial perceptions. In: Strategic Management Journal 27(2006)3, pp. 265-282.

Peteraf, M.A. (1993): The cornerstones of competitive advantage: A resource-based view. In: Strategic Management Journal 14(1993)3, pp. 179-191.

Peters, N. (2010): Inter-organisational design of voluntary sustainability initiatives: Increasing the legitimacy of sustainability strategies for supply chains. Diss. Wiesbaden 2010.

Pfohl, H. (2004): Logistiksysteme: Betriebswirtschaftliche Grundlagen. 7. ed., Berlin 2004.

Phan, M.C.T./Styles, C.W./Patterson, P.G. (2005): Relational competency's role in Southeast Asia business partnerships. In: Journal of Business Research 58(2005)2, pp. 173-184.

Pietrobelli, C./Barrera, T.O. (2002): Enterprise clusters and industrial districts in Colombia's fashion sector. In: European Planning Studies 10(2002)5, pp. 541-562.

Piore, M.J./Sabel, C.J. (1984): The second industrial divide: Possibilities for prosperity. New York 1984.

Podsakoff, P.M./MacKenzie, S.B./Lee, J./Podsakoff, N.P. (2003): Common method biases in behavioral research: A critical review of the literature and recommended remedies. In: Journal of Applied Psychology 88(2003)5, pp. 879-903.

Podsakoff, P.M./Organ, D.W. (1986): Self-reports in organizational research: Problems and prospects. In: Journal of Management 12(1986)4, pp. 531-544.

Polyanyi, M. (1967): The tacit dimension. London 1967.

Popper, K.R. (2002): The logic of scientific discovery. London 2002.

Porter, M.E. (1980): Competitive strategy: Techniques for analyzing industries and competitors. New York 1980.

Porter, M.E. (1985): Competitive advantage: Creating and sustaining superior performance. New York 1985.

Porter, M.E. (1990): The competitive advantage of nations. New York 1990.

Porter, M.E. (1991): Towards a dynamic theory of strategy. In: Strategic Management Journal 12(1991)2, pp. 95-117.

Porter, M.E. (1998a): Clusters and the new economies of competition. In: Harvard Business Review 76(1998)6, pp. 77-90.

Porter, M.E. (1998b): On competition. Boston 1998.

Porter, M.E. (2000a): Locations, clusters, and company strategy. In: Clark, G. L./Gertler, M. S./Feldman, M. P. (eds.): The oxford handbook of economic geography. Oxford 2000, pp. 253-274.

Porter, M.E. (2000b): Location, competition, and economic development: Local clusters in a global economy. In: Economic Development Quarterly 14(2000)1, pp. 15-34.

Porter, M.E. (2003): The economic performance of regions. In: Regional Studies 37(2003)6/7, pp. 549-578.

Powell, W.W./Koput, K.W./Smith-Doerr, L. (1996): Interorganizational collaborations and the locus of innovation: Networks of learning in biotechnology. In: Administrative Science Quarterly 41(1996)1, pp. 116-145.

Prahalad, C.K./Hamel, G. (1990): The core competence of the corporation. In: Harvard Business Review 68(1990)3, pp. 79-91.

Pred, A.R. (1976): The interurban transmission of growth in advanced economies: Empirical findings versus regional-planning assumptions. In: Regional Studies 10(1976)2, pp. 151-171.

Procter, M. (1996): Analysing other researchers' data. In: Gilbert, N. (eds.): Research social life. London 1996, pp. 255-286.

Punch, K.F. (2005): Introduction to social research: Quantitative and qualitative approaches. 2. ed., London 2005.

Quévit, M./van Doren, P. (1997): The problem of innovative milieux and territorial structural adjustment policies. In: Ratti, R./Bramanti, A./Gordon, R. (eds.): The dynamics of innovative regions: The GREMI approach. Brookfield 1997, pp. 343-366.

Ramaseshan, B./Yip, L.S.C./Pae, J.H. (2006): Power, satisfaction and relationship commitment in Chinese store-tenant relationship and their impact on performance. In: Journal of Retailing 82(2006)1, pp. 63-70.

Ratti, R./Bramanti, A./Gordon, R. (1997): The dynamics of innovative regions: The GREMI approach. Brookfield 1997.

Rauch, A./Wiklund, J./Lumpkin, G.T./Frese, M. (2009): Entrepreneurial orientation and business performance: An assessment of past research and suggestions for the future. In: Entrepreneurship Theory and Practice 33(2009)3, pp. 761-787.

Reinartz, W./Krafft, M./Hoyer, W. (2003): Measuring the customer relationship management construct and linking it to performance. INSEAD 2003.

Remenyi, D./Williams, B./Money, A./Swartz, E. (1998): Doing research in business and management: An introduction to process and method. London 1998.

Ricardo, D. (1817): On the principles of political economy and taxation. London 1817.

Richter, A.W./West, M.A./van Dick, R./Dawson, J.F. (2006): Boundary spanner's identification, intergroup contact, and effective intergroup relations. In: Academy of Management Journal 49(2006)6, pp. 1252-1269.

Ringle, C.M./Wende, S./Will, A. (2005): SmartPLS 2.0 (beta). Available at: http://www.smartpls.de.

Rocha, H.O. (2004): Entrepreneurship and development: The role of clusters. In: Small Business Economics 23(2004)5, pp. 363-400.

Roelandt, T.J./den Hertog, P./van Sinderen, J./van den Hove, N. (1999): Cluster analysis and cluster policy in the Netherlands. In: OECD (eds.): Boosting innovation: The cluster approach. Paris 1999, pp. 315-338.

Romanelli, E./Khessina, O.M. (2005): Regional industrial identity: Cluster configuration and economic development. In: Organization Science 16(2005)4, pp. 344-358.

Rosenfeld, S.A. (1995): Overachievers: Business clusters that work. Washington 1995.

Rosenfeld, S.A. (1997): Bringing business clusters into the mainstream of economic development. In: European Planning Studies 5(1997)1, pp. 3-23.

Rosenthal, S.S./Strange, W.C. (2003): Geography, industrial organization, and agglomeration. In: Review of Economics and Statistics 85(2003)2, pp. 377-393.

Rossiter, J.R. (2002): The C-OAR-SE procedure for scale development in marketing. In: Journal of Research in Marketing 19(2002)4, pp. 305-335.

Rumelt, R.P. (1974): Strategy, structure, and economic performance. Boston 1974.

Saaty, T.L./Vargas, L.G. (2001): Models, methods, concepts and applications of the analytic hierarchy process. Boston 2001.

Sabel, C.J. (1989): Flexible specialization and the re-emergence of regional economies. In: Hirst, P./Zeitlin, J. (eds.): Reversing industrial decline? Industrial structure and policy in Britain and her competitors. Oxford 1989, pp. 17-70.

Sabel, C.J. (1995): Turning the page in industrial districts. In: Bagnasco, A./Sabel, C. J. (eds.): Small and medium-sized enterprises. New York 1995, pp. 134-161.

Santoro, M.D./Chakrabarti, A.K. (2002): Firm size and technology centrality in industry-university interactions. In: Research Policy 31(2002)7, pp. 1163-1180.

Sarkar, M./Echambadi, R./Harrison, J.S. (2001): Alliance entrepreneurship and firm market performance. In: Strategic Management Journal 22(2001)6-7, pp. 701-711.

Sasuga, K. (2008): An Asian triangle of growth and cluster-to-cluster linkages. Institute of Developing Economies 2008.

Saxenian, A. (1990): Regional networks and the resurgence of Silicon Valley. In: California Management Review 33(1990)1, pp. 89-112.

Saxenian, A. (1994): Regional advantage: Culture and competition in Silicon Valley and Route 128. Cambridge 1994.

Schnell, R./Hill, P.B./Esser, E. (2008): Methoden der empirischen Sozialforschung. 8. ed., München 2008.

Schoonhoven, C.B. (1981): Problems with contingency theory: Testing assumptions hidden within the language of contingency "theory". In: Administrative Science Quarterly 26(1981), pp. 349-377.

Schrader, C.B./Lincoln, J.R./Hoffman, A.N. (1989): The network structures of organization: Effects of task contingencies and distributional form. In: Human Relations 42(1989)1, pp. 43-66.

Schreiner, M./Kale, P./Corsten, D. (2009): What really is alliance management capability and how does it impact alliance outcomes and success? In: Strategic Management Journal 30(2009)13, pp. 1395-1419.

Schreyögg, G./Kliesch-Eberl, M. (2007): How dynamic can organizational capabilities be? Towards a dual-process model of capability dynamization. In: Strategic Management Journal 28(2007)9, pp. 913-933.

Schröder, F./Waibel, M./Altrock, U. (2010): Global change and China's clusters: The restructuring of Guangzhou's textile district. In: Pacific News 33(2010), pp. 4-8.

Schumpeter, J.A. (1934): The theory of economic development. Cambridge 1934.

Schumpeter, J.A. (1964): Theorie der wirtschaftlichen Entwicklung. 6. ed., Berlin 1964.

Schumpeter, J.A. (1975): Capitalism, socialism and democracy. 3. ed., New York 1975.

Schumpeter, J.A. (1993): Kapitalismus, Sozialismus und Demokratie. 7. ed., Tübingen 1993.

Scott, A.J. (1988): New industrial spaces: Flexible production organization and regional development in North America and Western Europe. London 1988.

Scott, A.J./Storper, M. (1992): Industrialization and regional development. In: Storper, M./Scott, A. J. (eds.): Pathways to industrialization and regional development. London 1992, pp. 3-17.

Shane, S./Venkataraman, (2000): The promise of entrepreneurship as a field of research. In: Academy of Management Review 25(2000)1, pp. 217-226.

Shaver, M.J./Flyer, F. (2000): Agglomeration economies, firm heterogeneity, and foreign direct investment in the United States. In: Strategic Management Journal 21(2000)12, pp. 1175-1193.

Siggelkow, N. (2007): Persuasion with case studies. In: Academy of Management Journal 50(2007)1, pp. 20-24.

Simmel, G. (1950): The sociology of Georg Simmel. New York 1950.

Simmie, J./Sennett, J. (1999): Innovation in the London metropolitan region. Brokes School of Planning, Oxford 1999.

Simon, H.A. (1991): Bounded rationality and organizational learning. In: Organization Science 2(1991)1, pp. 125-134.

Simon, M.C. (2007): Der Internationalisierungsprozess von Unternehmen. Wiesbaden 2007.

Smith, A. (2007/1776): Wealth of nations. New York 2007.

Smith, D.F./Florida, R. (1994): Agglomeration and industrial location: An econometric analysis of Japanese-affiliated manufacturing establishments in automotive-related industries. In: Journal of Urban Economics 36(1994)1, pp. 23-41.

Smith, K.G./Di Gregorio, D. (2006): Bisociation, discovery, and the role of entrepreneurial action. In: Hitt, M. A./Ireland, D. R./Camp, M. S./Sexton, D. L. (eds.): Strategic Entrepreneurship: Creating a new mindset. Oxford 2006, pp. 129-150.

Sölvell, Ö./Lindqvist, G./Ketels, C. (2003): The cluster initiative greenbook. Stockholm 2003.

Spanos, Y.E./Lioukas, S. (2001): An examination into the causal logic of rent generation: Contrasting Porter's competitive strategy framework and the resource-based perspective. In: Strategic Management Journal 22(2001)10, pp. 907-934.

St. John, C.H./Pouder, R.W. (2006): Technology clusters versus industry clusters: Resources, networks, and regional advantages. In: Growth & Change 37(2006)2, pp. 141-171.

Staber, U. (2001): Spatial proximity and firm survival in a declining industrial district: The case of knitwear firms in Baden-Württemberg. In: Regional Studies 35(2001)4, pp. 329-341.

Stam, W./Elfring, T. (2008): Entrepreneurial orientation and new venture performance: The moderating role of intra- and extraindustry social capital. In: Academy of Management Journal 51(2008)1, pp. 97-111.

Starbuck, W.H. (1992): Learning by knowledge-intensive firms. In: Journal of Management Studies 29(1992)6, pp. 713-740.

Sternberg, R./Arndt, O. (2001): The firm or the region: What determines the innovation behavior of European firms? In: Economic Geography 77(2001)4, pp. 364-382.

Stevenson, H.H./Jarillo, C.J. (2007): A paradigm of entrepreneurship: Entrepreneurial Management. In: Cuervo, A./Ribeiro, D./Roig, S. (eds.): Entrepreneurship: Concepts, theory and perspective. Berlin 2007, pp. 155-170.

Stimpert, J./Duhaime, I.M. (1997): In the eyes of the beholder: Conceptualizations of relatedness held by the managers of large diversified firms. In: Strategic Management Journal 18(1997)2, pp. 111-125.

Stokes, K.M. (1995): Paradigm lost: A cultural and systems theoretical critique of political economy. Armonk 1995.

Storper, M. (1997): The regional world: Territorial development in a global economy. New York 1997.

Storper, M./Allen, S.J. (1989): The geographical foundations and social regulation of flexible production complexes. In: Wolch, J./Dear, M. (eds.): The power of geography. London 1989, pp. 19-40.

Strauss, A.L. (1987): Qualitative analysis for social scientists. Cambridge 1987.

Stuart, T.E./Sorenson, O. (2003): The geography of opportunity: Spatial heterogeneity in founding rates and the performance of biotechnology firms. In: Research Policy 32(2003)2, pp. 229-253.

Stuart, T.E./Sorenson, O. (2007): Strategic networks and entrepreneurial ventures. In: Strategic Entrepreneurship Journal 1(2007)3-4, pp. 211-227.

Sun, Y./Wen, K. (2007): Uncertainties, imitative behaviours and foreign R&D location: Explaining the over-concentration of foreign R&D in Beijing and Shanghai within China. In: Asia Pacific Business Review 13(2007)3, pp. 405-424.

Swann, G.M.P./Prevezer, M./Stout, D. (1998): The dynamics of industrial clustering: International comparisons in computing and biotechnology. Oxford 1998.

Tan, J. (2006): Growth of industry clusters and innovation: Lessons from Beijing Zhongguancun Science Park. In: Journal of Business Venturing 21(2006)6, pp. 827-850.

Tappeiner, G./Hauser, C./Walde, J. (2008): Regional knowledge spillovers: Fact or artifact? In: Research Policy 37(2008)5, pp. 861-874.

Taube, M./Ögütcü, M. (2002): Investment in China's regional development: Experiences from the coastal belt and policy challenges for the Western territories. Discussion paper No. 287 of the faculty of Economics and Management, Gerhard Mercator University, Duisburg 2002.

Teece, D.J./Pisano, G./Shuen, A. (1997): Dynamic capabilities and strategic management. In: Strategic Management Journal 18(1997)7, pp. 509-533.

Travica, B. (1998): Information aspects of new organizational designs: Exploring the non-traditional organization. In: Journal of the American Society for Information Science 49(1998)13, pp. 1224-1244.

Tzeng, C. (2010): Managing innovation for economic development in greater China: The origins of Hsinchu and Zhongguancun. In: Technology in Society 32(2010)2, pp. 110-121.

Ulrich, P./Hill, W. (1979): Wissenschaftstheoretische Aspekte ausgewählter betriebswirtschaftlicher Konzeptionen. In: Raffee, H./Abel, B. (eds.): Wissenschaftstheoretische Grundfragen der Wirtschaftswissenschaften. München 1979, pp. 161-190.

UN Department of Economic and Social Affairs (2008): The current status of industry and products classifications in China. Available at: http://unstats.un.org (accessed: 27.09.2010).

van de Vijver, F.J./Leung, K. (1997): Methods and data analysis for cross-cultural research. Thousand Oaks 1997.

van den Berg, L./Braun, E./van Winden, W. (2001): Growth clusters in European studies: An integral approach. In: Urban Studies 38(2001)1, pp. 185-205.

van Tulder, R. (1988): Small European countries in the international telecommunications struggle. In: Freeman, C./Lundvall, B. (eds.): Small countries facing the technological revolutions. London 1988, pp. 169-183.

Venkatraman, N. (1989): Strategic orientation of business enterprises: The construct, dimensionality, and measurement. In: Management Science 35(1989)8, pp. 942-962.

Venkatraman, N./Ramanujam, V. (1986): Measurement of business performance in strategy research: A comparison of approaches. In: Academy of Management Review 11(1986)4, pp. 801-814.

Verspagen, B./Schoenmakers, W. (2000): The spatial dimension of knowledge spillovers in Europe: Evidence from firm patenting data. Paper presented at AEA conference in intellectual property econometrics, Alicante (Spain), April 2000.

Vinzi, V./Lauro, C./Tenenhaus, M. (2003): PLS path modeling. Discussion paper of the faculty of HEC School of Management, University of Naples, Naples 2003.

Visser, E. (1999): A comparison of clustered and dispersed firms in the small-scale clothing industry of Lima. In: World Development 27(1999)9, pp. 1553-1570.

vom Hofe, R./Chen, K. (2006): Whither or not industrial clusters: Conclusions or confusions? In: The Industrial Geographer 4(2006)1, pp. 2-28.

vom Hofe, R./Chen, K. (2007): Method for identifying local and domestic industrial clusters using interregional commodity trade data. In: The Industrial Geographer 4(2007)2, pp. 1-27.

Wacker, J.G. (2008): A conceptual understanding of requirements for theory building: Guidelines for scientific theory building. In: Journal of Supply Chain Management 44(2008)3, pp. 5-15.

Walter, A./Auer, M./Ritter, T. (2006): The impact of network capabilities and entrepreneurial orientation on university spin-off performance. In: Journal of Business Venturing 21(2006)4, pp. 541-567.

Wang, C.C./Lin, G.C. (2008): The growth and spatial distribution of China's ICT industry: New Geography of clustering and innovation. In: Issues & Studies 44(2008)2, pp. 145-192.

Wennberg, K./Lindqvist, G. (2010): The effect of clusters on the survival and performance of new firms. In: Small Business Economics 34(2010)3, pp. 221-241.

Wernerfelt, B. (1984): A resource-based view of the firm. In: Strategic Management Journal 5(1984)2, pp. 171-180.

Whitford, J. (2001): The decline of a model? Challenge and response in the Italian industrial district. In: Economy and Society 30(2001)1, pp. 38-65.

Wiklund, J./Shepherd, D. (2003): Knowledge-based resources, entrepreneurial orientation, and the performance of small and medium-sized businesses. In: Strategic Management Journal 24(2003)13, pp. 1307-1314.

Wiklund, J./Shepherd, D. (2005): Entrepreneurial orientation and small business performance. In: Journal of Business Venturing 20(2005)1, pp. 71-91.

Winter, S.G. (2000): The satisficing principle in capability learning. In: Strategic Management Journal 21(2000)10-11, pp. 981-996.

Winter, S.G. (2003): Understanding dynamic capabilities. In: Strategic Management Journal 24(2003)10, pp. 991-996.

Wo-Lap Lam, W. (2006): Chinese politics in the Hu Jintao era: New leaders, new challenges. Armonk 2006.

Wolf, J. (2008): Organisation, Management, Unternehmensführung. 3. ed., Wiesbaden 2008.

Woodward, D.P. (1992): Locational determinants of Japanese manufacturing start-ups in the United States. In: Southern Economic Journal 58(1992)3, pp. 690-708.

Worldbank (2010): China quarterly update - June 2010. Beijing 2010.

Wright, P.M. (2001): Human resources and the resource based view of the firm. In: Journal of Management 27(2001)6, pp. 701-721.

Wu, W. (2007): State policies, enterprise dynamism, and innovation system in Shanghai, China. In: Growth and Change 38(2007)4, pp. 544-566.

Xu, K./Jayaram, J./Xu, M. (2006): The effects of customer contact on conformance quality and productivity in Chinese service firms. In: International Journal of Quality and Reliability Management 23(2006)4, pp. 367-389.

Yi, M.Y./Davis, F.D. (2003): Developing and validating an observational learning model of computer software training and skill acquisition. In: Information Systems Research 14(2003)2, pp. 146-169.

Yin, R.K. (2009): Case study research. 4. ed., Thousand Oaks 2009.

Yoshino, M.Y./Rangan, S.U. (1995): Strategic alliances: An entrepreneurial approach to globalization. 2. ed., Boston 1995.

Yu, Z./Xin, T. (2003): An innovative region in China: Interaction between multinational corporations and local firms in a high-tech cluster in Beijing. In: Economic Geography 79(2003)2, pp. 129-152.

Yusuf, S./Nabeshima, K. (2009): Growth through innovation: An industrial strategy for Shanghai. Beijing 2009.

Zahra, S.A. (1991): Predictors and financial outcomes of Corporate Entrepreneurship: An exploratory study. In: Journal of Business Venturing 6(1991)4, pp. 259-285.

Zahra, S.A./Covin, J.G. (1995): Contextual influences on the corporate entrepreneurship - performance relationship: A longitudinal analysis. In: Journal of Business Venturing 10(1995)1, pp. 43-58.

Zahra, S.A./Garvis, D.M. (2000): International corporate entrepreneurship and firm performance: The moderating effect of international environmental hostility. In: Journal of Business Venturing 15(2000)5-6, pp. 469-492.

Zander, U./Kogut, B. (1995): Knowledge and the speed of transfer and imitation of organizational capabilities. In: Organization Science 6(1995)1, pp. 76-92.

Zeitlin, J. (1992): Industrial districts and local economic regeneration: Overview and comment. In: Pyke, F./Sengenberger, W. (eds.): Industrial districts and local economic regeneration. Geneva 1992, pp. 279-294.

Zhang, S./Li, X. (2008): Managerial ties, firm resources, and performance of cluster firms. In: Asia Pacific Journal of Management 25(2008)4, pp. 615-633.

Zhang, Y. (2009): China's chip industry planners look to build 'headquarters economy' around R&D hotbed. In: Electronic Engineering Times (2009)1557, pp. 14-16.

Zhao, X./Flynn, B.B./Roth, A.V. (2006): Decision science research in China: A critical review and research agenda - Foundations and overview. In: Decision Science 37(2006)4, pp. 451-496.

Zhou, Y./Chuah, K.B. (2002): Computer-integrated manufacturing in China: A report of industrial field surveys. In: International Journal of Operations and Production Management 22(2002)3, pp. 271-288.

Zucker, L.G. (1986): Production of trust: Institutional sources of economic structure. In: Research in Organizational Behavior 8(1986), pp. 53-111.

Appendix 1: Detailed outline of this research study

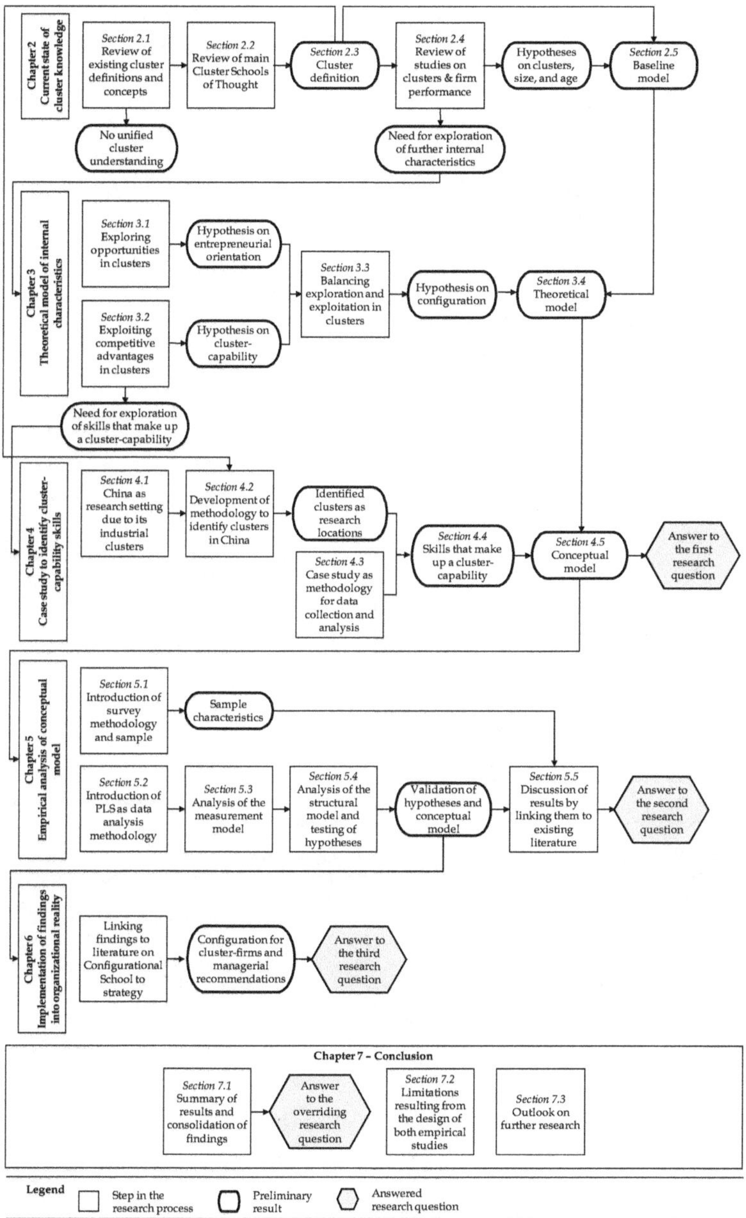

Appendix 2: Remaining Landscapes of regional cluster configurations

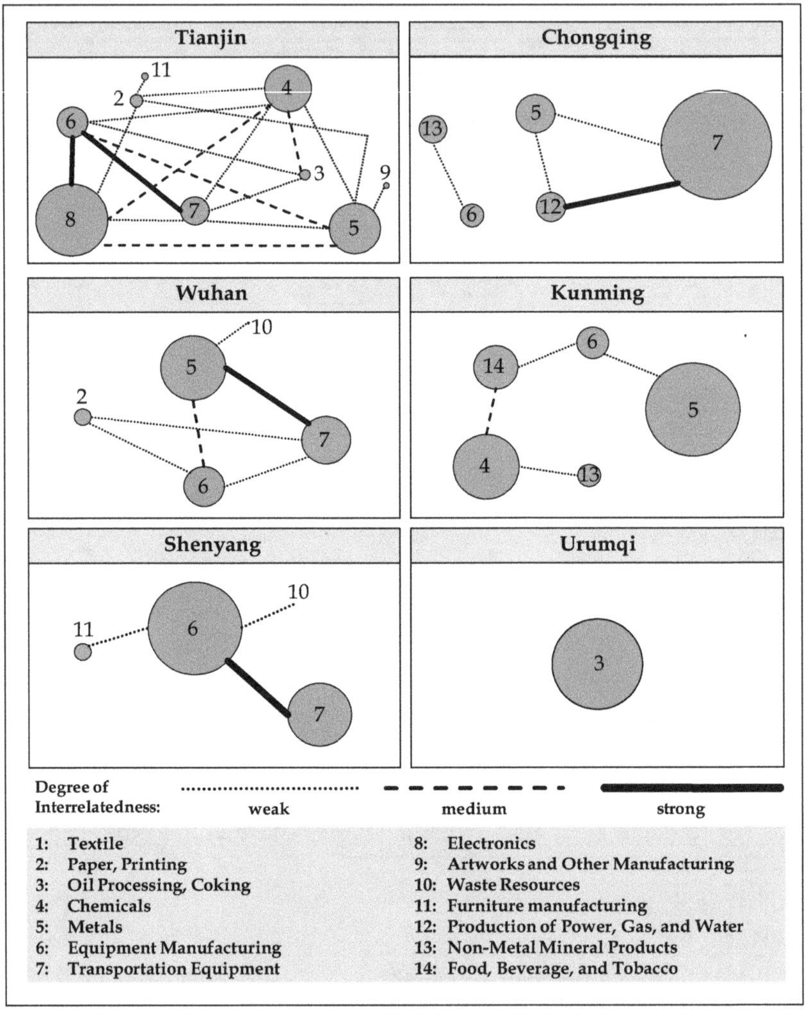

FSC
www.fsc.org
MIX
Papier | Fördert
gute Waldnutzung
FSC® C083411

Kolibri 360 GmbH
Ferdinand-Jühlke-Straße 7
99095 Erfurt, Deutschland
produktsicherheit@kolibri360.de